Machiavelli, Marketing and Management

This fascinating and cutting edge text provides insight into the meaning and interpretation of Machiavelli and his works for management, marketing and political thought, and highlights their particular relevance to the manager today. By bringing together contributions from authors ranging from Machiavelli's descendants, through prominent 'politicos' and writers on Machiavelli, to some of the leading management thinkers in the UK, this book addresses a number of common themes relating to the influences and arguments of perhaps the first political scientist and advocate of sound management and marketing principles. Topics covered include:

- modern management
- governance and ethics
- post-modernism
- marketing
- political communication and spin doctoring
- rhetoric and dichotomy of Machiavelli

Machiavelli, Marketing and Management will be of great interest to all students and scholars of management, marketing and political science.

Phil Harris is co-director of the Centre for Corporate and Public Affairs, Manchester Metropolitan University, and Chairman of the Academy of Marketing. **Andrew Lock** is Pro-Vice Chancellor and Dean of the Faculty of Management and Business, Manchester Metropolitan University. **Patricia Rees** is Senior Lecturer in Management, Manchester Metropolitan University.

Machiavelli, Marketing and Management

Edited by Phil Harris,
Andrew Lock and Patricia Rees

London and New York

First published 2000
by Routledge
11 New Fetter Lane, London EC4P 4EE

Simultaneously published in the USA and Canada
by Routledge
29 West 35th Street, New York, NY 10001

Routledge is an imprint of the Taylor & Francis Group

Typeset in Galliard by Taylor & Francis Books Ltd
Printed and bound in Great Britain by
TJ International Ltd, Padstow, Cornwall

British Library Cataloguing in Publication Data
A catalogue record for this book is available from the British Library

Library of Congress Cataloging in Publication Data
Machiavelli, marketing and management / edited by Phil Harris, Andrew
Lock, and Patricia Rees.
p. cm.
Includes bibliographical references and index.
1. Management. 2. Marketing. 3. Machiavelli, Niccolo, 1469–1527. I.
Harris, Phil. II. Lock, Andrew. II. Rees, Patricia.
HD31 .M28133 2000
658–dc21
                                                          00-021043

ISBN 0-415-21669-9 (hbk)
ISBN 0-415-21670-2 (pbk)

The book is dedicated to Irene, Monty and Sally.

Contents

AS FAR AS THE ACT GOES, THAT IT MAY BE
A SIN, IS A FABLE, AS WHAT SINS IS THE
WILL, NOT THE BODY.

MANDRAGOLA, 3.11M4.89[1]

Foreword

Beatrice Rangoni Machiavelli

As Machiavelli wrote in a famous letter to Francesco Vettori describing his solitary days of exile:

> ... Evening has fallen, I return home and enter my study; and ... so decorously clad I enter into the ancient courts of ancient men; where received amorously by them, I nourish myself of that food that is only mine and for which I was born; where I shame not to speak with them and ask them the reason for their actions.
>
> (Machiavelli 1961: Introduction)

Machiavelli turned to the great figures of the past to find answers to the problems of his day. Five hundred years later a group of university professors, historians and experts in social, economic and human sciences joined together in an international seminar organized by the Manchester Metropolitan University to discuss whether the author of *Il Principe* still had relevant answers to the many problems of our society. His masterpiece *Il Principe* is such a tour de force that his ideas have found applications beyond the political sphere, today as well as yesterday, in very different sectors of social and economic life, such as management and marketing. Against the contemporary view that history was governed by God and fate, Machiavelli affirmed *homo faber*'s free will to determine his own destiny, capable of matching his behaviour to the necessities of his times.

We must remember that Machiavelli's masterpiece was in reality a job application addressed to a contemporary prince that, however, never attained the desired results. On the other hand, the author was far too intelligent not to realize that success is not the same as reading a book about success. Since the criteria and yardsticks of its interpretation vary from person to person, one man's success could well represent another man's failure. It is not always easy to establish what personal success is: quite often a millionaire can be just as dissatisfied as a poor person.

The interest and passion Machiavelli dedicated to politics can be applied to the management of the complex world of business, where we can find all the elements of failure and success, courage and cowardice, not to mention the treachery, conspiracy and strategies that are described in *Il Principe*.

Some advice offered by Machiavelli to his Prince bears a striking resemblance to today's laws of marketing and advertising. He recommends fair and honest trading, because this is the key to success. Today's market economy is in fact based on the trust of the consumers and the stakeholders. Experience teaches us, however, that 'princes heedless of trust' often prevail, affirming that they can be fought in two ways: through the force of the law or by using force. The Prince must be ready to use both: he must know how to be a 'fox' (cunning, to detect snares) or a 'lion' (to scare away the wolves). Should he be forced to go back on his word for the sake of political advantage, he must clothe the breach with good reasons. Even simulation is in fact a princely quality, since men pay much attention to appearances.

In management, it is apparent that interpersonal skills and leadership are important to build a career, but in reality there are many other aptitudes scarcely taken into account in university teaching, since they seem too unconventional and unethical, exactly as Machiavelli's theories must have appeared to his contemporaries. He was also the first to develop theories of perception and communication where, in *Il Principe*, he distinguished between direct personal experience of reality and indirect secondhand experience, affirming that men, being generally disbelieving, do not trust novelties unless they have tried them through personal experience.

Machiavelli cannot be considered a champion of the free market, and yet it is true that he condemned those who 'idly live from the revenue of their possessions in abundance, with never a thought to tilling land or other necessary wearying tasks of living. These are pernicious fellows in every republic and in every province; but even more pernicious are those who, besides the aforesaid riches, rule the castle, and have subjects who obey them.' There are many of these two species of men, and where they are numerous 'never has a republic arisen nor any sort of political life; because such generations of men are totally hostile to any form of civilization' (Machiavelli 1971: Book 1, ch. 55.2). In matters of commerce and trade Machiavelli always advised allegiance to the law to restrain the mighty from manipulations contrary to the interest of share-holders and small investors.

To him, every decision in the lives of individuals, commerce or government was a political choice, the result of the evaluation of priorities and principles that govern our behaviour. The dynamics of modern politics, swaying within a context of competition and consent, find their intellectual foundation in the works of the Florentine Secretary.

Machiavelli never argued that the ends justified any means to achieve them, a sentiment arbitrarily attributed to him by his enemies. On the contrary, Machiavelli's political ideas identify the ruler (the Prince) as the means for reaching an end that was beyond his own grasp: the establishment of social order, which he considered to be an absolute necessity. He believed that a ruler should be loved and should govern by the consent of the people, but if he could not otherwise achieve this, then he would better be feared and respected.

Machiavelli was in many ways a modern thinker trying to theorize about human affairs, so it is little wonder that his work remains so fresh today, since the actors of the human comedy are always the same. Machiavelli was amused by mankind and by its perennial agitation, prompted by a variety of passions, never realizing how ridiculous that agitation can sometimes be. However, he felt neither detached nor superior but part of the human comedy. This is why he could laugh at himself, at his mirth and his tears.

Machiavelli died on 21 June 1527 at the age of 58. It is said that, while hearing his last confession, Friar Matteo exhorted him to condemn the devil and his pomp. He answered, 'Do you think this is the right moment to make enemies?' His wit, the key to his wisdom, never abandoned him, not even in the most difficult of moments. His sense of humour was a way not only to defend himself from life, but also to live it in the love of liberty and civil equality that was his true strength. In fact, he believed that only among free and equal men and women is it possible to smile upon human events with a profound and sincere sense of understanding.

Notes

1 Cited in De Grazia, S. (1989) *Machiavelli in Hell*, Princeton, NJ: Princeton University Press, p. 293.

References

Machiavelli, N. (1961) *The Prince*, trans. G. Bull, Harmondsworth: Penguin.
—— (1971) 'Discorsi sopra la Prima Deca di Tito Livio', in *Niccolò Machiavelli: Tutte le opere*, Firenze: M. Martelli. (Extract translated by author.)

1
Introduction

I THINK THAT THIS WOULD BE THE TRUE
WAY TO GO TO PARADISE: TO LEARN THE
WAY TO HELL IN ORDER TO FLEE IT.

LETTER TO GUICCIARDINI,
3 JANUARY 1526[1]

1 Introduction

This book resulted from the *Machiavelli at 500* conference held in Manchester in May 1998, which marked the 500th anniversary of Machiavelli becoming the Second Secretary in the Florentine Republic after the downfall of Savonarola. The conference was held in the evocative surroundings of the fifteenth-century Hall of Chetham's School. In the same building is the library founded by Humphrey Chetham with its chained books and the desk where Marx worked during his visits to Manchester to see Engels.

Why hold a seminar about an individual who, it was claimed in the seventeenth century, was the wickedest man who ever lived? The early idea came from our own interest in Machiavelli's ideas in relation to corporate lobbying and political marketing (Harris and Lock 1996; Lock and Harris 1996) and was stimulated by discussions at the Academy of Marketing conference which was held in Manchester in 1997. This gave birth to the concept of a quincentennial seminar to mark his emergence on the public stage as Second Secretary in Florence at the age of 29. Manchester, with its long tradition of radical politics, seemed a very suitable venue for the seminar. But where – in what is, architecturally, largely a nineteenth- and twentieth-century city – would be appropriate? Should we really have looked for a postmodern setting for such an event? Those who know his works would say he probably would have enjoyed that. Chetham's School, founded in 1653 and now a leading specialist music school, provided the ideal setting. We are very grateful to the headmaster, the Reverend Peter Hullah, for allowing us to use the Hall and to him and his staff for their excellent hospitality.

We were amazed and delighted by the widespread enthusiasm that was expressed for the concept of the seminar and the wealth of ideas and suggestions we received. Having started to ask for contributions, a letter arrived from Lord William Wallace of the London School of Economics suggesting that we contact the Contessa Beatrice Rangoni Machiavelli to see whether the family would like to participate. The Contessa Beatrice, her brother the Marchese Ludovico and his wife the Marchesa Avril Rangoni Machiavelli all agreed to attend the seminar – we were going to have 'three Machiavelli in Manchester'. We were surprised to learn subsequently that, despite Machiavelli's fame or notoriety, this would be the only event to mark this quincentenary, and that his fame is rarely celebrated in the land of his birth.

The enthusiastic response we received from the Rangoni Machiavelli family was matched by everyone we approached. The event received significant coverage in national newspapers in Britain, which is quite remarkable for a Renaissance writer, showing the modernity of Machiavelli's thinking and its continued relevance to politics and social life. Direct comparisons were drawn with the skills of Peter Mandelson, the then Secretary of State for Trade and Industry, who is widely credited with having masterminded the image transformation of the Labour Party ('New Labour'), laying the foundations for their 1997 General Election Victory. Peter had politely declined our invitation to attend. Media coverage culminated in the Contessa Beatrice Rangoni Machiavelli and Phil Harris being interviewed on the prime-time morning news programme *Today* on BBC Radio 4.

In many ways, we can describe Machiavelli as an early modern thinker. The fact that he is widely read today and remains highly readable sets him aside from his contemporaries. At this period Italian philosophers could still be classified as Aristotelians or Platonists, and science, or natural philosophy, had not emerged from the 'natural magic' phase. Indeed, Paracelsus, the alchemist, was a contemporary. Outside the fields of art and architecture, only Copernicus, amongst Machiavelli's contemporaries, can be said to have surpassed his influence across the centuries. Machiavelli is a shrewd observer, almost an empiricist, of politics and history, exhibiting a pragmatism which particularly endears him to Anglo-Saxon readers.

However, Machiavellianism as a description of individual conduct has acquired a life of its own, independent of Machiavelli's own thought. The term machiavellian has become a recognized word in English with a very distinct meaning. Measures of machiavellianism have been developed by psychologists and these have been tested across professions and across cultures. It is worth contrasting the concept as developed with George Bull's comment (see chapter 3) that 'for Machiavelli the act of governing is in itself a profoundly moral matter'.

The seminar itself proved a most fascinating and stimulating event. The diversity of backgrounds of the speakers and the audience gave it a multi-disciplinary character, which gave everyone new insights into Machiavelli, his work and its subsequent influence. Student actors read out excerpts from his works to set the scene for each session. Over two days we ranged across time, space, culture and history. Politicians met with academics, artists, business people and diplomats. The wide range of ages gave both old and young much upon which to reflect. Its very eclecticism produced a very special atmosphere and its own resonance. Amongst the many vivid memories is the wonderful debate between Alistair McAlpine and Gordon Heald about the reasons for the Conservatives' electoral debacle in 1997. We had a very stimulating after-dinner speech from Gerald Kaufman, whose book *How to be a Minister* was based on his own observations and experiences as a Minister and Member of Parliament.

Those attending felt that the ideas should be further developed into a book, which built on the event and focused on the influence of Machiavelli's writings on marketing and management. This book is the result. The original event had more contributions and ideas than could possibly be included in this work. We know that there is a great deal of potential for future symposia of this kind. At the time of writing it is planned to hold a further seminar on Machiavelli's own estate at Bibbione, near Florence, in May 2000.

The book is organized in parts based on a number of common themes that emerged from our initial discourse in memory of one of the founders of modern political thought. These are:

Part 1: Introduction

Part 1 contains three papers on Machiavelli's life and times. They show the variety and vitality of the man and his work. The first piece by Phil Harris, Andrew Lock and Patricia Rees provides the historical background to Machiavelli and his thought. It presents facts and leaves the reader to decide whether the myths are well-founded. Machiavelli lived in a remarkable age in which intellectual enquiry flourished. It would not have been thought odd that one individual who was a diplomat, playwright and poet should write, as he did, about politics, ethics, history, psychology, metaphysics, logic, military science, geography, statecraft, generalship, religion and philosophy. Like many Renaissance figures, his learning was very wide-ranging, though, as Beatrice Rangoni Machiavelli observes, he was not able to read Greek.

The myths surrounding Machiavelli began in the sixteenth century and continue to this day. What comes across from his works, however, is an image of a fervent patriot who is ultimately optimistic about the human condition, despite being trenchantly realistic about human frailties. Modern notions of principal and agent theory and the concept of moral hazard are modern versions of some of the ideas in *The Prince*.

George Bull, the eminent translator of Italian classics and also Japanese works, introduces the reader to Machiavelli's contemporaries and the contemporary influences and debates which would have affected him. He argues that Machiavelli has always attracted interest because *The Prince* is a guide to action. However, what rulers mostly did (and possibly still do) was to go to Machiavelli, or at least to quote from him, to find justification rather than inspiration for their action. He suggests that the same is probably true for the leaders of great modern business corporations.

Beatrice Rangoni Machiavelli traces the history of the family name and argues that Niccolò Machiavelli would have said 'never was I Machiavellian'. She also emphasizes that the Italian historical and political tradition is very different from the northern European one with which we are most familiar. It drew its inspiration from the republican models of Classical Rome rather than concepts of hereditary monarchy. He was a believer in his country and good government and, as he was later dubbed, a 'master of republican liberty'. She denies that he believed that the end justifies the means, or perhaps rather that any means are justified by particular ends.

Part 2: Marketing

The key to Machiavelli's popularity over time is his clarity of expression. The more we read Machiavelli the more we are left with a clearly stated vision of reality which is timeless – a sense of someone seeking to understand and to consider what is happening in times of turbulence. Five hundred years later his name is usually remembered for the wrong reasons. Machiavellianism has entered the language as a term to describe political cunning and duplicitous fixing. Sight is lost of the great political commentator and analyst of power politics. His observations also have relevance in the market place. Machiavelli was an acute observer of people and part 2 offers some analyses of the implications of Machiavelli's views for brands – truth, loyalty, stakeholders and 'spin'.

Marketing as a discipline emerged in the second half of the twentieth century in an increasingly complex world with consumers being presented with a growing range of choices. Thus the papers in part 2 reflect the desire to make sense of this. In the first piece, Richard Elliott explores the interpretations of reality in his article 'Contra postmodernism: Machiavelli on limits to the malleability of consciousness'. Elliott argues that Machiavelli was one of the first analysts of the realities of life rather than just reflecting authority and received wisdom. Lived experience is a continual immersion in events and actions along a path in time – the temporal reality of marketing in modern post-industrial society. Mediated experience, on the other hand, is an outcome of mass communication. We are introduced to the debate about the nature of marketing in a postmodern world. A Machiavellian model of consciousness is proposed to explore self-symbolism and social-symbolism as one possible answer. In Elliott's view, Machiavelli was the first communication theorist to identify lived experience as countervailing mediated experience.

Michael Thomas, in his article 'Niccolò Machiavelli as relationship marketing guru', argues the necessity for effective marketers to address the needs and concerns of stakeholders in society. He posits that one has to understand civil society to build long term relationships and therefore effective relationship marketing. He proposes that marketing thought is shifting from an emphasis on transactions and customer acquisition to relationships and retention. He argues in Miltonic terms for 'paradise regained' which reflects social justice, democratic renewal, community regeneration, a social market and equitable rewards for stakeholders globally. This vision is of a postmodern, post-marketing, post-consumerist society. The only future is to stimulate loyalty, win it, inculcate it and cultivate it – what marketing is all about.

Dominic Wring in his article outlines the recent emergence of the 'spin doctor'. He recounts the rise of Peter Mandelson and his grandfather Herbert Morrison within the Labour Party and that particular organization's usual contempt for the media, showing that Morrison was an exception in his enthusiasm for the effective use of publicity. He argues that Machiavelli would have understood both men and the way they have aroused the hostility of powerful rivals but retained the ear of the leader (or Prince). Marketing is at the heart of modern politics and its rejuvenation. Marketing is, however, more than 'spin'. Amongst other things, it can foster better communication between government and citizen or promote new leaders and ideas. Something Machiavelli five hundred years ago understood well, though he would not necessarily have recognized the term 'marketing'.

Part 3: Management

Machiavelli was a man who believed in action – getting things done – and thus his ideas lend themselves well as analogies in management. *The Prince* has become an alternative handbook for the modern manager. It was surprising to discover in our research how many management figures claim to have a copy of *The Prince* readily to hand. They are happy to admit this, while politicians may be more reticent. Part 3 deals with determination to succeed, the awareness of the reality of dark and light management skills and the virtues of good corporate governance.

The idea of the clear and consistent management of power is the essence of Machiavelli; to prevaricate or to vacillate wastes resources and leads to decline or oblivion. Boldness is to be encouraged. Supporters should be promoted, provided they have been picked for the right reasons. Those who remain neutral in tough situations should be seen as enemies for they do not support your cause and are therefore against you.

Lord Alistair McAlpine, the former Conservative Party Treasurer, international businessman and collector, argues in 'Renaissance realpolitik for modern management' that Machiavelli's approach to politics is as painstaking as that of his artistic contemporaries. *The Prince* is relevant to both business and politics (a point which is contested in part 4 by Terry Berrow). It highlights the importance of understanding human nature. Machiavelli understood the capacity for evil in humans. He studied those around him and then used the examples from the ancients to justify his conclusions.

Lord McAlpine has written two books concerning Machiavelli – *The Servant* (1992) and *The New Machiavelli – Renaissance Realpolitik for Modern Managers* (1997). He takes us through the latter. He notes a striking similarity between fifteenth-century Italy and the great corporations of the late twentieth century and points out the importance of circumstance and luck (using the 'luck as a woman' quotation from *The Prince*). He states that there is a need to organize people in business by providing leadership and puts forward the principles of leadership – loyalty, trust, fairness, ability and respect. Lord McAlpine expresses his disgust at the way in which Margaret Thatcher was treated, when she was ousted as Prime Minister.

McAlpine sees success as a state of mind and exhorts us not to fear failure, because we can learn from it. He advocates attack on the Establishment – whatever its form. The use of consultants also comes under attack (cf. Machiavelli's view of mercenaries). Success comes from the determination to succeed, not the determination to avoid failure.

'From the dark to the light: ranges of the real skills of management' by Brian Stone and Jayne Pashley is in the form of a dialogue between a business teacher and his former student who is now working with the realities of working life. This chapter echoes a point made by Beatrice Rangoni Machiavelli in the Foreword – that there are many attitudes not taken into account in university teaching. It also continues the theme of reality in business life from the preceding chapter. The dark skills of management are discussed – skills not usually explicitly considered in management and business courses in business schools. The authors suggest, tongue in cheek, that perhaps universities should teach 'Advanced Gender Manipulation' or 'Lying Part III'. More seriously they produce a taxonomy of management skills displaying the dark and the light sides. These skills are: truth handling; self-defence; self-promotion (in which the 'luck as a woman' quotation appears again); gender handling; the skill of 'bull'; networks; and politics. *The Prince* is drawn upon to guide the contents of the taxonomy. The idea is that students should be taught the light skills but be made aware of the dark skills. In this way they will be better prepared for the 'real world', whether it is business or any other.

In the light of the recent UK corporate governance review, Ken Simmonds, in his piece 'Corporate governance – real power, Cecil King and Machiavelli', puts forward the pros and cons of various ways of 'disposing' of underachieving directors. Simmonds is a professor at the London Business School and has held a number of major board positions. He argues against the use of 'Cecil King clauses' where the board of directors can remove a director. Instead, invoking Machiavelli and his regard for the rule of law, he comes to the conclusion (with some reservations) that fixed-term contracts for directors are the solution to the problem of underachieving directors.

Part 4: Political management

Power is at the heart of Machiavelli's thoughts, whether it be gaining it and keeping it in *The Prince*, its use in *The Discourses* or its impact in *The Art of War*. His letters are scattered with references to his desire, after falling from office, to come back and to serve his people, to return to government and to engage in politics which he saw as his métier. Machiavelli, after the return of the Medici, never regained his position either as political adviser or as senior Florentine official. However, that gave him the time to write, which has gained him more influence than he would have ever considered possible.

In part 4 a number of themes are explored – language, rhetoric and Machiavellian tactics in politics and of course the nature of 'humble servants' today. The historian Terry Berrow, in his piece 'Machiavelli, politics and modern language use in modern management' reminds us that Machiavelli wrote more than just *The Prince*. He argues that a business is not like a state. When Machiavelli talks of killing enemies he means it – it is not a metaphor. He further observes how eminently quotable Machiavelli is, rather like the modern day 'sound bites', and wonders if Machiavelli is popular amongst business writers because he gives credibility to a young discipline with his long pedigree. He contends that Machiavelli has great relevance to politics but not to management. Berrow exhorts people actually to read Machiavelli, rather than just quoting randomly from his work, making up something that Niccolò would not himself recognize as his thought.

Maureen Ramsay, who is a political theorist and lecturer in politics, observes in her article 'Are Machiavellian tactics still appropriate or defensible in politics?' that individuals and groups use a variety of arguments to justify immoral means in politics. She does not accept Machiavelli's version of the distinction between private and public morality and has problems in understanding Machiavellian tactics – especially the difference between just ends and just means. Ramsay argues from a feminist perspective with a concern about the democratic issues surrounding management. She, like Berrow, believes that businesses are not like states. This appears to be a common view amongst political scientists and historians which is not necessarily shared by business people or marketers.

The final piece in part 4 is by Kevin Moloney who lectures and writes on communications, especially political communication. In his piece 'Nicco and Charlie: a story of two political servants and of political management' he argues that Machiavelli would not have approved of 'spin doctors' but that he would have recognized some similarities with his own age. He then reviews modern 'spin doctoring' and argues that 'spin doctoring' is a sub-set of political marketing. He sees an important relationship between spin doctors and journalists and believes that it is good news for democracy that spin doctors' careers usually end in tears.

Part 5: Machiavellian management thought in modern times

The papers in part 5 consider some latter-day comparisons and parallels with Machiavelli and his thought. Even today the popular image of Machiavelli is in sharp contrast with the reality of the Florentine patriot. Despite his works being banned for over three hundred years by the Catholic Church, his ideas never ceased to be influential. Their consequent notoriety may even have fanned their resonance across the generations.

John Parkin suggests in 'Machiavelli and Powell: maximizing prophets' that both men were interested in ancient literature. Powell was a Greek scholar (but – as Beatrice Rangoni Machiavelli points out – Machiavelli was not, although he had very good access to Petrarch and the Latin classics). Comparisons are drawn between Powell and Machiavelli, such as their writing style. Each developed a highly epigrammatic style which made them eminently quotable, then and now. Both saw fortune as a woman. Parkin argues that neither Powell nor Machiavelli was a 'spin doctor' in the sense used by Wring or Moloney and that both used dichotomous arguments to make a point. Interestingly, both men were marginalized for the latter part of their lives.

'Butchers, bunglers and Machiavelli' by the High Master of Manchester Grammar School, Martin Stephen, compares the views of Machiavelli and the career of First World War general Field Marshal Earl Haig. Machiavelli was involved in planning for the defence of the Florentine Republic and argued for a regular militia to be set up, rather than for the use of less reliable mercenaries – thus allowing civic duties to include defending one's state. Haig, as the First World War progressed, relied more and more heavily on conscripts and the common man to win it – a 'Machiavellian' army. Neither man regarded technological developments in warfare as important; Machiavelli dismissed the power of artillery whilst Haig did not see a threat from a machine gun against a well-prepared cavalryman. Machiavelli and Haig lived in worlds where politics and soldiering were inseparable, and both were capable managers of politics and resources. They have both suffered from unfair myths comparing them to the devil or a bloodsucker. Populations as a whole, and politicians in particular, are quite willing to accept war when it appears not to require anyone's death or any sacrifice.

In the final piece in part 5, Robert Gutfreund in 'Machiavelli and human nature' argues for the preference amongst humans for fantasy. He sees three main reasons for the relevance of Machiavelli today. First, Machiavelli's concept of human nature retains an ongoing significance for contemporary thought. Second, his concept of and belief in the unchanging character of human nature is shared with the scientific and philosophical traditions of Hobbes and Freud. Third, the intrinsic disposition of human nature is a key foundation stone for individual liberty. Gutfreund contends that Machiavelli confirms our experiences that not everyone around us is predisposed to be good or virtuous at all times. We need, therefore, to learn how not to be good when the occasion demands otherwise – how to do so without the damaging feelings of guilt that often accompany 'unkind' acts.

At the end of the book is an 'End piece' by Phil Harris, dedicating the seminar and book to Niccolò Machiavelli for his contributions to marketing, management and politics. It is in the style of Machiavelli's original dedication of *The Prince* to Lorenzo de Medici.

Acknowledgements

We wish to take this opportunity to express our warmest thanks to all those who participated in the *Machiavelli at 500* seminar. They are as follows:

The Contessa Beatrice Rangoni Machiavelli, President of the European Economic & Social Committee
Terry Berrow, Southampton Institute
Viv Bingham, past President of the Liberal Party
George Bull, Central Banking Publications
Patrick Curry, co-author of *Machiavelli for Beginners*
Jorge Velazquez Delgado, Mexico City University

Richard Elliott, Exeter University
Nick Ellis, Derby University
His Excellency Ambassador Paulo Galli, Italian Embassy, London
Hanne Gardner, Manchester Metropolitan University
Robert Gutfreund, Manchester Metropolitan University
Helen Harrison, University of Kent
Gordon Heald, Opinion Research Business
The Reverend Peter Hullah, Headmaster of Chetham's School of Music
Allan Baktoft Jakobsen, Delta Software Engineering, Denmark
Rt. Hon. Gerald Kaufman, Member of Parliament for Manchester Gorton
Gordon Lishman, Age Concern
Richard Lynch, Manchester Metropolitan University
Lord Alistair McAlpine
Rob McLoughlin, Granada Television and now Precise Communications
Kevin Moloney, Bournemouth University
Andrew Mousley, Bolton Institute
Paul Nichols, Dibb Lupton Alsop
John Parkin, Bristol University
Jayne Pashley, Manchester Metropolitan University
Maureen Ramsay, Leeds University
Tony Proctor, Keele University
Ken Simmonds, London Business School
Martin Stephen, High Master, Manchester Grammar School
Brian Stone, Manchester Metropolitan University
Michael Thomas, Strathclyde University
Ted Wilson, Manchester Metropolitan University
Dominic Wring, Loughborough University

We would also like to thank all those who helped in the organization of the event and made it such a success: Heather Standeven, Irene Harris, Barbara Cousins, Nillan Fakira, Mark Fernandes, Audrey Roberts, Kate Cleevley, Julia Banks, Carol Reed and Semi Da-Cocodia and the staff at the Princess Hotel and Restaurant Simply Heathcotes.

We would also like to thank Professor Morris Holbrook, of Columbia University, for his most helpful comments on the original manuscript of this book, and countless others for their support. Finally we would like to thank our editor Michelle Gallagher, the initiator of the book Stuart Hay, and Allison Bell and others for their assistance in the conception and production of this book. Their attention to detail, professionalism and understanding have been greatly appreciated.

Note

1   Cited in De Grazia, S. (1989) *Machiavelli in Hell*, Princeton, NJ: Princeton University Press, p. 360.

References

Harris, P. and Lock, A. R. (1996) 'Machiavellian Marketing: the Development of Corporate Lobbying in the UK', *Journal of Marketing Management* 12 (4): 313–28.

Lock, A. R. and Harris, P. (1996) 'Political Marketing: Vive La Différence', *European Journal of Marketing* 30 (10/11): 21–31.

McAlpine, A. (1992) *The Servant: A New Machiavelli*, London: Faber & Faber.

—— (1997) *The New Machiavelli: Renaissance Realpolitik for Modern Managers*, London: Aurum.

FORTUNA

HAVE YOU EVER SEEN IN ANY PLACE
HOW A FIERCE EAGLE ACTS
DRIVEN BY HUNGER AND FASTING?

AND HOW IT TAKES A TORTOISE UP SO HIGH
THAT THE BLOW OF FALLING SHATTERS IT
AND IT FEEDS ITSELF ON THAT DEAD FLESH?

SO FORTUNE, NOT SO THAT ONE MAY REMAIN THERE
TAKES ONE UP HIGH, BUT SO THAT DESTROYING [ONE]
SHE ENJOYS IT, AND ONE CRIES AS ONE FALLS

THE TREATISES, 4–317–18[1]

2 Machiavelli through the ages: 500 years on

Enlightenment or obfuscation?

Phil Harris, Andrew Lock and Patricia Rees

Machiavelli: the first 500 years

Act 1 – the Great Hall, Chetham's, Manchester, 1998

A lone figure enters the stage and welcomes those gathered and explains the meaning of the gathering. He sets the scene thus:

The Truth as far as we know it: Niccolò Machiavelli – 1469–1527

Niccolò Machiavelli was born in Florence in 1469 of a very old Tuscan family. His ancestors originated from Montespertoli, a small commune, situated between the Val da Elsa and the Val di Pesa, a short distance from Florence. The Machiavelli also possessed properties in the quarter of Santo Spirito, near Santa Felicita, and the Ponte Vecchio in Florence, where they had been long established, and were among the most notable of the *popolani* (Villari 1888). It has been suggested that his father was illegitimate (for example, Jensen 1960) which precluded Niccolò from being a candidate in electoral politics but did not debar him from public service.

The young Machiavelli had a vigorous humanist education, was taught Latin by good teachers and had access to much of the best of classical history and ideas. Little is known about the rest of his life until, at the surprisingly young age of 29 in 1498, he was recognized by the *Signory and Secretary* for his administrative talents, and was elected to the responsible post of Chancellor of the Second Chancery. He is also given duties in the Council of the Ten of Liberty and Peace (formerly Ten of War), which dealt with Florentine foreign affairs (Villari 1888, Jensen 1960, Skinner 1979 and 1981).

During the next 14 years, Machiavelli served the republic faithfully, not only carrying out his secretarial and administrative duties, but also serving as a diplomat and as personal advisor to Pietro Soderini, Gonfalonier of Florence from 1502 to 1512. Thus he was closely involved in the turbulence of Renaissance Italy and the development of the city state. He was a contemporary of Cellini, Da Vinci, Galileo, Michelangelo and Raphael.

During his time in office, his journeys included missions to Louis XII and to the Holy Roman Emperor Maximilian in Austria; he was with Cesare Borgia in the Romagna; and, after watching the Papal election of 1503, he accompanied the newly elected Pope, Julius II, on his first campaign of conquest against Perugia and Bologna. In 1507, as a Chancellor of the recently appointed Nove di Milizia, he organized an infantry force which fought at the capture of Pisa in 1509. Three years later this force was defeated by the Holy League at Prato and the Medici returned to power in Florence. Machiavelli was almost immediately excluded from public life as a previous holder of high office under the former republican regime, where he had built up a number of powerful enemies who were determined he should not retain his post.

After being falsely implicated in a plot against the Medici, he was imprisoned in the Bargello and hideously tortured. He maintained his innocence and was eventually granted an amnesty on the election of the new pope, Leo X (Cardinal dei Medici), and retired to his farm six miles away from Florence just outside San Casciano, where he lived with his wife and six children and concentrated on study and writing. For much of the rest of his life his movements were restricted by one regime or another because of his past. He desperately wanted to return to government service to serve Florence and his countrymen, 'If only to roll stones' (*Letter to Vettori*, 10 December 1513, in Machiavelli 1961: Introduction), but never regained public office. At 43, Machiavelli's public career had ended, but his work as a writer, for which he is celebrated, was just beginning.

He wrote *The Prince* in just a few months in 1513. In it he attacked 'the writers' whose inconsistent moralism allows them to admire great deeds but not the cruel acts necessary to accomplish them. This small book came to be seen as the most notorious and shocking piece of literature of the Italian Renaissance and gave birth to the well-known negative epithet Machiavellian, now commonly used in many languages. But before starting to write *The Prince*, Machiavelli began a lengthy political commentary on Roman history – the *Discourses on Livy*. This work was never fully completed, but throws the most complete light on the development of Machiavelli's political thought. It shows that he was basically a republican, who saw the state as a secular and autonomous structure relying for its survival upon human skills and mass support. Mansfield and Tarcov (1996: xx) argue that, in comparison with *The Prince*, the *Discourses* is 'a long, forbidding, apparently nostalgic, obviously difficult, but decent and useful book that advises citizens, leaders, reformers, and founders of republics on how to order them to preserve liberty and avoid corruption'.

Machiavelli also wrote *The Art of War* (Gilbert 1958), whose essential unity of statecraft and warfare appealed to later military thinkers such as Frederick the Great, Napoleon and von Clausewitz. Other works included a number of plays, the best known of which is the comedy, *Mandragola* (Bondanella and Musa 1979), a satire on seduction. Numerous other minor works of both prose and poetry were written by him including *The Marriage of the Arch-Devil Belphagor* and many short discourses and much poetry. In 1520, Cardinal Giulio de'Medici secured him a commission to write a history of Florence, which he finished in 1525. After a brief re-emergence into Florentine society, he died in 1527.

Not many people read Machiavelli's wider works, which is a pity as they give a more measured view of his political thinking and intellect. *The Prince* was never published during its author's lifetime and, although circulating quite widely in manuscript form, it seems to have caused little if any controversy during Machiavelli's life. In 1532, five years after Machiavelli's death, it was published in Rome. Subsequently Cardinal Reginald Pole in his *Apologia ad Carolum V. Caesarem* (1536) vigorously attacks *The Prince* as a product of the devil and warns against its use by unscrupulous rulers to undermine the *Respublica Christiana* (he may have had Henry VIII in mind, as he had fled England to avoid the Reformation and imprisonment). With this, the Machiavellian mythology is born. In 1559 all of Machiavelli's works are condemned and placed on the Papal Index.

His words are direct, never boring (for example, Gilbert 1958, Jensen 1960, Bull 1961, Skinner 1981, Wooton 1994) and still readable today. He is one of the first modern writers to use the powerful stylistic device of the 'either/or' choice. In *The Art of War*, in discussing how to organize the troops so they cannot do harm, he writes that they 'can do harm in two ways; either among themselves or against a city'. De Grazia (1989) argues 'Each of these two he then divides in two subcategories, from each of which he selects the more pertinent and divides that one further in two'.

Machiavelli in *The Prince* abandons the moral teachings of the classical and biblical traditions for a new conception of virtue as the willingness and ability to do whatever it needs to acquire and maintain what one has acquired. It is this continuing reputation and influence of *The Prince* which has resulted in the use of the Machiavellian theme by modern management commentators such as Jay (1964), Calhoon (1969), Shea (1988), Curry (1995) and McAlpine (1992 and 1997). His epigrammatic prose lends itself to the production of high quality aphorisms, which transcend time and place and have been frequently borrowed by the management writer or politician. Examples are:

All armed prophets conquered, all the unarmed perished.

Men should be either treated generously or destroyed because they take revenge for slight injuries – for heavy ones they cannot.

Everyone sees what you appear to be; few experience what you really are.

... he who seeks to be honest among many bad men procures his own destruction.

(after Machiavelli 1961)

... success or failure lies in conforming to the times.

(Machiavelli 1996)

Wars begin when you will, but they do not end when you please.

(Machiavelli 1958: vol. 3)

Old injuries are never suppressed by new benefits.

(Machiavelli 1996: 216)

So, to return to our point, irresolute republics never take up good policies unless by force, because their weakness never allows them to decide where there is any doubt; and if that doubt is not suppressed by violence that drives them on, they always remain in suspense.

(Machiavelli 1996: 83)

Many of his official letters and reports still exist and provide a useful source of insight into his political views (for example, Gilbert 1958, Jensen 1960, Skinner 1981, Wooton 1994).

Machiavelli: the plot

Act 2 – the dining room, Chetham's, Manchester

The Scene
   There is a smell of warm toast and coffee in the air. A constant rattle of cups and mumbling from assorted characters can be heard. Rain is teeming down the window panes just as it does onto Sante Croce's roof 1,000 miles or so away.
   Two staff are engaged in animated debate over coffee and biscuits (the power of the biscuit is mightier than the sword in academic circles). Both staff are wearing gowns, which seem to have a touch of Florence and the Renaissance about them. The plot unfolds.

PROFESSOR LUCRETIA BORGIA *(FOR IT IS SHE)* But why hold a quincentenary seminar for Machiavelli in Manchester?
DOCTOR WILLIAM EWART GLADSTONE *(FOR IT IS HE)* Why not?
BORGIA Come on. Tell me why should we hold a celebration of a thinnish, bookish, slight-looking Florentine in Manchester? Who died 480 years or so ago? Who was supposed to be the devil incarnate if not Beelzebub? He was anti-Christian. Proscribed by the Pope and always held up in history as the hero of some of the nastiest people I know. What's it got to do with us?
GLADSTONE Power!
BORGIA Power?
GLADSTONE Yes, Niccolò Machiavelli was one of the first writers of modern history who wrote about the use and abuse of power. He said that states and power were not dependent on God for fortune and prosperity. As a

republican and humanist he believed in a strong set of democratic values and limitations. He saw the state as a secular and autonomous structure, dependent on human skills and mass support for its survival. This is articulated in his core writings like *The Prince* and *Discourses on Titus Livy*, which say power is dependent on people and how they are ruled and is not given to other human beings and their princes as of right. Quite a modern view of the state!

BORGIA You mean respect has to be earned and doesn't just come with the job? Good grief, that's powerful stuff. When was it published?

GLADSTONE His best-known work *The Prince* only took a few months to cobble together, but the *Discourses* were written over a longer period. *The Prince* was not actually published until 1532, long after his death. *The Art of War* is a piece of action research carried out whilst on government service and his *History of Florence* is written towards the end of his life after he eventually receives a grant from the Medici. He also wrote prose, poetry and a number of well thought of plays.

BORGIA Gladstone, do you know everything?

GLADSTONE No, but I did have Professor Pasquale Villari's *Life and Times of Savonarola* dedicated to me in 1888 with the inscription 'Champion of Italian Freedom, Master of Italian Learning, Author and Translator',[2] which was in recognition of a little knowledge.

BORGIA Show-off. Doesn't count towards your four double blind refereed articles that the government wants to see to prove that you are benefiting the Treasury and mankind.

Borgia picks up from the floor a pile of papers which is made up of a vast array of journal articles which seem to say nothing and are difficult to understand. Borgia looks boringly into Gladstone's eyes.

GLADSTONE True – but a university is supposed to be about the preservation of knowledge, not just its manufacture and transmission, even though that is all we get paid for! Anyway there is still a lot of mileage in Machiavelli's ideas for new papers in marketing and management. And mention of his name seems to make people take an interest.

BORGIA Are you plugging your dedication in the book again? I have told you before about 'false prophets'.

GLADSTONE Good use of Machiavelli there. It's from *The Prince*.

BORGIA What! He wrote about 'false prophets'?

GLADSTONE Yes. Machiavelli raised fundamental issues that every society has to address. Do its leaders know what they are doing? Will the state treat its citizens fairly? How can one build and develop a successful society that will sustain its citizens? How can one maintain freedoms and guarantee peace and security? He also was a great Italian nationalist, who could not understand why foreign powers kept playing various Italian states off against one another. He saw unity as the only answer.

BORGIA Good gracious, he was pretty far-reaching for a sixteenth-century Florentine. He is beginning to sound like a mixture of Bill Clinton, New Labour and Boris Yeltsin with a dash of Berlusconi and Murdoch for good measure.

GLADSTONE No, you don't understand, he bore no relation to them. No, he didn't even look like them. Villari (1888: 245) says he was 'of middle height, slender figure, with sparkling eyes, dark hair, rather a small head, a slightly aquiline nose, a tightly closed mouth: all about him bore the impress of a very acute observer and thinker, but not that of one able to wield much influence over others'.

He was if anything a practical government servant, who believed that a state could be run for the benefit of its people. All you had to do was organize things accordingly. The Renaissance in Italy was a pretty turbulent time for politics, however. He occasionally got it wrong. Apparently he once failed to organize a march of militia on a parade ground.

BORGIA So he observed what made things work and happen. In other words 'Don't rely on God then and good Fortune'.

GLADSTONE Quite so. He suggested that a strong state could emerge through organization and education and that belief in rituals and divine providence was not the best way of achieving goals and ends. He would have probably been quite keen on Samuel Smiles' ideas of self-help.

BORGIA So he wasn't a traditionalist or logical positivist then. He had a richer and more developed epistemological thought process which was empirically grounded positivism based upon a phenomenological paradigm shift. The actualization of which was the symbolic discourse using a contextual process to develop a typology of constructs to outline the use and abuse of power for civic society.

GLADSTONE Yes and he also wrote very clearly, which is why his ideas have weathered the test of time. He observed, analysed and then reported his findings and observations in a way in which they could be understood, applied and used. He was almost the patron saint of aphorisms and applied logic. That is the reason why his works are so often used by management and marketing academics.

BORGIA Surely you are not suggesting management and marketing staff are simple and inarticulate and that some disciplines use long words when short ones will do?

Now look here, hermeneutic circle observation is a well known, hypothetical, inductive, multivariate nomothetic a posteriori process. It could not be simpler really. It shows the use of a randomly operationalized triangulation theory which is dependent upon a grounded approach founded upon a post-Marxist fundamentalist refractive (data emic) which has contributed to an a priori event.

GLADSTONE Well. If you say so.

BORGIA Well if you want it simple and straight between the eyes. Why commemorate Machiavelli in Manchester?

GLADSTONE Well – Manchester was one of the first great industrial cities. Many argue that it was where the industrial revolution began. Its great wealth was founded on textiles much as Florence's was linked to the cloth industry.

It sucked in vast numbers of people from the countryside to be employed in its factories, much like Florence, where some early mass production techniques were developed.

It is cosmopolitan like Florence. It is a university city.

BORGIA (*interrupts*) Do I detect the use of the political three couplet meta technique in your argument, Gladstone! Look, I am not a politician, I am a simple ontological academic with scatological leanings, so don't be pompous with me, sunbeam!

GLADSTONE Oh really. You see, Manchester was at the forefront of the development of radical reform, popular democracy, where Cobden led the Anti-Corn Law League, championed the end of slavery and the abolition of the old corrupt form of placement in local government. It is where Bright advocated individual liberty and free trade. Economic and social liberalism went hand in hand. Engels was a business man and wrote 'The Conditions of the Working Class' here. Where, in Humphrey Chetham's Library, Marx regularly met Engels to plot revolution and pay him his grant.

The established order was based in Liverpool and tried to stifle Manchester's growth by curtailing access to the sea much as Florence's freedoms were neutered by powers controlling Pisa and access via the Arno to the sea or demands from warring states for protection money. Manchester stood as a parliamentary bastion in the north of England in the English Civil War surrounded by royalist areas. This is similar to Florence, its position in Tuscany and its contribution to the development of modern Italy.

There is a rebirth, a renewal going on in Manchester at the moment – almost, one could say, a renaissance. What more fitting place to celebrate Machiavelli and his elegant, humanist works than Manchester.

BORGIA Oh all right – I give up. There is good reason to reflect on Machiavelli's contribution to mankind in Manchester. But why now and 1498?

GLADSTONE Well one could celebrate the birth or death of the great writer and thinker. But the key date writers pick upon is Niccolò Machiavelli's emergence on the centre stage of Florentine life in May 1498, with the fall of Savonarola (Villari 1888). From then on Machiavelli observed the real world of politics as a participant, began to develop his ideas which emerge later as his intellectual heritage to the world.

BORGIA Gosh. A seminal event, Gladstone.

GLADSTONE Well, a seminar anyway.

BORGIA But come on, you haven't told me why Machiavelli has any connection with management or even marketing. I can see the research implications for politics, philosophy and the arts. But on management and marketing? Surely trying to measure the exchange process has nothing to do with Machiavelli's teachings. With managing businesses it must have the most tenuous of links?

Gladstone, hang up your axe. It's not as sharp as it used to be.

GLADSTONE Oh dear. You are beginning to sound like Father Loyola and some of the Spanish Jesuits who ensured Machiavelli got a bad press. You are being a bit traditionalist in propagating the perceived myth and wisdom that Machiavelli was not OK on politics, although a little anti-establishment – but with little relevance today.

There is a long history of borrowing from Machiavelli's core works and ideas and applying them to the management of science and its application in everyday life. Jay (1964) used Machiavelli to explore how to manage and survive in the corporate world. And the idea of *The Prince* has often been used as a metaphorical tool to parallel situations and roles in modern management. In marketing, the exploration of power in buying and selling behaviour is essential to the understanding of purchasing decisions. The interaction approach, relationship and services marketing have all borrowed basic concepts from Machiavelli and applied them in more modern times. The use of straightforward language to communicate complex ideas is deemed paramount. Picking the right message and the use of political marketing techniques to get over policy ideas and to communicate with the electorate have some of their early ideas in Machiavelli. Segmenting the market and understanding what people desire is the modern paramount praxis of marketing. *The Prince* and *The Art of War* are full of this type of fundamental consumer research and its application. Machiavelli used the case study method throughout his teachings, outlining cases based on the lives of Borgia, Savonarola, Medici, etc. which draw out distinct management issues and their implications. Fisher *et al.* (1994) even used him to outline effective negotiation strategy.

Machiavelli argued how to manage people and to build effective teams to achieve ends. His ideas are of particular relevance in understanding the internal processes in the higher echelons of major corporations. Christie and Geis (1970) even developed a scale to measure the personal beliefs of leaders who control the behaviour of others through manipulative means which seemed to coincide with *The Prince* and *The Discourses*. They observed that many leaders have the following characteristics: a relative lack of concern with conventional morality, a lack of gross psychopathology, a lack of ideological commitment. Hunt and Chonko (1984) even carried out a research project on marketing staff in American organizations using this scale to find out whether they were more manipulative and unethical than other members of society.

BORGIA Great, what did they find out?

GLADSTONE Not a lot really. Just that there are as many manipulative and unethical marketing people as there are amongst other realms of society.

Those at the top end of any group seem to have developed more manipulative and unethical skills than the others and this was reflected across all professions and groups in society. To get to the top there was a tendency for one to be – dare I suggest it – more Machiavellian than others. It was interesting stuff but I think distracts us from the reality of what Niccolò Machiavelli had to say.

For Machiavelli was a practical philosopher, who recommended actions and attempted to suggest ways in which mankind could improve society.

He therefore lends himself through his managerial approach and practical reality to being one of the first true marketers. A marketer of ideas that have lasted 500 years.

BORGIA Oh all right, you can have your seminar. I'll have another coffee. Now about that quality assessment exercise, have you got those 4,251 forms I put in your pigeon hole the other day? Simplicity is the answer.

Borgia marches off and leaves Gladstone reflecting. Gladstone picks up The Times *'Higher' of 20 March 1998 and starts reading Laurie Taylor's column:*

The explosion in the number of journals coupled with unpredictable price rises has created a Journals crisis (*THES* March 1998).

This week's new journals
GREED, EASIMONEY AND KLAWBACK proudly announce four new academic journals designed to meet the needs of those who wish to keep up to date in newly emerging areas of knowledge or simply cannot find anywhere else to publish their articles.

He looks up and thinks of Professor Lucretia Borgia who would not understand the meaning of Laurie Taylor, likewise Gentillet, De Rivadeneira, Clemente and others who damned Machiavelli and did not understand honesty. He remembers a quotation from The Prince: *'men are so simple, and so much creatures of circumstance, that the deceiver will always find someone ready to be deceived' (Machiavelli 1961).*

The key dates and events associated with Niccolò Machiavelli's life:

1469	3 May, born in Florence the son of a poor lawyer, who went to some trouble to ensure his son was given the best education available. He was introduced to the writings of Petrarch, Boccaccio, Bracciolini and benefited from the availability of non-secular writings and texts.
1494	The Medici were expelled from Florence. Machiavelli appointed clerk to Marcello Virgilio Adriani in the Second Chancery.

1498	February, Adriani nominated Secretary of the Republic. May, Girolamo Savonarola and two supporters hanged and burnt to death in Piazza della Signoria (ironically the location of his original Bonfire of Vanities). Machiavelli succeeded Adriani as Second Chancellor and Secretary.
1500	Sent to France where he met with Louis XII and the Cardinal of Rouen.
1502	Married Marietta Corsini. Sent to Romagna as envoy to Cesare Borgia where he witnessed the events leading up to the death of Borgia. Machiavelli's political philosophy was highly influenced by his study of Cesare Borgia.
1503	January, returned to Florence.
1504	Second mission to France.
1505/6	Accompanied Pope Julius II on his first campaign of conquest.
1506	December, submitted a plan to reorganize the military to Pierre Soderini, Florence's Gonfalonier, and it was accepted.
1507	As Chancellor of the newly appointed Nove di Milizia, he organized an infantry force which fought at the capture of Pisa in 1509.
1508	Mission to the court of the Emperor Maximilian at Bolzano, then in Austria.
1511	Third and last mission to France.
1512	The Medici, after the Victory of the Holy Roman League at Prato, returned with the support of a Spanish army. Florence deposed Soderini and welcomed the Medici. Machiavelli after a few days was dismissed from office as a Republican and retired to his estate near San Casciano.
1513	Imprisoned after being accused of participation in a conspiracy and failed coup. He was tortured on the *strappado* (a hoist-like device from which the roped-up prisoner with arms tied behind his back is violently dropped, resulting in broken shoulders), repeatedly and then released upon Cardinal Giovanni de Medici's election to the papacy. Returned to San Casciano and wrote *The Prince*.
1515	Wrote *La Mandragola*.
1519	Consulted by the Medici on a new constitution for Florence which he offered in his *Discourses*.
1520	Appearance of *The Art of War* and *The Life of Castruccio Castracane*. These, along with *Mandragola*, were the only three published works in his lifetime. Commissioned to write the *History of Florence*, which he finished in 1525.

1526	Clement VII employed Machiavelli to inspect the fortifications at Florence and then sent him to attend the historian Francesco Guicciardini.
1527	Died on 22 June.

Principal dates in the development of Machiavellian thought and mythology

1532	*The Prince* published in Rome five years after Machiavelli's death. Only three of his works were published in his lifetime, the most significant of these being *The Art of War*.
1536	Cardinal Pole condemned *The Prince*. The term 'Old Nick' and the devil was from Elizabethan times in England synonymous with Niccolò Machiavelli and his works.
1559	All Machiavelli's writings were placed on the Papal Index of proscribed works.
1576	The French Protestant Huguenot writer Innocent Gentillet's 'Contre-Machiavel' attacked Machiavelli and the influence of his ideas, which he saw being personified in Catherine de Medici's rule in France.
1595	The Spanish Jesuit assault on Machiavelli and his ideas began with Pedro De Rivadeneira's *Tratadoro de la religion*.
1598	William Shakespeare in *The Merry Wives of Windsor* refers to him as 'Murdrous Machiavel' and one of the characters replies, 'Am I politic, Am I subtle, Am I Machiavel'. Francis Bacon also commented 'We are much beholden to Machiavelli and other writers of that class who openly and unfeignedly declare or describe what men do, and not what they ought to do' (Wooton 1994).
1637	Claudio Clemente's *El machievelismo degollado (Machiavellism Decapitated)* was published. Both De Rivadeneira and Clemente were particularly fearful of Machiavelli because they saw him as a debaser of religion and glorifier of the development of the secular nation state.
1740	Frederick II of Prussia launched a notorious literary assault on Machiavelli and *The Prince – L'antimachiavel*. At the end of a long reign of office he subsequently changed his mind and said Machiavelli was right (Curry 1995).
1796	Vittorio Alfieri published *Del principe e delle lettere* which lauded *The Prince* as a satire and saw Machiavelli as the only true Italian philosopher. This view was further popularized by Spinoza and Rousseau.
1824	Leopold von Ranke, Hegel, Fichte and Herder saw Machiavelli as a nationalist writer whose philosophy is useful

	in post Napoleonic Europe and began to dream of German unity (Jensen 1960).
1827	Lord Macaulay wrote his *Essay on Machiavelli* which was published in the *Edinburgh Review* of March 1827 and argued that Machiavelli's depravity was symptomatic of his time and reflected life and conditions in Renaissance Italy.
1817–83	De Sanctis witnessed the final unification of Italy and praised Machiavelli as one of its noblest patriots who was devoted to country, reason, intelligence, and to manliness.
1888	Pasquale Villari wrote and published his *Life and Times of Savonarola* and saw in Machiavelli a nationalist philosopher for modern Italian aspirations. The full English translation was published in 1892.
1891	Burd argued that Machiavelli and his writings could only be applied to a particular time and location and that, taken out of the context of Renaissance Italy, his thought becomes distorted and meaningless. This argument was subsequently adopted and modified by many (Skinner 1981).
1918–24	Many studies published on 'war guilt', 'reparations', 'international morality' and 'self determination' used Machiavelli as a touchstone (Jensen 1960).
1924	Friedrich Meinecke's study of the concept of 'raison d'état' saw Machiavelli as the founder of the concept of the state and the emergence of 'realpolitik'.
1920s to 1940s	Mussolini saw *The Prince* as a guide for statesmanship. He never completed his thesis which was a study on Machiavelli. Stalin and other totalitarian leaders were known to admire *The Prince* and saw Machiavelli as a master of statecraft. Bernard Shaw suggested instead *The Prince* is a 'handbook for Gangsters' (for example, Curry 1995, Jacobi 1996).
1945	Leonardo Olschki (1945) argued that – more than those usually associated with the beginnings of modern science, Da Vinci and Galileo – Machiavelli possessed a detached, impartial, scientific mind and, just like Galileo, by his attitudes to method, laid the foundations of modern science. Thus Machiavelli by a similar approach to mankind and its institutions, founded the science of politics. Kraft (1951) subsequently criticized this assertion by suggesting that Machiavelli's objectivity must be questioned as his methods were as prejudiced as those of most of his contemporaries.
1958	Garrett Mattingley argued that *The Prince* was always meant as a satire and jokebook and devised to amuse Machiavelli and his cronies, but never delivered to the Medici.
1961	George Bull's popular translation of *The Prince* appeared in the UK.

1964	Antony Jay's *Management and Machiavelli*, the American Management Association award-winning best-seller, appeared and it sold over a quarter of a million copies in hardcover. It became required reading at Harvard and other business schools.
1965	Gilbert's *Machiavelli and Guicciardini*, a seminal study of the two leading writers of the Italian Renaissance, was published.
1981	Quentin Skinner's elegant and thorough *Machiavelli* was published.
1988	Michael Shea published *Influence: A Handbook for the Modern Machiavelli*.
1994	Wooton's refreshingly clear *Machiavelli* was published.
1994	The term 'Machiavellian marketing' was coined by Harris to describe the strategic influencing of decision and policy making in government (corporate lobbying) for commercial or organization gain (Harris and Lock 1996).
1997	Publication of *The New Machiavelli: Renaissance Realpolitik for Modern Managers* applies the teachings of Machiavelli to modern company management.

> The secret of success, if there is such a simple and singular secret, is the determination to succeed and not the determination to avoid failure.
>
> (McAlpine 1997: 176)

1998	Aspects of Machiavelli are likened to the Labour Government's Minister Without Portfolio, Peter Mandelson (*The Independent*, Thursday 5 March).

Notes

1 Cited in De Grazia, S. (1989) *Machiavelli in Hell*, Princeton, NJ: Princeton University Press, p. 202.
2 Dedication reads:

> To The Right Hon. William Ewart Gladstone,
> Champion of Italian Freedom,
> Master of Italian Learning,
> Author and Translator
> Dedicate this book
> In Token of friendship and respect
> Florence, 1888

References

Bondanella, P. and Musa, M. (1979) *The Portable Machiavelli*, Harmondsworth: Penguin.

Burd, L. A. (ed.) (1891) *Introduction to Machiavelli's Il Principe*, Oxford: The Clarendon Press.

Calhoon, R. P. (1969) 'Niccolo Machiavelli and the Twentieth Century Administrator', *Academy of Management Journal* June: 205–12.

Christie, R. and Geis, F. L. (1970) *Studies in Machiavellianism*, New York: Academic Press.

Curry, P. (1995) *Machiavelli for Beginners*, Cambridge: Icon Books.

De Grazia, S. (1989) *Machiavelli in Hell*, Princeton, NJ: Princeton University Press.

De Sanctis, F. (1960) 'Storia della Letteratura Italiana', vol. II, in Jensen, D. (trans.) *Machiavelli: Cynic, Patriot or Political Scientist?*, Lexington: D.C. Heath & Co.

Fisher, R., Kopelman, E. and Kupfer Schneider, A. (1994) *Beyond Machiavelli: Tools for Coping with Conflict*, Cambridge, MA: Harvard University Press.

Frederic II (1789) *Papers of the King of Prussia*, Berlin: 5–11, 86–94.

Gentillet, I. (1960) 'Discours sur les moyens de bien gouverner et maintenir en bonne paix un Royaume ou autre Principauté', in Jensen, D. (trans.) *Machiavelli: Cynic, Patriot or Political Scientist?*, Lexington: D.C. Heath & Co.

Gilbert, A. (trans.) (1958) *Machiavelli: The Chief Works and Others*, vols 1–3, Durham, NC: Duke University Press.

Gilbert, F. (1965) *Machiavelli and Guicciardini*, Princeton, NJ: Princeton University Press.

Harris, C. P. and Lock, A. R. (1996) 'Machiavellian Marketing: the Development of Corporate Lobbying in the UK', *Journal of Marketing Management* 12 (4): 313–28.

Hunt, S. D. and Chonko, L. B. (1984) 'Marketing and Machiavellianism', *Journal of Marketing* Summer: 30–42.

'The Face of Power', *The Independent*, 5 March 1998, p.15.

Jacobi, D. (1996) *Machiavelli for Beginners*, Cambridge: Icon Books Audio Cassettes.

Jay, A. (1964) *Management and Machiavelli*, San Diego, CA: Pfeiffer Press. (Revised paperback edition 1994).

Jensen, D. (ed.) (1960) *Machiavelli: Cynic, Patriot or Political Scientist?*, Lexington: D.C. Heath & Co.

Kraft, J. (1951) 'Truth and Poetry in Machiavelli', *Journal of Modern History* 22: 109–11, 116–21.

Machiavelli, N. (1958) 'History of Florence', in A. Gilbert (trans.) *Machiavelli: The Chief Works and Others*, vol. 3, Durham, NC: Duke University Press.

—— (1961) *The Prince*, trans. G. Bull, Harmondsworth: Penguin.

—— (1995) *The Art of War*, trans. P. Bondanella and M. Musa, Harmondsworth: Penguin.

—— (1996) *Discourses on Livy*, trans. H. C. Mansfield and N. Tarcov, Chicago, IL: Chicago University Press.

Mattingley, G. (1958) 'Machiavelli's Prince: Political Science or Political Satire?', *The American Scholar* 27: 482–91.

McAlpine, A. (1992) *The Servant: A New Machiavelli*, London: Faber & Faber.

—— (1997) *The New Machiavelli: Renaissance Realpolitik for Modern Managers*, London: Aurum.

Meinecke, F. (1924) *Machiavellism: The Doctrine of Raison d'État and its Place in Modern History*, trans. D. Scott, New Haven, CT: Yale University Press, 1957.

Olschki, L. (1945) *Machiavelli the Scientist*, Berkeley, CA: The Gillick Press.

Pearce, E. (1993) *Machiavelli's Children*, London: Victor Gollancz.

Pole, Cardinal Reginald (1536) *Apologia ad Carolum V. Caesarem*, Rome.

Shea, M. (1988) *Influence: How to Make the System Work for You*, London: Century.

Skinner, Q. (1979) *The Foundations of Modern Political Thought*, Cambridge: Cambridge University Press, 2 vols.

—— (1981) *Machiavelli*, Oxford: Oxford University Press.

Strauss, L. (1958) *Thoughts on Machiavelli*, Chicago, IL: Chicago University Press.

Villari, P. (1888) *Life and Times of Savonarola*, London: Unwin.

Wooton, D. (1994) *Machiavelli: Selected Political Writings*, Indianapolis, IN: Hackett Publishing Company.

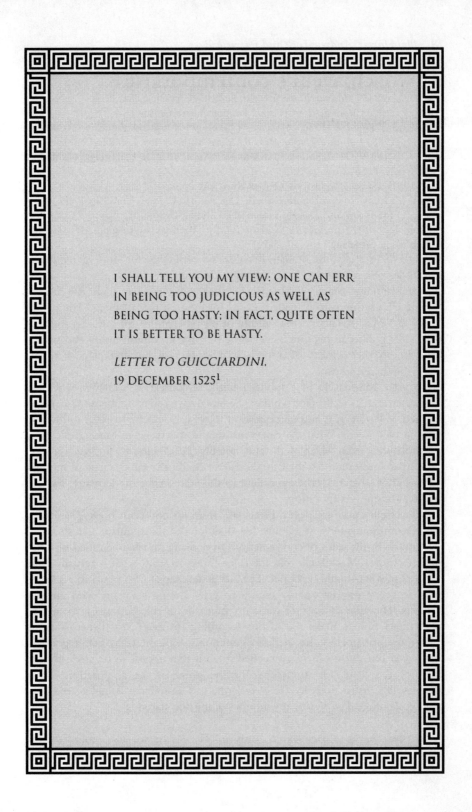

I SHALL TELL YOU MY VIEW: ONE CAN ERR
IN BEING TOO JUDICIOUS AS WELL AS
BEING TOO HASTY; IN FACT, QUITE OFTEN
IT IS BETTER TO BE HASTY.

LETTER TO GUICCIARDINI,
19 DECEMBER 1525[1]

3 Machiavelli's contemporaries

George Bull

Managers can study the Italian Renaissance profitably for both general and specific lessons relevant to the challenges they are meeting at the start of the new millennium. Many of them will already be familiar with the use of Machiavelli's writings to provide maxims for modern management. The genius of Niccolò Machiavelli and the validity of his perceptions for business today as well as for politics in his time need to be put, for maximum utility and understanding, in the context of a period of staggering intellectual and artistic creativity: the Renaissance.

To place Machiavelli in a modern business context is justifiable when we remember that, as well as for scholars, he has always had an immense fascination for men of action. It is an open question to what extent he has ever influenced them in their deeds. What the rulers mostly did was to go to Machiavelli, or at least to quote from Machiavelli, and notably *The Prince*, to find justification rather than inspiration for their methods. No doubt the same is true of modern rulers and of advisers to the equivalent of the State in the modern age: namely, the great business corporation.

Machiavelli's maxims, drawn principally from his notorious book *The Prince*, are of continuing interest if only for their power to stimulate the shock of recognition or the spirit of contradiction. In drawing up what he called his original set of rules, Machiavelli told the ruler always to study what is actually done rather than what should be done. 'The fact is that a man who wants to act virtuously in every way necessarily comes to grief among so many who are not virtuous. Therefore if a prince wants to maintain his rule he must learn not to be virtuous, and to make use of this according to need.' For this reason, the ruler must not possess the qualities commonly thought of as being good in themselves but those which are needed, even if they appear to be vices, for the good of the State. Or, therefore, for the good of the corporation. From Machiavelli's instructions in *The Prince* one can assemble a complete management code of conduct worth any number of mission statements.

Be decisive As an object lesson, early in *The Prince* we are reminded how Cesare Borgia sprang into action secretly, swiftly and mercilessly against his treacherous, mercenary troops and extremely unpopular commander.

One morning, Remirro's body was found cut in two pieces on the piazza at Cesena, with a block of wood and a bloody knife lying beside it. The brutality of the spectacle kept the people of the Romagna for a time appeased and stupefied.

(Machiavelli 1961)

Asking whether a leader ought to be thought compassionate rather than cruel, loved rather than feared, Machiavelli adds that 'Cesare Borgia was accounted cruel; nonetheless this cruelty of his reformed the Romagna, brought it unity and restored order and obedience.' 'Violence must be inflicted once for all ... benefits must be conferred gradually.' This is good advice both for national leaders and for CEOs slimming their companies down.

Build goodwill   Combining the ferocity of the lion and the cunning of the fox, successful rulers delegate to others the enactment of unpopular measures and keep entirely in their own hands the distribution of favours, to ensure personal support. Being feared is one thing, being despised is another. To safeguard against losing your power to outsiders or through an internal coup, Machiavelli advises that you must respect your people's property and ensure you have the right allies.

Watch your friends   If you annex new territory, you must disarm the inhabitants. But remember that rulers

> ... have found men who were suspect at the start of their rule more loyal and more useful than those who, at the start, were their trusted friends ... a prince will never have any difficulty in winning over those who were initially his enemies, when they are such that they need someone to lean on.
>
> (Machiavelli 1961)

The history of business, like that of war, is thick with reports of the reversal of alliances.

Keep independent   A new man, Machiavelli insists, 'should never join in aggressive alliance with someone more powerful than himself, unless it is a matter of necessity ... . This is because, if you are the victors, you emerge as his prisoner' (Machiavelli 1961). Modern business variants on this include the entrepreneur who parts with too large a share stake to a friend or financier.

Buy loyalty

> The first opinion that is formed of a ruler's intelligence is based on the quality of the men he has around him. When they are competent and loyal he can always be considered wise, because he has been able to recognize their competence and keep them loyal.
>
> (Machiavelli 1961)

And Machiavelli's 'infallible guide' for the assessment of your colleagues is simply to realize that 'when you see a minister thinking more of himself than of you, and seeking his own profit in everything he does … you will never be able to trust him.' On the other hand, to keep a man consistently up to the mark you must be considerate towards him, pay him honour, enrich him, put him in your debt, and so 'having riches and honours to the point of surfeit, he will desire no more; having so many offices, he cannot but fear changes.'

Fend off the flatterers   The Renaissance courts were full of flatterers; so are modern boardrooms. Machiavelli's advice is beware:

> Men are so happily absorbed in their own affairs and indulge in such self-deception that it is difficult for them not to fall victim to this plague; and if they try to avoid doing so they risk becoming despised. This is because the only way to safeguard yourself against flatterers is by letting people understand that you are not offended by the truth; but if everyone can speak the truth to you then you lose respect. So a shrewd prince should adopt a middle way.
>
> (Machiavelli 1961)

His tirade against flatterers concludes with a sound admonition to anyone running an organization from the top down. Make it known you are not offended by the truth; but don't let everyone have the right to tell you what he thinks. A shrewd ruler chooses wise men and allows only them the freedom to speak, and then only concerning matters on which he asks their opinions. 'But he should also question them thoroughly and listen to what they say; then he should make up his own mind as to how to act.'

Train for war   The leader must always be ready for war, says Machiavelli. He must always be thinking what the enemy may be about to do:

> Philopoemen the leader of the Achaeans … never in peacetime thought of anything else except military strategy. When he was in the country with his friends, he would often stop and invite a discussion: 'If the enemy were on top of that hill, and we were down here with our army, which of us would have the advantage? If we wanted to retreat, how would we set about it?'
>
> (Machiavelli 1961)

Many a victim of a take-over bid or boardroom coup would have saved himself if he had thought like that and adopted what we now call scenario planning.

Machiavelli used soft as well as hard criteria in his recommendations for effective State management. The ruler must never rob people of their property or their honour, he advises:

> A prince also wins prestige for being a true friend or a true enemy, that is, for revealing himself without any reservation in favour of one side against

another. This policy is always more advantageous than neutrality. For instance, if the powers neighbouring on you come to blows, either they are such that, if one of them conquers, you will be in danger, or they are not. In either case it will always be to your advantage to declare yourself and to wage a vigorous war, because, in the first case, if you do not declare yourself you will always be at the mercy of the conqueror, much to the pleasure and satisfaction of the one who has been beaten, and you will have no justification nor any ways to obtain protection or refuge. The conqueror does not want doubtful friends who do not help him when he is in difficulties; the loser repudiates you because you were unwilling to go, arms in hand, and throw in your lot with him.

(Machiavelli 1961)

In the end the leader must possess the necessary prowess, the Virtù, himself. Machiavelli comments: 'Good advice, whomever it comes from, depends on the shrewdness of the prince who seeks it, and not the shrewdness of the prince on good advice.'

In his time and after, Machiavelli was resented partly because he gave the game away; princes felt they should not be exposed as behaving in the manner he advised, even if they did.

Machiavelli's advice is usually compact common sense. For every manager it carries relevant instructions – too often disregarded until too late. The relevance of Machiavelli's writings to the principles and practice of modern business resides in more than its provision of a set of maxims. After his career as a diplomat in the service of the Florentine Republic had ended in dismissal when the Medici were forcibly restored to Florence in 1512, Machiavelli wrote *The Prince* in the belief that his experience as an envoy and his study of history (the actions of great leaders) could furnish the reasoned political discourse to prove his excellence as an adviser whose services would be invaluable to the Medici in power in particular and leaders in general. In his Dedication of *The Prince*, Machiavelli wrote that he could not give a ruler (a prince, or a chairman or a chief executive officer) 'a more valuable gift than the means of being able in a very short time to grasp all that I, over so many years and with so much affliction and peril, have learned and understood' (Machiavelli 1961).

Fortune, Machiavelli conceded, especially because of the tremendous pace of change in the world, suddenly raging like a violent storm, was the arbiter of half the things men did. Fortune triumphed when foresight had been lacking. Those who relied on their good fortune invariably in time came to grief. They needed to adapt their policy to the changing times. Few men could do so. No man was shrewd enough 'to know how to adapt his policy as needed; either because he cannot do otherwise than what is in character or because, having always prospered by proceeding one way, he cannot persuade himself to change.' Even for a circumspect leader, however, fortune could sometimes still be fatally adverse, Machiavelli conceded: Cesare Borgia's plans to carve himself out a kingdom in

Italy had collapsed because the life of his father Pope Alexander had been cut short, and Cesare himself had fallen sick at this critical time.

In his chief political works, *The Prince* and the *Discourses*, Machiavelli constructed an overarching – and inevitably oversimplifying – political philosophy of sharp relevance to business management. Isaiah Berlin (1979) has argued that, rather than being castigated for encouraging autocrats to act immorally, Machiavelli should be regarded to some extent as a forerunner of liberalism. He had created a self-contained systematic political philosophy distinct from and independent of religion. There are more than echoes of this in contemporary confusions over the nature of so-called business ethics as managers and directors try to make right choices between vigorous free-market prescriptions assuming total concentration on the bottom line and 'soft' business philosophies purporting to subordinate profit to people. For Machiavelli the act of governing is in itself a profoundly moral matter (as is business management today). Both are intimately concerned with the well-being of people: for Machiavelli, the nobles and the populace of Florence and, beyond that, of Italy in his time invaded, divided and oppressed: for modern managers, the so-called stakeholders, providing their money, their intellectual and physical labour, their custom. For the achievement of good business governance through the accepted principles of accountability, transparency and probity, we need Machiavelli's intellectual rigour and also his passion for seeing and reporting what really is, not what we would like to exist.

One of his close friends, Francesco Vettori, in correspondence with Machiavelli rejected his fundamental arguments on the validity of political discourse which, he claimed, was always problematic in a world where its surmises and inferences tended to be governed by the interpreter's own *fantasia*, his imaginings, rather than by reality. The warning reminds us to read Machiavelli with caution, to sift his remarkable insights into human nature before trying to apply them when engaged in the 'active process of determining and guiding the course of a firm towards its objectives' (see Ansoff 1965).

The achievements of Machiavelli's contemporaries, like those of Machiavelli himself (ironically literary rather than political), reward investigation partly as illuminating the diversity and energy of the Renaissance and the validity of the claim, albeit qualified, that it was above all an age of the flowering of the individual. Machiavelli was just such an individual of the Renaissance, versatile, creative, questioning and curious (Burckhardt 1960).

The often rapier-like thrust of Machiavelli's prose, like the sarcastic expression in his portrait, reveals just one sardonic facet of his complex character. Feverishly active by nature, Machiavelli nonetheless was devoted to reading, conversation and 'the pleasures of life'. When we look in the direction of Machiavelli, the image of a lean and hungry man standing isolated like Cassius is transformed by the appearance all around him of scores of fond relations, intimate friends and loyal colleagues. Like Michelangelo, who has also suffered misrepresentation from a gloomy reputation, Machiavelli cannot be properly understood without reference to his intricate network of significant relationships including great contemporaries such as the creative historian Francesco Guicciardini and the – until recently – too little appreciated Francesco Vettori.

Machiavelli enjoyed a big family and a socially catholic range of friendships and contacts. There are some disconcerting gaps. There are few if any artists in his group. In the autumn of 1506, when Machiavelli was aged 37 and on a mission to the court of the warrior Pope Julius II, Buonaccorsi wrote to him from Florence mentioning that Niccolò would just then have had some money delivered to him by the hand of the sculptor Michelangelo. Michelangelo as it happened, then aged 31, had ridden away from Rome in a fury early in 1506 abandoning the work he was meant to be doing for Julius's tremendous tomb, and efforts were being made to reconcile these two hot-tempered men, the divine artist and the terrible Pontiff. However, on 11 September, Biagio wrote to Machiavelli to say that Michelangelo had cut short his journey and returned to Florence. Later, Michelangelo was reconciled with the Pope in Bologna where he made his statue in bronze. His name never occurs again in connection with Machiavelli.

Machiavelli, after sending home several very telling and forthright dispatches, was recalled to Florence in October, a considerably more confident and experienced government figure, after this second mission to the Papal court. He had been making notes for a projected history of Florence. He had, since being elected to office as a Second Chancellor and Secretary in 1498, been on diplomatic missions to among others Caterina Sforza, ruler of Imola and Forli; Louis XII, King of France; Cesare Borgia, son of Pope Alexander VI, and then Pope Julius. He was honing his skills of observation, analysis and reportage.

I mention Michelangelo partly to emphasize that Machiavelli's contemporaries included many of Italy's greatest artists ever, including: Leonardo da Vinci, still active in 1506 and aged 54; Fra Bartolommeo, aged 34; Botticelli, 59; Carpaccio, 41; Piero di Cosimo, 44; Mantegna, who died in 1506, 75; and Benvenuto Cellini, just 6 years old.

This is just a small fraction of the Italian painters, sculptors and architects who were ensuring the continuance of the Renaissance into what the great art historian Vasari called its modern age, with its third style or period originated by Leonardo that would culminate in the achievements of Michelangelo, who would bring the arts to 'absolute perfection' (Vasari 1947: 254).

In *The Prince*, Machiavelli advises the ruler to show his esteem for talent, honour those who are professionally excellent, and keep taxes down to help the enterprising. In the *Discourses* Machiavelli mentions artists chiefly to praise them for honouring antiquity and copying antiques which fetch high prices, in contrast to politicians and rulers who neglect works of history. Nonetheless he was a man of wide culture and among the contemporaries whom he frequented were the mostly noble-born intellectuals and humanists who regularly met in the splendid Oricellari gardens during the opening decades of the sixteenth century, to discuss politics and history and literature. These included the historians Filippo Nerli and Iacopo Nardi; the poets Luigi Alamanni and Cosimo

Rucellai, the grandson of the wealthy friend of the Medici and patron of the arts who had cultivated and opened up the gardens in the previous century; Francesco da Diacceto, philosophy don; Donato Giannotti, political writer and theorist; Zanobi Buondelmonti to whom Machiavelli dedicated the *Discourses on Livy*, along with Cosimo Rucellai; and Battista della Palla, a famously sharp art dealer who was involved in the conspiracy of 1522 against the Medici which led to the break-up of the Oricellari circle. During the years when he was involved with this loosely connected group of mostly younger men, Machiavelli wrote many of his literary works: the *Discourses*, the satirical poem *The Golden Ass*, the *Dialogue on our Language*, the short story *Balfagor*, the ribald play *Mandragola* and *The Art of War*, based on discussions set in the gardens.

Writing to Ludovico Alamanni in 1517, Machiavelli grumbled that he resented being ignored in Ariosto's prize list of living poets in the *Orlando Furioso*. This illustrates a key Machiavelli dichotomy like that between fortune and virtue: the overlapping attractions of politics and literature with elements of the contrasted imperatives of action and contemplation. In a letter to Vettori, Machiavelli remarked how confusing it would be for someone reading the correspondence to find their thoughts and works alternating so abruptly between serious matters of state and the frivolities of sex and sentiment. This was the Machiavelli who, writing from Verona in 1509, with a characteristic splurge of grotesque exaggeration responded to Francesco Guicciardini's account of a sexual adventure with a nauseating description of his own tumble in the dark with a rank prostitute – 'Yuk! I almost fell dead immediately, she was so ugly' he said, telling what appeared when he lit his lamp. 'First thing I saw was a tuft of piebald hair, half black, half white with age, and a bald head with some lice scuttling about … ' (Hale 1960: 123–5). There are many more salubrious and significant one-to-one encounters in the story of Machiavelli to add to his crowded experiences in Chancery, in the gardens and in encampments where he was part of a team.

Some decisively affected his life, others his thought. Piero Soderini, nearly 20 years his senior, heading the government of Florence from 1502 until his ignominious exile in 1512, gratified by Machiavelli's eager assiduity, took him on almost as a personal assistant and ensured for him the 14 years of diplomatic employment that provided abundant raw material for his political writings.

Francesco Guicciardini, a greater historian than Machiavelli, more grandly born, more cynical with his stress on the basic importance of *il suo particulare* and less original, who became one of the efficient tools of Medicean power, seems to have been stimulated by *The Prince* in refining his own political views from as early as 1516 when he wrote a *Discorso* on how the Medici should govern securely. Familiarity between the two developed into a warm friendship in the 1520s when Machiavelli was on minor missions for the Medici and the Florentine wool guild, and Guicciardini was governing Reggio and Modena for the Medici Pope Leo X. Guicciardini was appointed Lieutenant General of the Papal army in 1526. With a turn in the political tide – the fall of the Medici regime in Florence – he, like Machiavelli before him, had to retire to his studies, but not to a life of frustration; soon he was advising the Medici again.

Guicciardini's political writing directly or indirectly took Machiavelli's views into account. *The Prince*, as we see from letters written in 1516 by Guicciardini's brother-in-law Ludovico Alamanni, through manuscripts circulating in and beyond Florence, was being used selectively in privately circulated works from 1516. Before it was published in 1532, about five years after Machiavelli's death, several printed works, by for example Agostino Nifo, the philosopher friend of Pope Leo X, signalled the start of a growth industry lifting from and/or lambasting *The Prince*. Thus Nifo in his *De regnandi peritia* adapted whole chapters from Machiavelli; unlike Machiavelli, prudently distinguished between tyrants and kings; and added pious comment to the more outrageous reports and recommendations in *The Prince*. Nifo used *The Prince* opportunistically 'to create a stir in Naples', comments Brian Richardson in his essay, '*The Prince* and its Early Italian Readers' (Coyle 1995).

Francesco Vettori, who did listen carefully to Machiavelli and pondered his ideas, was active in diplomacy but hardly influential at all in politics. He came from one of the great families or *ottimati* of Florence, related to the Guicciardini and the Rucellai and a few cuts above the Machiavelli family, a humanist and writer of stories who started to hold down legal and diplomatic offices in Florence from 1504 and first worked closely with Machiavelli in 1508 on a mission to the Emperor Maximilian, sharing responsibilities. In a meaty correspondence subtly salted with significant anecdotes about their own and their friends' sexual proclivities and pursuits, over two years from 1513 to 1515 when Vettori was basking as Ambassador in the Roman heat, the two friends exchanged critical views on the current course and fundamental nature of politics. This discourse to a large extent inspired and formed the content of *The Prince* (Najemy 1993).

In observing and analysing political behaviour past and present, Machiavelli, like Michelangelo bringing the images he had conceived out of the marble, created his own imagined world of memorable political protagonists. Cesare Borgia he studied closely, first with apprehensive fascination on his mission in 1502–3 when Borgia was potent and threatening, appearing to Machiavelli as '... splendid and magnificent ... victorious and formidable', and then with bemused contempt when he went to report on the election of Pope Julius II and found Cesare weak and distraught, full of 'poison and anger' against the Florentines. Machiavelli's Cesare Borgia is the contemporary who stands out most starkly as we look back to Niccolò's crowded contemporary world. Despite Cesare's fall and decline after the death of Pope Alexander, Machiavelli on reflection wrote in *The Prince* that he knew no better precepts to give a new prince than ones derived from Cesare's action; 'and if what he instituted was of no avail, this was not from his fault but arose from the extraordinary and inordinate malice of fortune' (Machiavelli 1961).

Cesare's great deeds are immortalized in Machiavelli's chapter VII of *The Prince*. To illustrate them he tells how the leaders of his unreliable mercenaries, including the Orsini, were lured by Cesare to Sinigaglia (Senig allia) where, after they had been trapped and arrested, the captains Vitelli and Oliverotto were strangled and the Orsini held fast. It was, comments Michael Mallett (1969), biographer of the Borgias, 'a classic and perfect vendetta'.

The Borgia Pope left the political prestige of the Papacy riding high, its spiritual repute irreparably tarnished. The Borgia's aim to establish a dynastic state failed, but the members of the Borgia family were left in securely powerful positions in Naples, France and Spain. Today Machiavelli's impression of his contemporary Cesare Borgia in *The Prince* still has the force to hold and horrify. Born the same year as Michelangelo, Cesare Borgia, through Machiavelli, still personifies the dark sinister side of the Italian Renaissance.

This rapid introduction to some of Machiavelli's contemporaries is best rounded off with a glance in the direction of signora Machiavelli, to lighten the gloom. Niccolò married Marietta Corsini in 1501 and they had six children. He had himself grown up with two older sisters and a younger brother. From the little we know about Marietta we can be sure that Niccolò, an often absentee and sometimes it seems faithless husband, was a lucky man. In November 1503 Marietta wrote to Rome telling Niccolò that their newly born and baptized son was well and looked like him – his 'spitting image', a friend had said.

> He is as white as snow, but he has what looks like black velvet on his head, and he is as hairy as you are, and since he is like you I find him handsome. He looks as if he had already been in the world for a year, and he opened his eyes before he was hardly born and filled the whole house with noise.
>
> (cited in Hale 1961: 77)

The widely appreciated relevance of Machiavelli's writings, especially *The Prince*, nearly five centuries since he lived, is the consequence partly of his literary skill and his power to horrify, but also the result of the accessibility to us today of the culture of Renaissance Italy in contrast to the apparent opaqueness of medieval civilization. Despite our post-Enlightenment flight from Christianity, we still respond to and understand the humanism of the Renaissance in whose atmosphere Machiavelli flourished intellectually. The sprouting of early capitalism and civic independence in Italy has something to do with this; so too does the existence in Italy's city states – Florence, Venice, the Papacy – of formidable patronage and sometimes ferocious competition (Vasari 1947). The Renaissance scholar John Hale has drawn attention to a 'scattering of opinions' from Petrarch to Cellini which

> ... does suggest that between the mid-fifteenth and the early seventeenth centuries thoughtful men – at different times and in different places and with different reasons – came to see themselves as living in a period which, for all its dovetailing into the previous centuries, felt different. For some this meant a participation in a period of cultural rebirth and in the fascinating maturity that followed. For most, the sources of awareness were

more various. However posterity describes this century and a half, whether selectively as 'the Renaissance' or blandly and neutrally as the 'early modern' phase of European history, to contemporaries it was, cumulatively and naturally enough, 'our age'.

(Hale 1993: 585–9)

'Our age' too surely feels 'very different' and this may be another reason for studying this period of the Renaissance and its spread through space and time.

Note

1 Cited in De Grazia, S. (1989) *Machiavelli in Hell*, Princeton, NJ: Princeton University Press, p. 371.

References

Ansoff, H. I. (1965) *Corporate Strategy*, Harmondsworth: Penguin (and successive editions). (Ansoff anticipated current debates on 'corporate governance' continuing the perennial discussions on profitability as the 'corner-stone of business'. Another distinguished writer on management, Peter Drucker, is quoted by Ansoff as insisting that, rather than profit maximization, survival is the 'central purpose' of the firm (p.39). This brings him close to Machiavelli's stress on how to keep as well as acquire a State.)

Berlin, I. (1979) 'Against the Current' in *The Originality of Machiavelli*, London: The Hogarth Press.

Burckhardt, J. (1960) *The Civilisation of the Renaissance in Italy: an essay*, London: Phaidon (and successive editions), Part II. (The classic exposition of the nature of Renaissance man and the emergence of individualism.)

Coyle, M. (ed.) (1995) *Niccolò Machiavelli's The Prince: New Interdisciplinary Essays*, Manchester: Manchester University Press.

Hale, J. R. (ed.) (1961) *The Literary Works of Machiavelli*, Oxford: Oxford University Press.

—— (1961) *Machiavelli and Renaissance Italy*, London: English Universities Press.

—— (1993) *The Civilisation of Europe in the Renaissance*, London: HarperCollins.

Machiavelli, N. (1961) *The Prince*, trans. G. Bull, Harmondsworth: Penguin. (Used for all quotations from *The Prince*. The most convenient Italian text of *The Prince* is published by Feltrinelli (Milan) in the *Opere* containing *Il Principe e Discorsi*.)

—— (1996) *Discourses on Livy*, trans. H. C. Mansfield and N. Tarcov, Chicago, IL: Chicago University Press. (Another recent translation of the *Discorsi* into English is the revised Penguin edition from L. Walker.)

Mallett, M. (1969) *The Borgias, The Rise and Fall of a Renaissance Dynasty*, London: Bodley Head.

Najemy, J. (1993) *Between Friends: Discourse of Power and Desire in the Machiavelli–Vettori Letters of 1513–1515*, Princeton, NJ: Princeton University Press. (Especially valuable for his comment on Machiavelli's agonized thinking about the feasibility of discovering rational prescriptions for successful political practice. Najemy decides that:

The Prince was the culmination of Machiavelli's year-long argument with Vettori about the very possibility of a correspondence between *cose* and the *discorsi et concetti che si fanno*; about the process of interpretation itself; and about the controlling and generative power of language over the otherwise capricious unpredictability of events.

Vasari, G. (1947) *Lives of the Artists*, vol. 1, trans. G. Bull, London: Penguin. (The importance of competition in stimulating excellence is especially emphasized by Vasari in his lives of the artists of the Renaissance. In his biography of Pietro Perugino, for example, he claims that artistic perfection was achieved in Florence because of the spirit of judicious criticism; the high cost of living which made people work hard; and the thirst for glory and honour generated in all the professions so that no able man would allow others to equal him.)

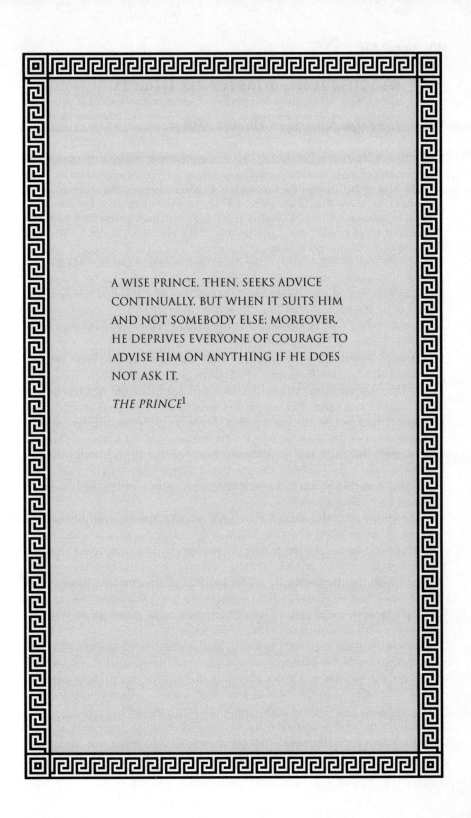

A WISE PRINCE, THEN, SEEKS ADVICE
CONTINUALLY, BUT WHEN IT SUITS HIM
AND NOT SOMEBODY ELSE; MOREOVER,
HE DEPRIVES EVERYONE OF COURAGE TO
ADVISE HIM ON ANYTHING IF HE DOES
NOT ASK IT.

THE PRINCE[1]

4   Machiavelli, master of liberty

Beatrice Rangoni Machiavelli

Machiavelli had six children. His last direct descendent, Francesco Machiavelli, died in 1727 leaving the heritage of his name and possessions to his cousin, the Marquis Giovanni Battista Rangoni. Subsequently, the Rangoni family added the name of Machiavelli to its own. Niccolò's estate – a palace on the Lungarno in Florence, the Castle of Bibbione and surrounding farmlands – belongs to the Rangoni Machiavelli family to this day.

Giuseppe Prezzolini, while in exile in Paris during the fascist period, wrote a renowned and brilliant biography of Machiavelli (Prezzolini 1926). He maintained that, like Socrates, Voltaire, Galileo and Kant, Niccolò Machiavelli was born with his eyes open. Machiavelli has been hated, feared, imitated, denied, honoured, misrepresented, even insulted. There are many Machiavellis: one for philosophers, one for patriots, one for Protestants, one for Catholics, one for official discourses and, the most famous, the one for all those who did not understand him. Machiavellianism was born. Niccolò Machiavelli would have surely declared, 'Never was I Machiavellian'; how many of his public opponents followed his teachings in private.

'The ends justify the means': ever since jesuitical morality introduced the concept of 'raison d'état', Niccolò Machiavelli's image has been haunted by the false belief that he was the creator of this proposition. Throughout the centuries that followed the first edition of *Il Principe*, two phenomena have been repeatedly observed: on the one hand, politicians of all persuasions have never ceased to use it as a 'livre de chevet', while, on the other hand, detractors from all sides have split hairs trying to give a 'moral' interpretation to the essay, in every case concluding with an implicit or explicit condemnation.

By analysing the method by which Machiavelli arrived at expressing the concepts that were the origin of so much scandal, we see that this method is based on the clearest and most objective observation, a scientific approach which, when applied to the study of medicine or astronomy, not only does not shock, but gives us a sense of pride in modern man's free spirit.

In order to better understand his analysis, however, we must bear in mind and reconstruct the historical context in which *Il Principe* was conceived. During the period from the birth of the author in 1469 to the publication of the work in 1513, the great European monarchies were being consolidated. Their polity allowed much greater political and territorial room for manoeuvre than feudalism and the free communes which had been characteristic of the preceding period. In Europe there were areas – especially France and Spain – in which we find the unity of population, territory and government which is the feature of the modern state. The government had one single head, almost always a hereditary king, following the custom of the barbaric peoples who had .invaded the Roman Empire, but were free from conditioning and interference from local vassals, the feudal nobles – ergo absolute power (from the Latin *ab-solutos*).

This royal autonomy had been constructed gradually and at a very high price (the case of France is exemplary) and allowed the government, identified in its king, the power to make rapid decisions and the economic means to put them into effect. Moreover, all the wealth and power were concentrated into one person: through direct taxation, vassals became subjects while military forces originated from the people, owed obedience to their sovereign and were recruited directly without passing through the mediation of the aristocracy. The sword and the purse, the two basic ingredients of the State, were placed at the service of territorial expansion ambitions.

In 1513 a conflict between two giants, France and Spain, was taking place, while Italy, the coveted quarry, was at that time little more than the expression of a geographical region.

Italy was already familiar with the systems of state in its own territory, although it was not a unified state, but a host of small states whose government was limited to the city walls and considered surrounding lands as territory to be conquered. Already in Machiavelli's time, these 'city' governments had evolved into some elective forms, which we could define as republican, or else to more authoritarian forms such as the Signorie (Lordships). Their territories had grown at the expense of conquered lands that became the property of the winners, but in no way were they part of an organic whole.

In these Italian realities, very different from the great states mentioned above, the power of government tended to become hereditary and despotic, in parallel with the prevailing political model elsewhere, giving rise to the period of the Principalities.

It would be well to remember, however, that in Italy, as it was in the Roman tradition, the concept of a sacred king and of the right of birth were unknown. In every city state, the memory and awareness that the authority of government derives from the consensus of the people was still very much alive. Even the Pope, whose person is considered sacred as long as he lives, owed his dignity to his election, in ancient times by acclamation, later by a college of cardinals.

On the other hand, the defence of selfish interests pushed the Italian cities to wage war against each other and maintained the custom of hiring mercenary troops, always ready to betray by passing on to the highest bidder.

In Machiavelli's time, the expansionist aims of the five major Italian powers (Venice, Milan, Rome, Naples and Florence) were threatened by the great foreign powers waiting for their chance to attack. In 1494 the army of Charles VIII subjugated the rich and cultivated inhabitants of the Italian states.

Machiavelli saw the situation with the clear vision of a citizen living in a town that had preserved its republican system and the exercise of political participation for a long time. Florence had also known the respectful and intelligent Lordship of the Medici, prelude to the Principality, despite holding onto the very Florentine characteristic of continuous strife among the political factions. Machiavelli had personally experienced what the fight for power meant in a city state. Thus he blended his personal political experience with the knowledge of history of the humanist scholar, steeped in the contemplation of the deeds of the ancient fathers through the meditation of their texts. Understanding history for Machiavelli was one and the same as understanding people and the passions that drive them to act. The aim of this study was to produce effective action that could dominate the course of events, forcing the hand of inconsistent fortune.

At the dawn of modern times, his ideas seem to have anticipated by at least a century the interest in rational control of reality that led to the foundation of natural sciences in the seventeenth century of Descartes and Galileo. The laws his investigation proposed to discover, however, were not those that govern the movement of physical bodies but those that dominate society; a body that was totally circumscribed by the restraints of natural laws, regulated by the same forces that preside over the development and decay of every living organism. In the early sixteenth century we find Machiavelli investigating the laws men use to govern themselves. These are laws of motion that tend to form a constant oscillation between social order and disorder.

His knowledge of history as well as national and international politics convinced him that, unless a strong unified state capable of defending itself from external enemies were formed, Italian city states would never survive what he defined as 'the second barbarian invasion'. But it had taken centuries for the great monarchies to be formed: Italy did not have the time. In order to survive, defend and establish itself (Machiavelli knew that defence and attack are synonymous in politics as well as in war) it had only one generation, or, in any event, a very short time, to mould a unified state. There was no time for the development and internalization of the mystical ideal of power that would lead to the establishment of an absolute monarchy, as in other European states, and furthermore it was in itself totally alien to the notions of government and authority inherited from the ancient Romans.

It was imperative to confront the task with a lucid mind and be able to design, plan and implement an initiative. A clear knowledge of the nature of power and a daring and ambitious leader were necessary, guided by an equally clear vision of the final objectives, since he knew that a second occasion would never return. We know that the author of *Il Principe* thought he had found the right man in a figure of his times, but fate impeded his initiative. The invaders once again crossed the Alps and the 'Italy Project' was delayed for three and a half centuries. We must emphasize that Niccolò Machiavelli was a man of letters and not a man of arms, and his project was a precise outline of the steps to follow, a rapid guide to the path towards solid and lasting power.

Keeping in mind this background, the style of *Il Principe* is logical and has a clear sequence:

- The work is concise and easy to read, thanks to its precise subdivision into logically progressive chapters. (The future prince has no time to waste reading through or subsequently consulting the manual.)
- The language style is direct, quite similar to a dialogue between the author and the reader (the prince needs to find a wise counsellor who sometimes is not ready at his side, he must be able to 'speak' with him).
- All abstract theorizing is eliminated (the prince must not be bored or tempted to skip a page or a paragraph, or reject the book feeling that it is more adapted to a philosopher than to a man of action).

The last is the crucial point: Machiavelli is not, and above all he does not want to be, a philosopher (remember that, although he had a refined knowledge of Latin, he did not know Greek; an exception in the humanist environment in Florence which excluded him from the contemporary speculation connected with Neoplatonism). He categorically affirmed repeatedly in his work his wish to restrict himself to the *verità effettuale* (factual truth), to truth that derives from facts: *e facto*.

If we consider *Il Principe* as a text uprooted from its context, we could easily fall into the temptation of analysing and comparing it with the abstract parameters of a political 'ought to be' to which it is very noble to aspire. The need to reach an immediate political objective, the historical 'haste' that moved Machiavelli, induced him to limit himself as closely as possible to a policy of what it is, disdaining as a waste of time and energy the consideration of what it should be. Hence his terse realism, his lack of abstract moralism, even though whoever has read the whole of Machiavelli's work knows that he never lacked for solid morality: in his straight language, evil is named evil and good is clearly good.The time has come to jettison the saying that the end justifies the means, which Machiavelli never pronounced, but came from his false pupils, and whoever has read the book by the great Florentine knows that never do we find this phrase, nor can we in any of his writings, because it would be contrary to the logic of his mentality. On the contrary, Machiavelli's political ideas indicate the Prince himself as the means for reaching an end that exceeds him: the establishment of social order, which he felt to be an absolute necessity.

The fiercest arguments against Machiavellianism came from King Frederick II of Prussia, poised to sacrifice every single ideal of liberty to the overall power of the State. But his abuse was not inferior to that of the theologians of the French royal court or the writers of the seventeenth century against the 'master of diabolical thoughts' (*Maître du penser diabolique*).

Meanwhile, the Jansenists at the end of the eighteenth century honoured him as the 'master of republican liberty' and Hegel, in an early writing (1913), exalted the thesis of *Il Principe* as the highest and truest conception of a synthetic political mind animated by the noblest sentiments. Nowadays, quite a few scholars affirm that without any doubt *Il Principe* is the book that contributed more than any other to ushering Europe out of the Middle Ages. Others hold that Machiavelli's thesis is a form of 'social anthropology' that, carrying forward ancient models, scrutinizes how forms of 'civilized living' take root in human institutions within the limits of nature and, at the same time, is attentive to deceit, self-deceit, illusions and appearances, which humans, shaped by their nature, perpetrate against their institutions, corroding them from the inside. The fact that human societies and their political forms are conceived as natural bodies permits the analogy with medicine and, keeping in mind how essential the role of medicine was in the Renaissance humanist culture, we can imagine the politician as the one who recognizes and treats the conflicts and lacerations that affect the social body.

Thus, Machiavelli's teaching can be considered modern in the most essential way: because we should consider politics as treatment, as medicine against the evils of society, as a levee against its 'ruin', as a search for its equilibrium with nature, overcoming an altered and destructive relationship. Machiavelli, cornerstone of the Renaissance, was the first 'scientist' in Europe, but he was never forgiven for having turned his spirit of observation onto man himself.

Five hundred years after the first voyage of Christopher Columbus, much has been said about Italian influence on America. It would be unjust not to assign a parallel discovery in the realm of politics to Niccolò Machiavelli. In the foreword to the first volume of his *Discorsi* he asserted that 'The quest for new ways and orders is no less dangerous than that for unknown waters and lands'. Columbus' search for new commercial routes culminated in the discovery of an inhabited continent. Stressing his desire to tread unexplored paths, Machiavelli made a decisive contribution to political thought, shaking his contemporaries out of their medieval lethargy.

In dealing with the development of republican tradition from Aristotle to the foundation of the United States, the American scholar John Pocock in *The Machiavellian Moment* (1975) underscores the importance of civic virtues for the fulfilment of human beings. He defines 'civic virtues' as the tradition in which Machiavelli played a decisive role by taking up the Aristotelian image of the essential character of virtuous political participation, thus enlarging the Greek philosopher's concept of citizenship. Pocock also argues that the Machiavellian version of civic humanism had a long and influential life thanks also to the work of James Harrington who, in the first half of the seventeenth century, made the Florentine's work known in England and expressed English political philosophy in the language and perspective that the world inherited from Machiavelli (Harrington 1988). Philosophers of the seventeenth century were thus influenced and they in turn influenced American revolutionaries.

Machiavelli considered himself the spiritual heir to the classic idea that only people able to manage themselves are worthy of managing the '*res publica*'. This legitimization weds power with wisdom in the conviction that who is able to repress the forces of passion within himself can control the passions of the 'polis' as well. The idea that there is an analogy between the government of the polis and that of the soul is implied in this ancient wisdom, indicating a continuity between individual and social ethics. In separating the public sphere from the private one, Machiavelli held that the morals of a man of politics are not and can never be the same as those of a common citizen. And yet, the ruler and his subject are similar in a way, since both are in pursuit of the same vital desire for self assertion.

Machiavelli is not just a political engineer; his investigation delves into the mechanisms that support politics in a dimension that goes beyond politics itself. It is in this wider horizon that the more modern traits of his thought emerge. He was the first to voice the profound need for renewal that pervaded Italian society to write a 'social' history, or history 'of the classes' , in which the nobility, the bourgeoisie and the common people are participants for the first time. The flow of events is intricately bound to the particular actions of single individuals.

The objectives of political action have their roots in 'social happiness': the happiest society possible for the greatest number of individuals, because

> ... not the particular good, but the common good is the maker of great cities. And there is no doubt that this common good cannot exist but in the republics: because whatever is done to achieve this purpose is accomplished: and although it may turn into damage for this or that person, yet they are many for whom this does good.
>
> (Machiavelli 1532: Book 4, ch. 1)

This is a powerful ambition, typical of modern philosophy, which achieves its complete expression in the American Declaration of Independence of 1787, where the pursuit of happiness is considered a fundamental right for all. At the dawn of capitalism this 'happiness' was connected with the economic affluence that renders the spirit enterprising and is based on the growth of markets and labour. Machiavelli condemned those who 'idly live from the revenue of their possessions in abundance, with never a thought to tilling land or other necessary wearying tasks of living. These are pernicious fellows in every republic and in every province; but even more pernicious are those who besides the aforesaid riches rule the castle, and have subjects who obey to them' (Machiavelli 1971: Book 1, ch. 55.2). There are many of these two species of men, and where they are numerous 'never has a republic arisen nor any sort of political life; because such generations of men are totally hostile to any form of civilization.'

Machiavelli invites us to consider the bonds between happiness and our affluent society, so rich and wealthy yet so impoverished in joy. His thoughts are pitted against the great questions that still torment us today.

At present, the world is divided into two parts: one distinctly headed toward modernization, within which the rules of the game of politics are beginning to change, the other strenuously trying to emerge from an underdeveloped agricultural age in which the rules of the game remain very similar to those of the past. The agricultural civilization took a long time to expand throughout the world; the industrial age spread more rapidly but it still needed more than two centuries to become established. Once again we are in a phase of transition passing from the industrial age to a postmodern society. In a way, a similar situation was present in the latter half of the nineteenth century. Around 1870, wondering what could still be considered alive in Machiavelli's work, the great historian of Italian literature, Francesco de Sanctis (1958) documented the modernity of the author of *Il Principe*, maintaining that he had at last established the 'autonomy and the independence of the State' as opposed to theocracy, demolished the Middle Ages and initiated 'awareness and meditation on life.' Among Machiavelli's greatest merits, according to De Sanctis, was the subordination of the world of imagination to the world of reality: 'What is important is not that something is reasonable, or moral or beautiful, but that it is real. The world can be like this or like that; take it as it is, and it is useless to try to see whether it could or should be otherwise.' Machiavelli taught us to see things for what they are and not for what they ought to be. He indicated that 'the means must be founded on intelligence and the calculation of the forces that move men'. He demonstrated that political science is based on the balance between the means and the ends and that the intellectual energies capable of making men and nations great spring from this balance.

Man's desire for Utopia is recurrent in history: 'Since human nature has this common basis, that desires and appetites are infinite, and weak and hesitant is the virtue to attain them, there is disproportion between the ends and the means; whence arise the oscillations and disorders of history', wrote De Sanctis more than a century ago, recapitulating Machiavelli's teachings.

The relationships between ethics and politics, public and private actions, licit and illicit actions in public administration, reality and projects, are still open questions that the Florentine Secretary fathomed with an extraordinary critical sense, balancing the cold detached attitude of the scholar with the lively and sometimes passionate one of the politician.

Just as the sword serves the gentleman to defend himself while the outlaw uses it to kill, so can his political science be of use to democrats and dictators alike. He well knew this when he affirmed: 'Though it is true that I have taught dictators how to conquer power, I have taught the people how to bring them down as well.'

It is in the *Discorsi sulla Prima Deca di Tito Livio* and in the *Istorie fiorentine* above all that Machiavelli studies the actions best suited to guarantee the citizen the establishment and the defence of his rights. Of course, in a context that was laboriously trying to free itself of the legacy of feudalism the concept of 'human rights' must not be taken in the sense we mean today. Machiavelli was inspired by the vision – albeit idealized by the classic authors – of the ancient Roman society to propose it once again as a model of liberty, respect for civil and human rights because:

> When it comes to pass that, for the good fortune of the city, there arises a wise, good and powerful citizen, who orders laws for which the passions of

the nobles and populous are placated, or in a way are so restrained that they work badly or cannot work at all, it is then that that city can call itself free, and that state can deem itself firm and stable. Since it is upon good laws and good orders founded, it needs not the virtue of one man, as occurs elsewhere, to maintain it.

(Machiavelli 1532: Book 4, ch. 1)

Maurizio Viroli, professor of Political Theory at Princeton University, maintains (1995) that for the Florentine Secretary love of his country was not only one of his most profound sentiments, but that he would have liked to see it flourish in the hearts of his compatriots as well. One of the main intents of the *Discorsi* is to urge young people to imitate the virtues of the Romans, while the central theme in the *Istorie fiorentine* is corruption and his end is to illustrate that the lack of civil virtues was the cause of the loss of common liberty and the decline of Florence. When he speaks of virtue he means patriotism, or the love of common liberty that makes men generous, and helps them see benefit as part of the common good of the republic.

Certainty of equal dignity for everyone represents the essence of justice and the ultimate goal in respect for human rights and citizenship: it is this concept that Machiavelli intends in his 'republican patriotism' formula that for four centuries nourished the Roman population who 'loved the glory and the common good of their country'. The 'love of common good' and 'love of country' that Machiavelli describes as the core of Roman patriotism is nothing more than their loyalty to the laws that protect their own freedom. The many good laws supporting 'public freedom' enacted during the Republican period were largely the result of the determination of the plebeians to resist the insolence of the patricians. The common good of the nation to whom the ancient Romans were so devoted was therefore first and foremost their attachment to their individual liberties, or the freedom to pursue their own interests and enjoy their own rights without hindrance from the powerful and the arrogant rulers. The patriotic citizens that Machiavelli so praises in his *Discorsi* serve their country, and the liberty and the laws of the city, because they know that common good is all one with each one's individual interest.

The Roman people, according to Machiavelli, deserve to be taken as a model for modern men and women because they were virtuous and civil; they were often in a state of turmoil through the streets of the city, they shut down their shops and abandoned Rome en masse, but all this never became a threat to liberty. They loved their common liberty and were able to withstand ambitious and arrogant rulers; but they were obedient to magistrates and the laws and respectful towards morality and religion. They loathed subjugation, but had no inclination to oppress other citizens. Virtue and urbanity went hand in hand in the free German cities as well, where citizens were ready to kill 'idle' nobles, because they caused corruption and scandal. At the same time they were disciplined and respectful of the laws, they obeyed the magistrates and paid their taxes punctually. When love for country declines, however, civil life becomes wholly corrupt. Where there is no civil virtue, ambitious citizens manage to pass laws that are against the common good, and bad laws in turn corrupt both public life and private lives. When love for one's country languishes it leads to the loss of liberty and the decline of civil customs.

For Machiavelli, therefore, political institutions and values cannot be decoupled from customs and ways of life. He speaks of 'free living' or of 'free life' as a particular way of life and particular culture as opposed to 'abject living' or another way of life and another culture. One's country is also a way of life and a culture founded upon values of freedom and civil equality.

Love for one's country brings citizens together and leads them to consider that the benefits they have in common are more important than the goods that each person possesses individually. Nothing is more individual than one's own soul, and yet the love for one's country can bring us to place common good above it, or to consider liberty as much our own as everyone else's.

On the other hand, in *Il Principe* he points out how 'There are two ways to fight: one through the laws, the other using force: that first belongs to men, that second to the beasts: but because the first is sometimes inadequate, 'tis better to resort to the second.' The totalitarian regimes of the twentieth century have given new momentum to the analysis of *Il Principe*, studied both by dictators and by their opponents. We must remember, however, that Machiavelli constantly advised the Prince to rule with the consent of the people: 'He must never be compelled to carry a knife in hand, but he must see to the well being of his subjects ... the friendship of his people, otherwise when times are adverse he will be lost' (Machiavelli 1961).

In the Social Contract by Jean-Jacques Rousseau (1994), Machiavelli was depicted as an honest man and a good citizen forced by circumstances to hide his love for liberty and to 'give lessons to the king', imparting a 'great lesson to the people' instead. In other words, Rousseau asserts that he used the ruse of seemingly instructing sovereigns while in reality he shed light on their bad deeds, therefore he considered *Il Principe* to be none other than the 'Book of Republicans'. In a way, Foscolo took up this idea in the *Dei Sepolcri* (1807). Contemplating Machiavelli's tomb in Santa Croce, the poet wrote that there lay 'The corpse of that great man / who sharpening the sceptres of rulers / their laurels he defoliates and to the people he reveals / of what tears they weep and what blood they shed.'

In his times, times of giants, his work was neither considered scandalous nor was it read in secret. His acceptance of reality with such a cool and serene spirit was his way of feeling part of the free minds of Renaissance times, a period of which the Florentine Secretary was one of the most illustrious representatives. One of the greatest scholars of the Italian Renaissance, the Swiss historian Jacob Burckhardt, affirmed (1960) that in that time Florence was 'the most turbulent and original city in the world'. It was without comparison 'the most important centre of modern Italian, indeed European spirit' and was 'the first among all the states of the modern world'. In Florence humanist culture was triumphant, placing man at the centre of the universe, restoring his earthly vigour and delivering him from the ascetic evasions of the Middle Ages. Machiavelli was a typical product of this cultural revolution. Humanism affirmed the autonomy of individuals. Machiavelli went so far as to affirm the autonomy of politics.

He taught us that, when adverse times come, 'only those defences are good, are certain, are durable that depend on you alone and on your virtue' and the letter that, in the sad days of exile, he addressed to his friend Francesco Vettori describing his days is testimony to his humanist faith:

> Evening has fallen, I return home and enter my study; on the threshold I divest myself of my daily attire, covered with mud and dust, and I don my regal and curial robes; and so decorously clad I enter into the ancient courts of ancient men; where received amorously by them, I nourish myself of that food that is only mine and for which I was born; where I shame not to speak with them and ask them the reason for their actions; and I feel no boredom for four hours, I forget every worry, I fear not poverty, death does not dismay me: everything I transfer in them. And since Dante says that there is no science without the memory of what we learned, I have taken note of everything of which I have gleaned through conversation with them and I have composed a pamphlet 'De Principatibus' ....
>
> (Machiavelli 1961: Introduction)

The German historian, Gerhard Ritter (1972), published an essay during the Nazi period in which he sought to reveal the demonic aspects of Hitler's dictatorship. With this in mind, he dedicated a chapter to Machiavelli's philosophy affirming that he deserved the highest praise for clearly revealing and unmasking the demoniacal face present in Hitler's power.

Utopians dream of a renewed humanity where everyone is potentially altruistic and endowed with good qualities. Their first objective is to assign vast powers to a 'good prince', wise people or an honest party to hasten the renewal of the world. The practical result has almost invariably proved disappointing and sometimes catastrophic.

We must not ask ourselves 'Who will govern us', as Karl Popper (1966) explained, but rather how we can organize politics and the institutions to bar evil, corrupt or incompetent rulers from doing serious damage. Relentlessly, realists bear the limits of our human condition in mind. This is an additional reason why, after nearly 500 years, we still need to meditate in the company of Niccolò Machiavelli.

Note

1 Taken from Gilbert, A. (trans.) (1989) *Machiavelli: The Chief Works and Others*, vol. 1, Durham, NC: Duke University Press, p. 87.

References

Burckhardt, J. (1960) *The Civilization of the Renaissance in Italy: an essay*, London: Phaidon, 1st edn.

De Sanctis, F. (1958) *Storia della Letteratura italiana*, Torino: N. Gallo.

Frederico II di Prussia (1741) 'Antimachiavel', in l'abbé de Saint-Pierre, *Réflections sur l'Antimachiavel de 1740*, Rotterdam: Jean Daniel Berman.

Foscolo, U. (1987) *Dei Sepolcri – Poesie e Carmi*, Milan: Rusconi Editor.

Harrington, J. (1988) *Ideal Commonwealths: comprising More's Utopia, Bacon's New Atlantis, Campanella's City of the Sun, and Harrington's Oceana*, Cambridge: Dedalus Ltd.

Hegel, G. W. F. (1913) *Lineamenti di filosofia del diritto*, Bari: Laterza.

Machiavelli, N. (1532) *Istorie Fiorentine*, Firenze: Bernado di Gunta. (Extract translated by author.)

—— (1961) *The Prince*, trans. G. Bull, Harmondsworth: Penguin.

—— (1971) 'Discorsi sopra la Prima Deca di Tito Livio', in *Niccolò Machiavelli: Tutte le opere*, Firenze: M. Martelli. (Extract translated by author.)

Pocock, J. G. A. (1975) *The Machiavellian Moment: Florentine political thought and the Atlantic Republic*, Princeton, NJ: Princeton University Press.

Popper, K. R. (1966) *The Open Society and its Enemies*, vol. 1, London: Routledge & Kegan Paul, 5th edn.

Prezzolini, G. (1926) *Vita di Niccolò Machiavelli fiorentino*, Milano: Mondadori.

Ritter, G. (1972) *The Sword and the Sceptre: the problem of militarism in Germany*, London: Allen Lane.

Rousseau, J.-J. (1994) 'Il Contratto sociale' in *Scritti politici*, vol. II, Roma: Bari.

Viroli, M. (1995) *For love of country: essay on patriotism and nationalism*, Oxford: Oxford University Press.

2
Marketing

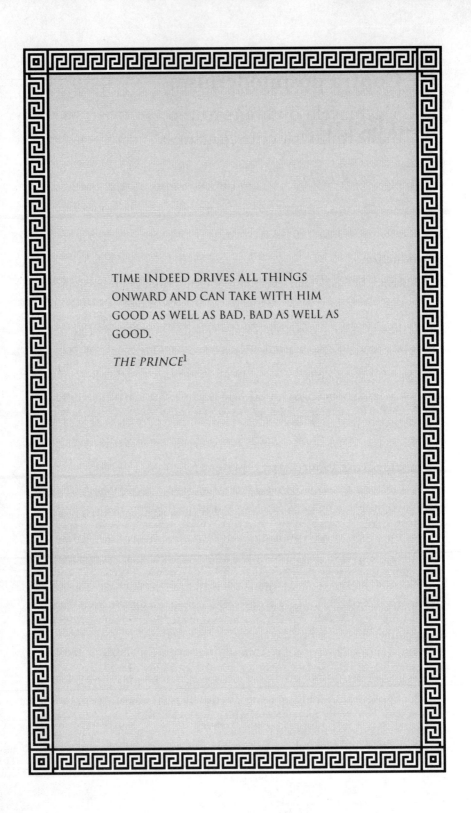

TIME INDEED DRIVES ALL THINGS
ONWARD AND CAN TAKE WITH HIM
GOOD AS WELL AS BAD, BAD AS WELL AS
GOOD.

THE PRINCE[1]

5 Contra postmodernism
Machiavelli on limits to the malleability of consciousness

Richard Elliott

Introduction

The influence of media representations on interpretations of reality is proposed as an irresistible process of the postmodern world (Featherstone 1991). Baudrillard (1983) goes so far as to propose that we now live in 'hyperreality' where the real and the simulated become confused so that images are indistinguishable from reality, and in fact become 'more real than the real'. The individual in postmodernity is depicted as a powerless victim of an 'hallucination of reality'. The postmodern condition, then, is one in which the 'aestheticisation of everyday life' has led to symbolic overload as the individual is bombarded with 'floating signifiers' and is unable to resist the hegemonic power of the mass media.

Lived experience vs mediated experience

In contrast to this postmodern perspective on the unlimited power of persuasion through media imagery, Machiavelli was the first communication theorist to identify the countervailing effects of lived experience. In *The Prince*, Machiavelli makes it clear that he sees a separation between mediated experience and lived experience: ' ... men are generally incredulous, never really trusting new things unless they have tested them by experience' (1961: 51) and 'it is easy to persuade them of something, but difficult to confirm them in that persuasion' (1961: 52). He was therefore a poststructuralist *avant la lettre*, anticipating by some 500 years the distinction made by Thompson (1995), who suggests that lived experience concerns the practical activities and face-to-face encounters in our everyday lives, which are situated, immediate, and largely non-reflexive, in that we take them for granted as 'reality'. Lived experience is a continual immersion in events and actions along a path in time. This historical aspect of lived experience is cumulative in that all past life and current situation are constantly in need of integration, which is largely a non-conscious process.

This should be distinguished from mediated experience which is an outcome of mass-communication culture and the consumption of media products and involves the ability to experience events which are spatially and temporally distant from the practical context of daily life. Machiavelli made this distinction long before the electronic age when he suggested that: 'Men in general judge by their eyes rather than by their hands; because everyone is in a position to watch, few are in a position to come in close touch with you. Everyone sees what you appear to be, few experience what you really are' (ibid.: 101). Certainly, there is considerable empirical evidence that attitudes formed through direct experience are stronger, more accessible, held more confidently and are more predictive of behaviour than those derived from mediated experience through advertising (e.g. Fazio and Zanna 1978; Smith and Swinyard 1988).

Viscous meaning and mediated experience

The meanings of mass communications start from reception by the individual, emerge in the interpersonal communication among people and may later become socially shared meaning: 'Shared meanings involving media content will arise among participants in the social action performances of reception and subsequent accommodation' (Anderson and Meyer 1988: 47). Yet these meanings are not solid, but remain viscous and tentative. Anderson and Meyer note that:

> ... sense making is an ongoing process in which meanings emerge in layers of time and circumstance and the development of one meaning does not preclude the development of others. We are prolific in our sense making, developing a depth and complexity of meaning.
>
> (Anderson and Meyer 1988: 17)

In order for the viscous meanings derived from mediated experience to become permanent and part of our consciousness, we must expose the meanings socially through the process of 'discursive elaboration' (Thompson 1990), which involves the social consumption of meanings, as they are described, discussed, argued about, laughed at, accepted or rejected. Anderson and Meyer (1988) note that mass media are often a source of interpersonal debate and, until meanings from mediated experiences have been subjected to discursive elaboration in a social context and interwoven with behavioural significations derived from everyday lived experience, they remain viscous, liable to be rejected or just forgotten. Only after this discursive elaboration can symbolic meanings be fully concretized and become what Eco (1979: 14) calls 'realised text'.

Symbolic meaning and ritual

Central to postmodern theory is the proposition that consumers no longer consume products for their material utilities but consume the symbolic meaning of those products as portrayed in their images, products in fact become commodity signs (Baudrillard 1983). 'The real consumer becomes a consumer of illusions' (Debord 1977) and 'the ad-dict buys images not things' (Taylor and Saarinen 1994). The functions of the symbolic meanings of products operate in two directions: outward in constructing the social world – *Social-Symbolism* – and inward towards constructing our self-identity – *Self-Symbolism* (Elliott 1997).

Machiavelli prefigured this 'symbolic turn' in the first *Discourse* where he identifies the consumption of symbolic meaning as the prime source of social stability, suggesting that religious worship can be used to 'inspire the populace to prefer the goods of their community to all other goods' (Skinner 1981). Machiavelli (1965: 234) goes on to valorize ritual as a vital element sustaining symbolic meaning suggesting that religious worship must be 'well used', anticipating McCracken's (1988) suggestion that ritual is the prime means for the transfer of symbolic meaning from good to person.

We engage in ritual partly to create or confirm socially shared meaning: 'the performers and the listeners are the same people. We engage in rituals in order to transmit collective messages to ourselves' (Leach 1976: 45). However, as pointed out by Mill (1875: 469), 'the laws of social phenomena can be nothing but the laws (actions and passions) of individual human nature' so individuals may have their own reasons, viewpoints and motives for ritualistic action which allow for contested meanings as well as shared meanings (Parkin 1992). Social rituals involve the valorization of shared meanings but we also engage in personal rituals which allow us to develop significations which are not reducible to language and will remain viscous and inchoate until expressed and validated in a social situation.

At the individual level, ritual behaviour can be a source of potent meaning creation and maintenance through the repetitive performance and valorization of even the most mundane of everyday lived experience, for example self-care rituals such as hair-washing and grooming (Rook 1985). It can also act as a defence mechanism against impulsive behaviour by requiring the rejection of socially harmful instincts and unconscious drives (Freud 1949). Individual rituals can also contribute to the 'individuation' process where the mature adult integrates the unconscious into consciousness and thereby gains control of his/her personality (Jung 1983).

Following in Machiavelli's footsteps, Durkheim (1912/1961) maintained that, through the exercise of religious rituals, high levels of emotion are expressed and these expressions work through 'collective effervescence' to develop and maintain social bonds. This ritual emotional experience occurs at the individual embodied level but often precedes and energizes social action (Lyon and Barbalet 1994). Turner (1969) agrees that ritual can have an integrative effect but proposes that it can also have an 'anti-structural effect'. In what he terms a 'liminal' phase, ritual engenders a feeling of 'communitas' which itself can be deviant, for example as central features of political resistance and confrontations.

The social practices of the 'kula' inter-tribal exchange cycles described by Malinowski (1922) provide an anthropological perspective on ritual behaviour that at first appears purely economic. Twice a year, the inhabitants of the Trobriands and other Melanesian islands would launch a canoe party to visit other oceanic islands carrying gifts and objects for barter. However, the main objective of these voyages was to obtain objects which were of no immediate practical use: white shell armlets and red shell necklaces. On arrival there would be much ritualistic entertainment followed by gift-giving and bartering, but the leading men in the party would seek out their permanent partners who would give them with much ceremony either armlets or necklaces which they would not possess for long before they were given away in turn. Although no individual islander appears to have been aware of it, the necklaces travelled from island to island in a clockwise direction and the armlets anticlockwise in an unchanging cycle linking thousands of people over a distance of hundreds of miles. Malinowski emphasized the social functions of the 'kula' in that it ensured that isolated peoples maintained contact with others and gave them an incentive for perilous journeys which, although they were accompanied by trade and barter, they would otherwise have had little need to undertake.

The social functions of 'kula' were developed by Mauss (1925/1990) in his theory of the Gift. Mauss proposed that the act of giving creates simultaneously a twofold relationship between giver and receiver, a relationship of solidarity and a relationship of superiority: the act both brings people together and pushes them further apart (Godelier 1999). Thus gift-giving rituals create obligations and can be simultaneously or successively an act of generosity or of violence and are replete with ambiguity and emotional potency. Machiavelli identified this strange bi-directional power of the gift long before anthropology: 'The nature of man is such that people consider themselves put under an obligation as much by the benefits they confer as by those they receive' (1961: 73).

The social effects of ritual have been explored in the area of broadcast media where televised ceremonies can be seen as a form of 'civil religion' which is laden with ambiguity that requires resolution by the audience (Dayan and Katz 1988). The acceptance and performance of ritual does not require total understanding, and television offers only partial explanations, often only 'suggesting an attitude towards events rather than spelling out their signification'. The place of reception, the private home, is no longer a separate domain from the public arena as public spaces invade the home. In traditional ritual ceremonies the witnesses validate it by their presence; similarly media events, through the shared experience of audiences, are validated and legitimized by the active television viewer, often watching as part of a small social group, who engage in discursive elaboration to arrive at the shared meaning of mediated events. Mediated ritual through television is an excellent example of Boorstein's 'The Image' (1972), having the power to lead us towards 'image thinking' which blurs out the outlines of reality and creates 'pseudo-events'. Our ability to distinguish between knowledge and ignorance is displaced by a multiplication of images, particularly advertising which finds its power through the three principles of pseudo-events: the appeal of the neither-true-nor-false; the appeal of the self-fulfilling prophecy; and the appeal of the half-intelligible. All this cyber-ritual contributes to a 'blurring of meaning' and a diminution of our power over the world (Boorstein 1972).

Language, thought and social representations

> Languages are systems of categories and rules based on fundamental principles and assumptions about the world. These principles and assumptions are not related to or determined by thought: they *are* thought ... . Such assumptions are embodied in language, learnt through language, and reinforced in language use.
>
> (Hodge and Kress 1993: 7)

Language performs a variety of functions in the world and does not just represent it for, as Foucault (1972) pointed out, we are only able to think within the constraints of discourse. Discourse is defined here as a system of statements that constructs an object, supports institutions, reproduces power relations and has ideological effects (Parker 1990). The fundamental assumptions of a poststructuralist perspective are that language is a medium oriented towards action and function, and that people use language intentionally to construct accounts or versions of the social world, this active process of construction being demonstrated in language variation (Elliott and Ritson 1998). Multiple meanings are inherent in poststructuralism, e.g. Barthes' classic description of language's inevitable 'overflows, leaks, skids, shifts, slips' (Barthes 1977). This freedom for language (and the individual) is evident in the lack of a unitary discourse found in empirical studies of everyday conversation where 'people frequently argue with each other, and often aloud with themselves' (Billig 1996). In their social practices individuals are faced with 'ideological dilemmas' as to how to categorize information into the multiplicity of alternative schemas they possess (Billig *et al.* 1988).

However, to paraphrase Marx: although we make our own history, we do not do so in circumstances of our own choosing. Symbolic freedom is severely constrained by social structure and by ideological limits to that which we are able to imagine. Discourse is socially determined through relationships of power extending through class and society. But this is not a uni-directional process as discourse also constructs social structures in a dialectical relationship, and individual acts of symbolic creativity are socially constitutive in that they cumulatively restructure orders of discourse (Fairclough 1989).

A concept that helps us link the individual domain with the social and individual freedom with social influence is that of social representations, shared images that permit us to give objects, persons and events 'a definite form, locate them in a given category and gradually establish them as a model of a certain type, distinct and shared by a group of people' (Moscovici 1984). Because they provide models for categorization and evaluation, social representations are behaviourally prescriptive and function on a psychological level, but are social in the sense that they are only constructed through social interaction. Although totally individual experience is part of our development of consciousness, almost all that we know we have learned from another, through their accounts, through the language that is acquired or through the objects which are used (Moscovici 1998). The significant knowledge and beliefs that enable us to live our lives have their origin in mutual interaction, and are located in specific structures such as families, churches, social movements and are adopted by the individuals who are part of them. 'The meaning which they communicate and the obligations which they recognize are profoundly incorporated in their actions and exercise a constraint which extends to all members of the community' (Moscovici 1998).

This introduces the important reciprocity of structure and action. Because it is only in behaviour that we interact with others, this is the way that representations of social structure are formed and so to focus only on structure ignores the reciprocity between social practice and structure. The structural dimension is the knowledge and beliefs, social relations and social identities that are formed by social practice but which also in turn guide and constrain social practice. Analysis in the structural dimension involves the analysis of social representations. Analysing the practice dimension requires an examination of the way in which the knowledge and beliefs, social relations and social identities are expressed and negotiated in behaviour and a search for evidence of uncertainty of or struggle over their form. Thus there is a constant interplay between the multiple contexts in which individuals are 'simultaneously embedded' and social representations at the individual level are meaning-making structures, but at the same time at the group level are the framework which allows individuals from the same social milieu to be able to predict and make sense of the behaviour of others (Oyserman and Markus 1998).

Narratives and experience

It has been proposed by Bruner (1990: 45) that there is a human predisposition to 'organise experience into a narrative form' and that through the construction of narratives we construct an orderly world, locate ourselves within it, and make ourselves meaningful and understandable to others. Four features differentiate narrative from other forms of discourse: its sequentiality, its 'indifference' to reality, its ability to merge the ordinary and the extraordinary and its dramatic quality. Narrative is inherently sequential in that it links together human beings, actions, events and experience into a story. A story can be based on reality or be entirely imaginary, be true or false without loss of the power of the story to organize events into a coherent sequence. One function of narrative is to provide a means of incorporating the extraordinary into the everyday by providing causal explanations that are within local cultural expectations. Bruner's final feature of narrative, its 'dramatism', posits that stories usually have a moral content, they relate to what is morally valued, morally appropriate or morally uncertain. To these elements of narrative can be added the dimension of movement or direction through time and the idea that narrative constructions can never be entirely a private matter, but are social constructions – the meaning of which requires negotiation between the individual and the social (Gergen and Gergen 1984).

Narrative identity theory (Ricoeur 1984, 1992) suggests that, in order to make time human and socially shared, we require a narrative identity for our self, that is, we make sense of ourselves and our lives by the stories we can (or cannot) tell. Thus we come to know ourselves by the narratives we construct to situate ourselves in time and place. This task can be greatly aided by symbolic resources; the main one articulated by Ricoeur (1978) is literature, which gives structure and meaning to the complexity and confusion of life by providing a causal model for the individual, linking disparate life events into a coherent sequence.

Dilemmas of the self

The individual in postmodern society is threatened by a number of 'dilemmas of the self' (Giddens 1991: 201): fragmentation, powerlessness, uncertainty and a struggle against commodification. These dilemmas are driven by the 'looming threat of personal meaninglessness' as the individual endeavours to construct and maintain an identity which will remain stable through a rapidly changing environment. Although the individual may on the one hand fear mass commodification because it threatens to remove choice and replace it with standardization, in fact, through ever-growing plurality of consumer choice, the individual is offered resources which may be used creatively to achieve 'an ego-ideal which commands the respect of others and inspires self-love' (Gabriel and Lang 1995: 98). The development of individual self-identity is inseparable from the parallel development of collective social identity, and this problematic relationship has been described as the 'internal–external dialectic of identification' by Jenkins (1996), who maintains that self-identity must be validated through social interaction and that the self is embedded in social practices.

The performative nature of social identity entails 'impression management strategies' where we endeavour to validate our self-identity in social interactions as we struggle to find the 'correct' signals to send and how to interpret others (Goffman 1959). For Goffman, there is a distinction between the 'all-too-human self' and the 'socialized self' or the 'self-as-character' and the 'self-as-performer' where the individual self has to be constructed through 'the all-too-human task of staging a performance'. This is similar to the concept of discursive elaboration where self and meaning must be subjected to social negotiation before becoming concrete. The use of a dramaturgical metaphor helps us recognize that in much of social life, we must all act to maintain the flow of social activity by accepting the impressions others attempt to impart regarding their identities and the meaning of their actions (Branaman 1997). A key issue here is that the self cannot be separated from the performance of self: 'To *be* a given kind of person, then, is not merely to possess the required attributes, but also to sustain the standards of conduct and appearance that one's social grouping attaches thereto' (Goffman 1959). Machiavelli was also concerned with impression management strategies, arguing that a Prince 'should appear to be compassionate, faithful to his word, guileless, and devout. And indeed he should be so' (1961: 100) and 'To those seeing and hearing him, he should appear a man of compassion, a man of good faith, a man of integrity, a kind and religious man' (1961: 101).

A Machiavellian model of the malleability of consciousness

We can now assemble a conceptual model of the development of consciousness based on Machiavelli's poststructuralist theory of persuasion and the importance of lived experience through narrative and ritual:

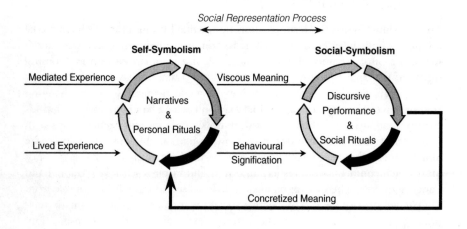

Figure 5.1   A Machiavellian model of consciousness

In this model, Machiavelli's emphasis on the political importance of symbolism and ritual is extended to include their role in the construction and maintenance of identity against the 'dilemmas of the self' inherent in postmodernity.
    Machiavelli wrote:

> Many have dreamed up republics and principalities which have never in truth been known to exist. [He is prefiguring here the world of Oxo's 'Katie' and Trollope's 'Aga saga'.] The gulf between how one should live and how one does live is so wide that a man who neglects what is actually done for what should be done learns the way to self-destruction rather than self-presentation. [Here he is anticipating self-bricolage.]
>
> (Machiavelli 1961: 90)

When writing this he had not been subjected, as we have, to the drenching effect of the mass media, so he still had the idea of a 'real' world and real ends to be achieved by purposive action. Thus his justification for a Prince learning 'not to be virtuous' is that this is to be used 'according to need' (1961: 91) and 'need' implies the existence of a desirable end. This form of pragmatism can easily be a euphemistic opening of the door to moral relativism, one of the most haunting fears of critics of postmodernism (Oram 1998). We should bear in mind, as a corollary to our awareness of the hegemonic voices whispering in our subconscious, that:

> The mind is its own place,
> and in itself
> can make a heaven of hell,
> a hell of heaven
> (John Milton, *Paradise Lost*, Book 1: line 253)

And we should seize the resources for empowerment which are to hand in the minutiae of everyday lived experience. Even if we only imagine freedom, imagined concepts can have real effects, and if we flag in our resolve, Nietzsche will spur us on:

> We have not truly got rid of God if we still believe in grammar.
> (Nietzsche 1977)

Note

1   Taken from Gilbert, A. (trans.) (1989) *Machiavelli: The Chief Works and Others*, vol. 1, Durham, NC: Duke University Press, p. 17.

References

Anderson, J. and Meyer, T. (1988) *Mediated Communication: A Social Action Perspective*, London: Sage.

Barthes, R. (1977) *Roland Barthes*, Basingstoke: Macmillan.

Baudrillard, J. (1983) *Simulations*, New York: Semiotext.

Billig, M. (1996) *Arguing and Thinking: A Rhetorical Approach to Social Psychology*, Cambridge: Cambridge University Press.

Billig, M., Condor, S., Edwards, D., Gane, M., Middleton, D. and Radley, A.R. (1988) *Ideological Dilemmas: A Social Psychology of Everyday Thinking*, London: Sage.

Boorstein, D. (1972) *The Image: A Guide to Pseudo Events in America*, New York: Atheneum.

Branaman, A. (1997) 'Goffman's Social Theory', in C. Lemert and A. Branaman (eds) *The Goffman Reader*, Oxford: Blackwell.

Bruner, J. (1990) *Acts of Meaning*, Cambridge, MA: Harvard University Press.

Dayan, D. and Katz, E. (1988) 'Articulating consensus: the ritual and rhetoric of media events', in J. Alexander (ed.) *Durkheimian Sociology: Cultural Studies*, Cambridge: Cambridge University Press.

Debord, G. (1977) *Society of the Spectacle*, Detroit, MI: Black & Red.

Durkheim, E. (1912/1961) *The Elementary Forms of the Religious Life*, London: Allen & Unwin.

Eco, U. (1979) *The Role of the Reader: Explorations in the Semiotics of Texts*, London: Hutchinson.

Elliott, R. (1997) 'Existential Consumption and Irrational Desire', *European Journal of Marketing*, 31 (4) 285–96.

Elliott, R. and Ritson, M. (1997) 'Poststructuralism and the Dialectics of Advertising: Discourse, Ideology, Resistance', in S. Brown and D. Turley (eds) *Consumer Research: Postcards from the Edge*, London: Routledge.

Fairclough, N. (1989) *Language and Power*, London: Longman.

Fazio, R. and Zanna, M. (1978) 'On the Predictive Validity of Attitudes: The Role of Direct Experience and Confidence', *Journal of Personality*, 46: 228–43.

Featherstone, M. (1991) *Consumer Culture and Postmodernism*, London: Sage.

Foucault, M. (1972) *The Archaeology of Knowledge*, London: Tavistock.

Freud, S. (1949) *Inhibitions, Symptoms and Anxiety*, London: Hogarth Press.

Gabriel, Y. and Lang, T. (1995) *The Unmanageable Consumer: Contemporary Consumption and its Fragmentations*, London: Sage.

Gergen, K. and Gergen, M. (1984) 'The Social Construction of Narrative Accounts', in K. Gergen and M. Gergen (eds) *Historical Social Psychology*, London: Lawrence Erlbaum.

Giddens, A. (1991) *Modernity and Self-Identity: Self and Society in the Late Modern Age*, Cambridge: Polity Press.

Godelier, M. (1999) *The Enigma of the Gift*, trans. N. Scott, Cambridge: Polity Press.

Goffman, E. (1959) *The Presentation of Self in Everyday Life*, Garden City, NJ: Anchor.

Hodge, R. and Kress, G. (1993) *Language as Ideology*, London: Routledge, 2nd edn.

Jenkins, R. (1996) *Social Identity*, London: Routledge.

Jung, C. (1983) *Selected Writings*, ed. A. Storr, London: Fontana.

Leach, E. (1976) *Culture and Communication: The Logic by which Symbols are Connected*, Cambridge: Cambridge University Press.

Lyon, M. and Barbalet, J. (1994) 'Society's Body: Emotion and the "Somatization" of Social Theory', in T. Csordas (ed.) *Embodiment and Experience: The Existential Ground of Culture and Self*, Cambridge: Cambridge University Press.

Machiavelli, N. (1961) *The Prince*, trans. G. Bull, Harmondsworth: Penguin.

—— (1965) *Discourses on the First Decade of Titus Livius*, trans. A. Gilbert, Durham, NC: University of North Carolina Press.

Malinowski, B. (1922) *Argonauts of the Western Pacific*, London: Routledge & Kegan Paul.

Mauss, M. (1925/1990) *The Gift: The Form and Reason for Exchange in Archaic Societies*, trans. W. Hall, London: Norton.

McCracken, G. (1988) *Culture and Consumption: New Approaches to the Symbolic Character of Consumer Goods and Activities*, Bloomington, IN: Indiana University Press.

Mill, J. S. (1875) *Dissertations and Discussions: Political, Philosophical and Historical*, London: Longmans Green.

Milton, J. (1998) *Paradise Lost*, Books 1 and 2, ed. A. Baldwin, Oxford: Oxford University Press.

Moscovici, S. (1984) 'The Phenomenon of Social Representations', in R. Farr and S. Moscovici, *Social Representations*, Cambridge: Cambridge University Press: 3–69.

—— (1998) 'The History and Actuality of Social Representations', in U. Flick (ed.) *The Psychology of the Social*, Cambridge: Cambridge University Press.

Nietzsche, F. (1977) *A Nietzsche Reader*, ed. R. Hollingdale, Harmondsworth: Penguin.

Oram, C. (1998) Personal communication, unpublished.

Oyserman, D. and Markus, H. (1998) 'Self as a Social Representation', in U. Flick (ed.) *The Psychology of the Social*, Cambridge: Cambridge University Press.

Parker, I. (1990) 'Discourse: Definitions and Contradictions', *Philosophical Psychology*, 3 (2): 189–204.

Parkin, D. (1992) 'Ritual as Spatial Direction and Bodily Division', in D. de Coppet (ed.) *Understanding Rituals*, London: Routledge.

Ricoeur, P. (1978) *The Rule of Metaphor: Multi-disciplinary Studies of The Creation of Meaning in Language*, trans. R. Czery, London: Routledge & Kegan Paul.

—— (1984) *Time and Narrative*, vol. 1, trans. K. McLaughlin and D. Pellar, Chicago, IL: Chicago University Press.

—— (1992) *Oneself as Another*, trans. K. Blamey, Chicago, IL: Chicago University Press.

Rook, D. (1985) 'The Ritual Dimension of Consumer Behaviour', *Journal of Consumer Research* 12: 251–64.

Skinner, Q. (1981) *Machiavelli*, Oxford: Oxford University Press.

Smith, R. and Swinyard, W. (1988) 'Cognitive Response to Advertising and Trial: Belief Strength, Belief Confidence and Product Curiosity ', *Journal of Advertising* 17 (3): 3–14.

Taylor, M. and Saarinen, E. (1994) *Imagologies: Media Philosophy*, London: Routledge.

Thompson, J. B. (1990) *Ideology and Modern Culture*. Cambridge: Polity.

—— (1995) *The Media and Modernity: A Social Theory of the Media*, Cambridge: Polity.

Turner, V. (1969) *The Ritual Process: Structure and Anti-Structure*, Chicago, IL: Aldine.

IT IS THE NATURE OF MEN TO FEEL AS
MUCH OBLIGATED FOR BENEFITS THEY
CONFER AS FOR THOSE THEY RECEIVE.

THE PRINCE[1]

6 Niccolò Machiavelli as relationship marketing guru

Michael Thomas

Introduction

My invitation to speak at the Machiavelli seminar stimulated me to reread *The Prince* and to see how useful parallels between his advice to the Prince and some of my current concerns about the future of marketing could be made. I have dwelt on the following topics, drawn from Machiavelli's chapter headings:

I   How many are the kinds of marketing and in what modes they are acquired
II   Of mixed marketing
III   How marketing should be administered
IV   Of those who have acquired marketing power through crimes
V   Of civil society
VI   In what mode marketing should be measured
VII   Of those things for which marketing is to be praised or blamed
VIII Of liberality and parsimony
IX   What a marketer should do to be held in esteem

Machiavelli offered me one challenge:

> It must be considered that there is nothing more difficult to carry out, nor more doubtful of success, nor more dangerous to handle than to initiate a new order of things. For the reformer has enemies in all those who profit from the old order, and only lukewarm defenders in all those who would profit by the new.
>
> (Machiavelli 1995: 51)

Jane Jacobs offered me another. She has written about right and wrong in business and politics. Her extraordinary book, *Systems of Survival* (Jacobs 1994), is written in the form of a Platonic dialogue about the moral foundations of commerce and politics. Jacobs explores two moral value systems. The dialogue that she constructs is based on two opposing moral syndromes, shown in table 6.1.

Table 6.1

The commercial moral	The guardian moral
Syndrome A	*Syndrome B*
Shun force	Shun trading
Come to voluntary agreements	Exert prowess
Be honest	Be obedient and disciplined
Collaborate easily with strangers and aliens	Adhere to tradition
Compete	Respect hierarchy
Use initiative and enterprise	Be loyal
Be open to inventiveness and novelty	Take vengeance
Be efficient	Deceive for the sake of the task
Promote comfort and convenience	Make rich use of leisure
Dissent for the sake of the task	Be ostentatious
Invest for productive purposes	Be exclusive
Be industrious	Show fortitude
Be thrifty	Be fatalistic
Be optimistic	Treasure honour

Source: Jacobs (1994: 214)

This clearly suggests a conflict between marketers' value systems and the guardian moral syndrome (defended and advocated by Machiavelli). I have been stimulated to explore the possibilities of convergence.

Jacobs refers to Machiavelli in her book:

> Machiavelli's famous advice to the Prince seems to cover many topics, and its ostensible theme is prowess, but its gist is loyalty: its indispensability to a successful prince. He dwells on it from every angle. How to deserve loyalty. How to win it, buy it, inculcate it, cultivate it, terrorize people into it. How to subvert loyalty to rival princes and States. How to sniff out disloyalty and deal with it. All his digressions lead back to loyalty ....
>
> (ibid.: 68)

The very stuff of marketing and marketing management. But alas, now my problem is exposed. For it is Jacobs' contention that in contemporary civil society there is a conflict between two moral syndromes: the first of which, the commercial syndrome, arises from trade and production unique to human beings; the second of which, the guardian syndrome, derives from behaviour which we share with other animals, protecting our territories, the ethical basis for the existence of armed forces, the police, government ministries and their legislatures, courts and organized religions. Two modes of survival with contradictory ethical systems.

What I will attempt to do is to explore my world, the world of markets and marketing, using some of Machiavelli's concepts, to see if reconciliation between the guardian syndrome and the commercial syndrome is possible.

I How many are the kinds of marketing and in what modes they are acquired

Free markets are an instrument of capitalism, but capitalism itself is an artefact created by legal artifice and political intervention, as table 6.2 demonstrates.

This leads me to speculate about the nature of what we will call the stakeholder society and the social market paradigm.

Table 6.2

	United Kingdom and United States	*Germany and Japan*
Time factor	Early industrializers.	Late industrializers.
Development strategy	Innovate across a broad front of entrepreneurship and management.	Catch up in technological sectors seen as the most valuable.
Historical role of governments	Generally ignorant of new business developments. Interfere after the fact to 'reform' wealth creators, who have adversarial roles to regulators.	Generally informed about strengths of leading economies. Co-operate before the fact to facilitate industrialization, playing a constructive role.
Education	Extremely broad and generalist, with stress on pure science and management studies.	More focused on successful technologies and science applied to key sectors.
Economies	Divided between macroeconomics (the whole economy) and microeconomics (the individual firm).	Organized around meso-economics (the dynamics of particular industries and sectors).
Social policies	Left behind in the leads to innovate. Government may seek to reimpose social 'burdens' on business retroactively.	Included in concerted efforts to industrialize. Government sees social benefits as key to winning popular consent.
Development philosophy	Laissez-faire, free-trade, and Anglo-American empiricism toward what markets demand, eschewing grand designs or 'picked winners'.	Managed competition, early protection, and teleology – a logic of ends – already accomplished by leading economies. Target key niches, 'pick teachers'.
Transition from feudalism	Slow and largely complete. Industry built on middle-class values of individualism and self-interest.	Rapid and partly unfinished. Industry built on collective concepts of feudal obligations and reciprocities.
Approach to financing industry	Domination by shorter-term equity markets and risk-taking profit-oriented individuals with high uncertainty, limited knowledge, fleeting relations.	Domination by longer-term bank financing and lower-risk industry-oriented institutions with lower uncertainty, deeper knowledge, closer relations.

Source: Hampden-Turner and Trompenaars (1993)

II   Of mixed marketing: the social market paradigm and the stakeholder society

The social market paradigm highlights the following factors:

1   Market institutions are not forms of spontaneous order – they are human artefacts created by legal artifice and political intervention.
2   Market institutions are justified by their contribution to individual and collective well-being and their structure is perpetually open to revision and reform.
3   Market institutions must be complemented by other institutions, and modes of public policy:

  - economic policy to create stability of both employment and prices
  - control instruments such as Company Law, Monopolies Commissions, Securities and Exchange Commissions, the World Trade Organization, the World Bank and the International Monetary Fund
  - market institutions are rooted in particular cultural traditions with an underpinning framework of law. These cultural traditions are diverse, as, to a degree, are the frameworks of law – individualistic in the Anglo-American tradition, solidaristic and familial in East Asia.

There is no universal or ideal typical market institution – all are rooted in cultural and historical forms. Markets that do not express the underlying national culture will be neither legitimate nor stable.

Markets will not have popular acceptance nor political stability if they do not meet the standards of legitimacy set by their underlying cultures. They must satisfy pervasive and deep seated norms of equity and fairness. Markets have a role as an important instrument of economic development – but only as an instrument.

Contemplate the following comparison in table 6.3, between the dominant social paradigm, and the environmental paradigm which is gathering support.

1   These two paradigms expose the tensions implicit in contemporary society. The stakeholder debate illustrates these tensions. It is the tension between personal autonomy and the need for membership and inclusion in the organization of civil society. Stakeholding is about the rights of ownership, the nature of trust relationships and political rights. All three exist and are defined in three contexts:

  i   At the micro level, concerning the rights and relationships of individuals in the workplace, in the household and in the neighbourhood.
  ii At the next higher level, in communities and organizations – companies, schools, hospitals, churches, trades unions, management and professional organizations, and voluntary associations.

Table 6.3

	Dominant social paradigm	Alternative environmental paradigm
Core values	Material (economic growth) Natural environment valued as a resource Domination over nature	Nonmaterial (self-actualization) Natural environment intrinsically valued Harmony with nature
Economy	Market forces Risk and reward Rewards for achievement Differentials Individual self-help	Public interest Safety Incomes related to need Egalitarian Collective/social provision
Polity	Authoritative structures (experts influential) Hierarchical Law and order	Participative structures (citizen/worker involvement) Nonhierarchical Liberation
Society	Centralized Large-scale Associations Ordered	Decentralized Small-scale Communitarian Flexible
Nature	Ample reserves Nature hostile/neutral Environment controllable	Earth's resources limited Nature benign Nature delicately balanced
Knowledge	Confidence in science and technology Rationality of means Separation of fact/value, thought/feeling	Limits to science Rationality of ends Integration of fact/value, thought/feeling

Source: After Routley (1982)

    iii   At the highest level, in national parliaments and in supranational orga-
nizations such as the European Union.

The tension, as reflected to a large degree in the social paradigm and the alternative paradigm, is the tension between the individual and the collective.

2   Being a stakeholder may imply autonomy and choice, freedom to enter and
exit jobs, organizations and relationships. On the other hand, stakeholding
implies collective obligations and rights conferred by membership of organizations. A stakeholder should have an interest in the decisions and actions
of all the organizations that affect the stakeholder's life and well-being, a
claim to the rights of consultation, access to all relevant information and,
most importantly, participation in decision making.

We may conclude that a stakeholding society must differ from the free market model, since it places implicit limits on the way the free market works because the rights defined in the stakeholder model require direct concern with the problems of polarization of society, concern with the marginalization of groups within society (the unemployed, the unskilled, the old, those who have not made it in the competitive market place), with the 'winner takes all' mentality of unfettered market competition.

III   How marketing should be administered

A new marketing paradigm is emerging which may hold rich possibilities for reconciling the dominant social paradigm with the environmental paradigm, the commercial moral syndrome with the guardian moral syndrome. These are questions that need to be addressed.

How do customers and consumers behave?

Much marketing thinking is guided by the belief that customers are rational value maximizers. What do we really know about how choices are made and exchanges consummated, in an era of proliferating choices and rapid technological and social change, and how these choices are influenced by persuasive efforts? What do we know about understanding customer needs – current, latent, and emerging?

What are the most appropriate models for describing and explaining the processes of search, preference formation and choice, and the resulting customer experience? Why are customers satisfied or dissatisfied, loyal or defectors? Further, what do we need to know about the influence of social trends, demographic shifts and market reforms on individual behaviour?

How do markets function and evolve?

The concepts of market segmentation, positioning and product life cycle are central to marketing. Yet serious doubts have been raised about the validity and utility of these foundation concepts. Are they adequate to the task of describing and explaining the function, structure and evolution of contemporary markets, or are new concepts and models needed? Issues that need to be addressed include: Are market boundaries distinct and stable, or shifting and overlapping? Is segmentation meaningful when it is possible to address and respond to segments of one? How do new products diffuse into new markets? How are patterns of market growth and evolution shaped by the forces of globalization, rapid information diffusion, and competitive consolidation? How do vertical market structures shift and how does value flow between levels?

How do firms relate to their markets?

In today's complex and dynamic global environment, firms increasingly relate to one another in the multiple roles of customer, competitor and collaborator. This raises questions concerning how firms should and do relate to their customers (and, by extension, to their customers' customers), to their suppliers and partners and to their competitors.

Marketing thought is shifting from an emphasis on transactions and acquisition to relationships and retention. Meanwhile, developments in information technology and networks facilitate interactive communications and help tighten relationships. There is a pressing need to understand the sources and implications of these evolving forms of linkages: why do the parties participate, how are conflicts resolved in a web of relationships and how do they evolve and adapt in global markets? How will electronic commerce and interactivity transform markets?

Co-operative relationships are also changing the competitive landscape. Suppliers, customers and channels – and even rivals – are entering into alliances and partnerships, greatly extending the complexity of inter-firm relationships. How will increasingly disaggregated firms manage the total value or supply chain? What competitive advantages are gained, and how are they sustained? A related issue is: how do firms come to understand and anticipate the reactions of competitors? How should they deal with the emergence of competition?

What are the contributions of marketing to organizational performance and societal welfare?

The role and value of marketing has been repeatedly challenged. Within the organization there have been pointed queries about the productivity of marketing expenditures, the appropriate organizational role and influence of the marketing function and the contributions to financial performance.

Where and when do marketing processes and activities need to be performed? There is also wide acceptance of the value of a marketing orientation to the organization. What is known and should be known about how this orientation is achieved and leads to better performance?

From a societal perspective, what is the net contribution of marketing societies and economies as a whole? What criteria should be used to judge their societal value? Who are the stakeholders? What theories and evidence can be used to objectively examine both the benefits as identified by it advocates and abuses seen by its critics? How might society seek to preserve the benefits and minimize the negative aspects?

All of those questions, when answered, will provide us with insights as to how marketing should be administered. We can point to a current development in marketing thought that suggests the direction of movement.

Relationship marketing is:

The consistent application of up-to-date knowledge on individual customers, to product and service design, which is communicated interactively, in order to develop a continuous and long-term relationship, which is mutually beneficial.

> Marketing needs to switch from current to lifetime value of customers. Indeed it could even open up an intriguing debate about whether or not excess returns are appropriately allocated to shareholders instead of customers. After all, shareholders only provide the commonest commodity – funds – whereas customers potentially provide the rarest loyalty.
>
> (Brady 1996: 10)

Loyalty, that lovely Machiavellian word.

The lifetime value of the customer. That has a resonance with loyalty. Brady also challenges us to think about stakeholders. Table 6.4 explicates the contrast between transactional and relationship marketing.

Table 6.4

Transactional marketing	Relationship marketing
Do the deal and disappear	Negotiate a win–win sale situation and stay around, being a resource for better results
Push price	Promote value
Short-term thinking and acting	Long-term thinking and acting
Build the business on deals	Build the business on relationship
Getting new customers	Keeping all customers and clients
No structure for ongoing business	Structure created to support relationship; special clubs and memberships for frequent user–buyers
Selling-focused	Relationship-focused for results
Short-term empathy	Long-term empathy and rapport
Incentive for doing the deal	Incentive for long-term relationships and revenue
Foundation of sale – telling and selling	Foundation of revenue – trust
Race for a sale result	Swift, strong and enduring in results through relationship building
After-sales support and service poor – seen as cost	After-sales support and service strong – seen as an investment in the relationship
Product–service-focused	People-expectations and perception focused
Rewards – incentive for 'doing deals'	Rewards – incentive for maintaining and growing relationship and revenue
'The deal is the end'. Pursuit of deal	The sale – just the beginning. Pursuit of long-term relationship and results

IV   Of those who have acquired marketing power through crimes

There is no doubt that many people have distrusted those who are involved in marketing. There is a curious paradox here. We are all of us consumers and, as consumers, we have power – the power to withhold our custom. We disapprove of selling refrigerators to Eskimos, we believe, rightly, that pyramid selling is exploitation, we disguise salesmen as commercial travellers. The carpet-bagger mentality supposes that consumers have short memories – my experience is quite the contrary. A cheated or short-changed customer never forgets. Nonetheless we should recognize, certainly historically, that there has been a lack of trust between buyers and sellers. One of the real benefits of globalizing business and the emergence of global brands, is that consumers are exposed to best practice, by which they may judge all competitors. That said, it would be myopic to believe that best practice is pervasive. We believe that the relationship paradigm does propose a long-term relationship as the way for buyers and sellers to relate, reducing the pay-off from short-termism. Whether caveat emptor will be replaced by caveat vendor is arguable, perhaps not even desirable. I have a particular interest in the economies in transition in the former Soviet empire. In parts of that empire there is today visible evidence of crime driving good business practice out and Mafiosi values ruling in many areas of business activity. Further, we are witnessing what Kapuscinski has called enclave development:

> In a highly developed European country, in Holland, for example, or Switzerland, the entire material world around us is developed at more or less the same level: the houses are neatly painted, there are panes in all the windows, the asphalt on the roads is smooth and the traffic lines well demarcated, the stores everywhere are well stocked, the restaurants are warm and clean, the street lamps are lit, and the lawns are evenly mowed. In a country with enclave development, however, the landscape looks different. An elegant bank stands amid shabby apartment buildings; a luxurious hotel is surrounded by slums; from a brightly illuminated airport one plunges into the darkness of a grim, squalid city; beside the glittering display window of a Dior boutique, the dirty, empty, and unlit windows of local shops; next to impressive cars, old, stinking, crowded city buses. Capital (largely foreign) has constructed its fragrant and shining sanctuaries, these excellent enclaves, but it has neither the means to nor any intention of developing the rest of the country.
>
> (Kapuscinski 1994: 328–9)

That is a depressing picture of current reality in the former Soviet Union and contains an indictment of Western capitalists. In Poland, to which I am a frequent visitor, the juxtaposition of local Coca-Colonization and the creation of MacWorld values stand alongside growing income disparities and a still fairly chaotic infrastructure. It is a situation where crimes and misdemeanours as drivers of trade and personal wealth creation outside the law flourish. We need not travel to Poland, however, for criminal economic and marketing activity are readily observed in the high-rise housing estates of Manchester, Liverpool, Edinburgh – the list goes on. And on a grander scale we cannot understand what is causing concern in the Pacific Rim, from which I have just returned, without understanding that criminal and conspiratorial behaviour is not unrelated to the problem. Covering clients' losses was the downfall of a major Japanese securities firm, just as Nick Leeson's greed (and those of his masters in London) led to the downfall of Barings Bank. That sort of marketing power is criminal and should be punished. It has no place in a responsible marketing environment, no place in a relationship marketing environment, though it clearly was part of the pathology of the transactional marketing environment.

V   Of civil society: glimpse of paradise lost and paradise regained

New productive technologies are raising the importance of human skills, of innovative technology based on research and development and of infrastructure, including virtual reality infrastructure like the Internet. All three are social investments.

Technology is a social process of human creativity and innovation. Social investment in education and research, and in infrastructure, leads to increased productivity. Yet we live at a moment when the current emphasis is on individual consumption and hence acquisition is the centre, the core of the value system – it is the pursuit of hedonism encouraged by market freedom. Can we shift capitalism from consumption ideology to a builder ideology? Success in the future will be based on building, on building brain power industries such as the bio-technology, pharmaceutical and chemical industries, the semi-conductor industry, telecommunications, aerospace, robotics, information technology – man-made brain-power industries, all are transforming our lives. The educational system and the healthcare delivery system are essentially public goods and their quality is an acid test of civil society. Both depend on builder ideology, both depend on human skills, advancing technology and infrastructure. Both are under threat from market forces, both are being seduced by the ethics of unfettered market capitalism. Hedonism and profit maximization should have nothing to do with education and healthcare. To temper the market we must reclaim civil society and government – we must again embrace the idea that government and civic vitality are allies not adversaries.

Paradise lost

1   Consumerism rules. The consumer and the person have become synonymous.
2   Civic alienation and spiritual poverty are widespread.

3   The nation state yields all power to global corporations and global financial markets.

4   Global companies seek out market freedom, but market freedom does not equal democracy. The biggest loser from globalization is labour, especially unskilled labour in the First World.

5   The invisible hand pays no attention to full employment, to environmental protection, to social safety nets, to personal protection.

6   Markets are not guarantors of the public good.

7   Increasing global production will lead to growing surpluses of goods because of the present and foreseeable maldistribution of income. Global production also endangers cultural identity – cars look alike, pop music and MTV are all persuasive, and English, peppered with Americanisms, is the world language.

The threats to the future of civil society:

1   Individual greed, unenlightened self-interest.
     Untrammelled individualism corrupts a nation. It leads to an emphasis on rights, with no regard to duties or responsibilities. It breeds distrust and jealousy – and lots of lawyers. If we can leave families when we feel like it, live free to ignore or insult our neighbours, treat organizations as stepping stones on a personal trip, and only make friends who will be useful contacts, to be discarded when no longer needed, we will erode that 'social capital' which more and more people are recognizing as the bedrock of a successful and prosperous society. The first principles of a civil society should be inclusion and self-restraint.

2   Global warming.

3   Nuclear weapons and international arms traffic.

4   Competing nationalisms.

5   Species extinction/habitat destruction.

6   Population pressures and mass refugee migration.

7   Poverty both in the Third World and at home (3 million people sleep on the streets of western Europe).

8   Disaffection with politics and political parties.

9   Pervasive loss of community. Loss of cohesion and stability in society.

10   Spread of restrictive, condemnatory religious fundamentalism.

11   Rising unemployment.

The architecture of paradise regained:

1   Social justice.

2   Democratic renewal.

3   Community regeneration.

4   A social market economy.

5   Equitable rewards for all stakeholders.

6   Cultural benefits (presently enjoyed by only a minority).
7   A peaceable global society.

VI   In what mode marketing should be measured: sophisticated measurement instruments will be revealed

It follows from what has preceded, that marketing and business activity needs to be measured in a much more sophisticated way than presently institutionalized by the accounting profession under the euphemism 'generally accepted accounting principles'. I have written extensively on this topic, but here I can only highlight the principles that I have elaborated elsewhere.

I have argued that successful companies add value more efficiently and more effectively than their competitors, judged primarily by the attitudes and behaviour of their customers.

I advocate that an organization's ability and success in adding value requires measurement of leadership (ability to deliver customer value), of marketing professionalism (market share, return on marketing investment, brand development, brand strength performance, the customer management process, customer retention performance), innovation management (customer and product development processes), supply chain management, financial management (investor satisfaction, price, relative cost of capital), employee management (investment in people, motivation, empowerment, turnover, value added per employee) and community relations.

VII   Of those things for which marketing is to be praised or blamed

Some would be brave enough to argue that marketing was responsible for the collapse of communism. The Ossies knew what was available to the Wessies on the other side of the Berlin Wall, so one day in 1989 they decided to break down the wall. Others will argue that the Soviet system imploded. Yes, its inability to deliver worldly goods was undoubtedly an important factor.

Less controversially, consider the following factors, all of which are market and marketing related. The internationalization of business is market driven – the search for customers. Nationally separate markets are no longer relevant. Where markets are not growing (characteristic of western Europe) competition between producers (of both products and services) leads to a search for better value for money strategies, for customer retention and loyalty strategies. Time-based competition (JIT) leads to 'faster to market' and 'first mover' strategies, which accelerates innovation rates. Market and performance assessment become more critical. The marketing concept (the whole business seen from the point of view of its end result – the consumer or customer) is now seen as relevant to all organizations – giant multinationals, SMEs, universities, theatres, symphony orchestras, the Salvation Army, the Boy Scouts – all have to be managed but none will survive unless what they offer to the market is perceived by consumers as having value.

VIII Of liberality and parsimony

We can identify the things that make managers' lives difficult. The sheer scale of contemporary management change; the frequency of management failure; the tension between business and the environment; the tension between business's need for innovation and the community's need for stability; the tension between the changing nature of knowledge and the limited capacity of the human mind; the tension between business's need to compete internationally and society's interest in the common good. How do we reconcile these tensions?

IX What a marketer should do to be held in esteem

Though we must beware of millennial pessimism, recent events in the Pacific Rim have reminded us that the global economy is not as robust as we might like to think. We, in Europe, are to a degree surrounded by economic, social and ideological uncertainty. Rising unemployment here (not mirrored in the USA) carries the threat of social instability. Global competition and the IT revolution have forced industrial restructuring, and are accelerating the process of techno-logical change. Concerns about job security, about crime, about healthcare create social insecurity, at a time when it has been popular to reduce or dismantle the welfare state and to privatize. Pro-market ideology has been triumphant for the last twenty years.

As a marketer I react in this way. Companies, organizations and indeed governments should be in the business of delivering value – if they do so, they inculcate loyalty. In western Europe we must be clear as to where our compara-tive advantage lies. We have a relatively well-educated middle class, so I must believe that technological innovation remains a major source of adding value. The pharmaceutical companies of Europe are world-class players. We have the capability of adding more value in the semi-conductor industry (we must reduce our dependence on America and Japan). We surely can add (global) value to the arts, culture and music (both pop and classical!) and in the fields of fashion goods and design. In the field of education, our quality standards are still highly regarded worldwide. We will still make things like refrigerators, auto-mobiles and aircraft, but the growing markets are elsewhere and there will be continuing pressure to take manufacturing closer to those markets.

We are left to speculate about the future relationship between marketing and politics. I detect some reaction against pro-market ideology. Let us talk about the politics of moderation. Will a reaction develop against our harried and congested lives? Will the growth markets be associated with leisure, relaxation and healthcare? Might we become bored with material possessions (and their acquisition) and consumerism *per se*? Will increasing emphasis on personal qualities, on knowledge (and knowledge acquisition), on health, lead politics toward the environmental paradigm? That paradigm holds the promise of self-actualization, of the public interest, of communitarian values, of mutual interdependence.

If there is a move in this direction, then we may begin to understand the relationship between excessive inequality and political instability, between over-consumption and environmental degradation, between social values and economic performance.

Perhaps I am contemplating a postmodern, post-marketing, post-consumerist society. But if you believe, as do I, that marketing is about delivering value, then companies, organizations and politicians will have to deliver value to sovereign consumers and citizens. If we demand a change – in our life styles, in our society's values – then in the market for ideas there will be responses and those who respond appropriately will be rewarded with our loyalty. How to deserve loyalty, how to win it, inculcate it, cultivate it, is what marketing is all about.

Note

1   Taken from Gilbert, A. (trans.) (1989) *Machiavelli: The Chief Works and Others*, vol. 1, Durham, NC: Duke University Press, p. 44.

References

Brady, J. (1996) 'The Future of Marketing: old age or second adolescence?', *Journal of Marketing Practice* 2 (4): 7–10.

Hampden-Turner, C. and Trompenaars, A. (1993) *The Seven Cultures of Capitalism*, New York: Doubleday.

Jacobs, J. (1994), *Systems of Survival*, London: Hodder & Stoughton.

Kapuscinski, R. (1994) *Imperium*, London: Granta Books.

Machiavelli, N. (1995) *The Prince*, ed. G. Bull, London: Penguin.

Routley, R. (1982) *The Basic Philosophical and Semantic Theory*, Co. Alaschdero, CA: Ridgeview Publications.

WE ARE MORE INCLINED TO MAKE A
RETURN FOR AN INJURY THAN FOR A
BENEFIT, FOR GRATITUDE IS LOOKED ON
AS A BURDEN, REVENGE AS A GAIN.

HISTORY OF FLORENCE[1]

7   Machiavellian communication

The role of spin doctors and image makers in early and late twentieth-century British politics

Dominic Wring

Introduction

A major and recurrent theme of reports about the new Labour government is the way in which the administration is obsessed with the image it presents. It is a theme implicit throughout *The Prince*, Machiavelli's pioneering study of statecraft:

> ... for as those who wish to delineate countries place themselves low in the plain to observe the form and character of mountains and high places, and for the purpose of studying the nature of the low country place themselves high upon an eminence, so one must be a prince to know well the character of the people, and to understand well the nature of a prince one must be of the people.
>
> (Machiavelli 1997: 4)

In modern political discourse the same phenomenon is evidenced by the many references to the ability of the so-called 'spin doctors' and focus groups to influence the development of policy. In his book *The Unfinished Revolution*, leading Blair strategist Philip Gould (1998) describes how he believes the self-styled modernizers (of which he was one) 'saved' the party from the despair and defeat to which it succumbed during the 1980s and early 1990s. At the heart of Gould's book is a concern to show how the marketing techniques he used were central to the rejuvenation and alleged reinvention of the party as 'New' Labour. Widely accepted in the media and by many political analysts, the concept of 'new' Labour is nevertheless a contested one. Eric Shaw (1995) questions whether a broad range of party members as varied as James Callaghan and Tony Benn can be collectively labelled 'old'. Others, such as former Millennium Dome adviser Stephen Bayley (1998), have written about what they believe to be the cosmetic communications strategy that hides the vacuous and muddled thinking at the heart of government.

The criticisms of Shaw, Bayley and others apart, it is instructive how successful Blair and his leadership team have been in restructuring the media's discourse in relation to their party. And yet they were not the first, nor even the most important, Labour pioneers of image management. Before, during and after the Policy Review of the late 1980s, the Kinnock leadership assiduously used marketing expertise in their overhaul of party policy and organization. Arguably it was these changes that created the political environment in which those like Tony Blair could flourish. Going further back Harold Wilson showed himself to be very adept at crafting and managing his own and his party's image in a series of campaigns, including the 'Let's Go with Labour' and eerily familiar 'New Britain' offensives that culminated in the 1964 Labour victory. As in 1997, these strategies aided Labour's return to office after a prolonged period of Conservative government and showcased the importance of good political communications.

The work of the Kinnock and, to a lesser extent, the Wilson leaderships is relatively well known. However, largely absent from discussion of Labour political communications is any reference to some of the innovative and highly sophisticated work done by key party strategists during the inter-war years. This was a particularly significant period, marking as it did Britain's transition to mass democracy and the emergence of affordable and highly pervasive mass media. In the 1920s the party branded itself, by adopting its first proper logo 'Liberty'. In 1922 senior strategist Sidney Webb also devised an ingenious system for identifying voters, called 'stratified electioneering':

> We should, as far as possible, 'stratify' our electioneering; appealing to each section of the electorate in the language which that section understands; emphasising just the points in which that section is interested; subordinating the questions that each section finds dull or unpleasant; addressing to each section the literature most appropriate to it; and generally seeking to substitute, for the 'greyness' of mass propaganda, the warmer and more individual colours of each man's speciality.
>
> (Wring 1996)

Webb's formulation was an attempt to segment this particular 'market'. Whatever the name, it was groundbreaking analysis. In addition to this, other Labour organizers sought to develop new and imaginative ways of using visual media. One enterprising local party tried to court young people with a film 'Love and Labour', combining romantic adventure and political conversion on a day out to Southend (Wring 1997). In 1935 the party even considered using an advertising agency. Though it did not, there was informal contact between marketing executive and party supporters, notably Herbert Morrison. And it is the 'Machiavellian' contribution of Morrison that will be explored in detail. More than any other Labour figure of the early twentieth century he saw the need to use and manage mass communications in the pursuit of political goals. In this there is also a fascinating and striking parallel between the work of Morrison and that of his grandson and fellow partisan Peter Mandelson. Like his famous relative, Mandelson is often identified as being the central figure behind the renewal of Labour's political communications strategy during his period of influence in the 1980s and 1990s. Before turning to discuss Morrison's pioneering work, the role of Mandelson in constructing and consolidating the 'new' Labour Party will be assessed.

The rise of Peter Mandelson

Since he first came to prominence in the mid-1980s as the Labour Party's Director of Campaigns and Communications, Peter Mandelson has excited considerable public controversy. Initially debate was concerned with his role as a key lieutenant of Neil Kinnock during the latter's sometimes turbulent period as Labour leader. In the post Kinnock became intent on, as he saw it, 'reforming' the party. For his part, the Campaigns Director played a prominent role in assiduously promoting the leader's agenda by briefing and advising selected press contacts. On these occasions critics and allies alike recognized Mandelson's ability to cultivate journalists and yet simultaneously infuriate politicians and officials who not uncommonly belonged to his own party.[2] Indeed Mandelson has been one of the political actors whose work has become synonymous with the term 'spin doctoring', a phrase which entered the political lexicon in the early 1990s. Besides his role as a press officer, Mandelson also played a part in developing Labour's use of marketing expertise, most notably by helping to organize and sustain the so-called 'Shadow Communications Agency'.

Mandelson's reputation for attracting controversy carried over into his first, successful attempt to win the Labour nomination and then the Hartlepool constituency in the 1992 general election.[3] Despite his personal victory, the party suffered a fourth national defeat at an election that ended Kinnock's career at the helm of the party. With his ally gone, Mandelson fared less well during the leadership of John Smith. His moment of triumph came with the election of Tony Blair as Smith's successor following the latter's death in 1994. Blair, a long time associate of Mandelson and fellow protégé of Kinnock, duly acknowledged the Hartlepool MP's part in his campaign for the leadership during a victory speech to his supporters. Conscious of the controversy that accompanied the mere mention of Mandelson's name, the new leader thanked his friend in code referring only to the debt of gratitude he owed to 'Bobby'. 'Bobby', it turned out, had played a key role as a confidant and adviser throughout a largely surefooted and competent leadership campaign (Jones 1995).

Blair's patronage secured Mandelson a prominent place within the 'New' Labour government elected in 1997. His success came, however, at a price. In giving covert aid to Blair, Mandelson succeeded in thwarting the political ambitions of Gordon Brown, the other main protégé of Neil Kinnock. Long considered as a serious contender for the leadership, Brown withdrew as a contender for the post after receiving a generally lacklustre press in the few weeks following Smith's death. By contrast Blair received plaudits and endorsements from journalists and then nominations of support from several MPs

(Franklin and Larsen 1994, Wring 1998). With Mandelson's part in the Blair campaign revealed, it was too much for some and Brown allies, such as Labour Consumer Affairs spokesperson Nigel Griffiths, made statements critical of the Hartlepool backbencher. The episode aided Mandelson's career but did little to dispel his image as a 'fixer' and 'manipulator' steeped in the supposedly unhealthy arts of the public relations professional.

More than one journalist has referred to his reputation for being an 'evil genius', 'prince of darkness' and, more pointedly, Mandelson's 'Machiavellian' ways (McSmith 1996). This label dogged his high-profile tenure as the supposedly 'behind the scenes fixer' Minister without Portfolio with responsibility for co-ordination of government policy. Speculation and interest in Mandelson continued following his promotion to the Cabinet as Secretary of State for Trade and Industry in 1998. A 'proper' job, the appointment signalled the beginnings of a serious attempt by the incumbent to establish a public reputation as a politician rather than as a creature of media fascination and Blair acolyte. The strategy proved short-lived following a highly detailed and uncomfortable assessment of Mandelson's private life. More devastatingly, press speculation over the Secretary of State's financial affairs ended in embarrassing revelations about his mortgage which ultimately led to his resignation after only a few months in high office (Routledge 1999, MacIntyre 1999). Several media opponents could barely contain their gloating over Mandelson's dramatic downfall. A major part of the subsequent reportage returned to the subject of his supposed deviousness and media skills. Others have developed or managed to cultivate such reputations, none more so than Mandelson's fellow Labour MP, Herbert Morrison.

Two things directly link the experiences of Morrison with those of Mandelson. First, the two men relate to each other not just as Labour strategists but, more literally, as grandfather and grandson: 'spinning' as it were could be 'in the blood'. Second, both politicians were committed to using public relations and advertising to get their message across. Far from being a superfluous activity, the two recognized professional advice and techniques to be an integral part of a carefully planned campaign. Furthermore, both succeeded in courting attention as well as animosity through their work as political communicators. However, whilst Mandelson's activities are widely known about and have been discussed in most recent accounts of the Labour Party (Hughes and Wintour 1990, Heffernan and Marqusee 1992, Shaw 1994, Anderson and Mann 1997), relatively little is known about the pioneering work of his grandfather over sixty years ago. It is to this case that discussion will now turn.

Herbert Morrison: 'spin doctor'

Herbert Morrison is more commonly remembered for being a highly influential Labour figure of the mid-twentieth century who served as a senior Cabinet minister before rising to become Foreign Secretary. Less remarked upon, he was also a keen proponent of good presentation. As early as 1920 he was castigating

party publicity for being 'dull, heavy and badly displayed' (Morrison 1920:
201). Partly to compensate for this, Morrison argued that good press relations
should be an important aim of every party organizer:

> Discretion is always desirable, but generally speaking it is best to assume
> that newspapermen are your friends, and to send Party publications to the
> Press, treating all papers equally. Newspapermen often write things we do
> not like and capitalism is as bad for journalism as it is for other occupations,
> but it is no more a reason for treating journalists with personal discourtesy
> than the need for housing would justify a housing reformer abusing a
> building trades operative engaged in the erection of a cinema.
>
> (Morrison 1920: 202)

Evidently people took Morrison's ideas seriously because he was elected to the
National Executive Committee in 1920, becoming a diligent and industrious
member of its Literacy and Publicity Sub-committee (Donaghue and Jones
1973). The following year he sought to lead by example when he wrote *The
Citizen's Charter*. Published to accompany his own parliamentary bill,
Morrison's 1921 pamphlet was concerned with protecting the rights of the
public against unscrupulous private business interests intent on monopolizing
local markets in food and other essential items (Morrison, 1921). If the title of
this plan is Morrison's rarely acknowledged legacy to governmental public relations in the 1990s, his wider work in the field of political communication
helped introduce innovative methods to Labour Party organization.

Morrison's unusual attention to publicity set him apart from Labour
colleagues. This approach did not, however, stem from his London County
Council (LCC) career. In 1912 he had started working for the *Daily Citizen* as
a circulation traveller before rising to become deputy manager of the section
(Edelman 1948). The job proved useful to his political career: Morrison gained
an insight into aspects of the trade such as layout and advertising in addition to
his formal responsibilities. As biographer Maurice Edelman noted: 'With his
experience which, though small, had been intensive he saw the value of what
later came to be known as public relations but which was then known quite
bluntly as propaganda' (ibid.: 30). Later, as Mayor of Hackney in the 1920s, he
demonstrated an acute concern for providing journalists on the local *Spectator*
paper with countless stories about his endeavours (Donaghue and Jones 1973:
55).

Having served on the borough authority, Morrison embarked upon a career
in city-wide politics by winning a seat on the LCC and then the group leadership. From this position he helped orchestrate a Labour victory. Morrison took
great personal interest in promoting the authority. In 1934 he proved to be
instrumental in first initiating and then co-ordinating Council use of professional advertising and public relations techniques.[4] Morrison issued briefings for
journalists and held press conferences at which sherry, not tea, was served. In
good Machiavellian fashion and, not unlike his grandson, he also used off-the-

record briefings and fed favourable stories to sympathetic columnists like Preston Benson of *The Star*, a paper which became known as 'Herbert's anchor'.

Other image-conscious projects followed, including the introduction of floodlighting at County Hall. Morrison also expanded the LCC publicity department, and directly involved himself in its work in such a way that: 'Presentation sometimes became more important than content, and he would judge an official's memorandum by its usefulness for reporters' (Donaghue and Jones 1973: 207–8). On one occasion, when the authority's Auxiliary Fire Service was launching an appeal for more volunteers, Morrison called in an advertising agency and organized a press conference at County Hall at which he used a ladder to climb down from a window onto a fire appliance below. He then proceeded to address the crowd. This early example of a 'photo-opportunity' was a great piece of political theatre and huge public relations success (ibid.: 208).

Morrison: 'market researcher'

Like Machiavelli in the quote at the beginning of this paper, Morrison showed himself to be preoccupied with understanding public opinion. In 1923 he wrote one of the most interesting and influential papers on the new electoral arithmetic. Posing the question: 'Can Labour win London without the middle classes?', he answered with an emphatic 'No'. In doing so, Morrison encouraged fellow organizers to gain the confidence and votes of what he called 'brainworkers', citing statistics based on the 1921 census in London showing the existence of an estimated 2.32 million working-class and 1.23 million middle-class voters living in the capital. From this Morrison argued the concentration of the proletariat in safe Labour parliamentary and council seats made it necessary for the party to pursue the affluent electorate, a group he admitted had tended to be regarded by sections of the organization as a 'psychological problem'. Besides their size, concentration in marginal constituencies and relationship to the 'Balance of Power', Morrison believed middle-class support was needed to compensate for what he estimated to be the quarter to a third of workers who voted Conservative. In conclusion, he argued Labour need to cultivate professional and self-employed people:

> ... by careful propaganda, by talking to them in a language which they understand rather than in some of our classic phrases which may be unintelligible or repugnant to them, there is no insurmountable difficulty which prevents us in due course securing a considerable number of supporters from among the middle classes and those are 'workers on their own account'.
>
> (Morrison 1923)

During the early 1940s Morrison returned to the theme of class, warning Labour against falling into the trap of using what he called the rhetoric of 'prefabricated slogans' presumably lest they detract from gaining the votes of discerning non-manual workers. By moving from his safe seat in proletarian Hackney to stand for the more middle-class East Lewisham constituency at the 1945 election, Morrison underlined the strength of his personal commitment to winning non-traditional supporters and warned Labour to be conscious of being seen to appeal only to 'sectional interest' (Morrison 1945). Recognizing the essentially 'workerist' appeal of the Party, Mass Observation executive Charles Madge nevertheless noted Labour made a serious attempt to appeal to the middle-class electorate in 1945 (Madge 1945). Significantly the subsequent landslide victory was in part built on 'blackcoated' voters' support and excellent results in areas such as Lewisham. This line of thinking was not lost on the organizers of the 1950 election campaign and they made a serious attempt to appeal to non-traditional supporters such as the middle classes as well as rural dwellers and Liberals. Significantly, the indefatigable Herbert Morrison proposed the paper that urged the NEC to develop: 'propaganda for the consumer and the housewife' (*Labour Party NEC Minutes* 1950).

Morrison: image maker

The re-organization of LCC's publicity department brought Morrison into close working relationship with several business executives sympathetic to Labour. In planning his party's campaign for re-election in 1937, the leader recruited a team of professional advisers prepared to advise him on a voluntary basis. The group included luminaries from the London Press Exchange and other agencies, principally Robert Fraser, George Wansborough and Clem Leslie who acted as chairman of the group.[5] Backed by comparatively large sums of money from wealthy supporters and the T&GWU and NUGMW (now GMB) trades unions, the strategists concentrated their efforts on promoting the key themes of housing, education and the leader himself. As George Jones comments, these advisers' 'unanimous recommendation was to personalise it (publicity) in Morrison' (Jones 1972). For his part, Leslie was greatly impressed by his client: 'We were responsible for the strategy of the publicity, the writing, the layout and some of the ideas. Herbert was a good client. He didn't interfere. He told us the message and I could see that housing offered a good theme' (Donaghue and Jones 1973). The main messages of the Labour campaign were condensed in arresting poster images featuring Morrison alongside children or against a backdrop of newly built LCC flats. These images were adorned with slogans such as 'Labour is Building Healthy Britons', 'Labour Puts Human Happiness First', 'Let Labour Finish the Job', 'Labour Gets Things Done' and 'Let Labour Build the New London' (ibid.: 209–11). The team even devised an advert for inclusion in hostile newspapers such as the *Daily Express* featuring two wavering Conservatives declaring their intention to support Morrison. Naturally enough this campaign was promoted in the

Labour press, notably the *Daily Herald* which duly reproduced the key themes from the party's campaign manifesto together with one of the stylish posters featuring Morrison and two youngsters (*Daily Herald* 1937).

The election result helped vindicate the innovative Morrison campaign plan. Overall the party won an improved 51 per cent share of the vote, nearly doubling the Labour majority on the LCC. The marketing press of the day, as represented by trade journal *Advertising Monthly*, praised the Labour strategy claiming it had 'set the standard' for commercial operatives (*Labour Organiser* 1937). Similarly, in their biography of Morrison, Donoghue and Jones conclude that the London campaign had been 'the most professional ever fought in Britain' (1973: 209). In an early survey of political communication in Britain, academic Ralph Casey argued the campaign was a highly significant landmark. Casey (1944) noted the use of: 'young liberal-minded advertising men and public relations specialists ... marked a departure from the usual labour-movement tradition of relying on a staff of journalists for propaganda services'. It should, however, also be noted that the victory served to highlight the internal tensions that existed within the Labour Party over the direction and pursuit of electoral strategies.

In planning for the 1937 election, Morrison had been very guarded about his use of voluntary publicity advisers. Though nominally accountable to the London Labour Party (LLP) executive, the leader kept his strategic formulations largely secret, fearing a potential backlash from committee members hostile to the proliferation of techniques more commonly associated with capitalist enterprise. Led by educationalists in the LLP hierarchy like Joan Bourne, many of these same critics also objected to professional advertising because they believed it encouraged the emergence of personality-based campaigning. Given the growing leader cult of European fascism at the time, it is highly probable that such views found resonance with many in the party. Bourne herself confessed to being 'nauseated' at the personification of party campaigning, given the rise of the 'Führer' principle (Donaghue and Jones 1973).

In spite of its apparent success, the London campaign did not trigger a strategic revolution within the national Labour party organization. That would not happen for twenty years. Most obviously, limited financial resources militated against headquarters' use of advertising techniques and professional agencies in general elections. Neither did the fact that the 1937 campaign innovations were associated with such an imposing personality as Morrison recommend their immediate adoption by a central party apparatus containing influential elements hostile to him. As Kenneth Morgan notes, the image of the London leader as both a 'Tammany right-winger' and a 'professional machine man' combined to help alienate potential allies on ideological as well as organizational grounds (Morgan 1992). The latter point is most graphically illustrated by the poor relationship that existed between Morrison and the formidable bureaucrat and future General Secretary Morgan Philips (Morrison 1960: 285 and Stewart 1974: 48). However headquarters' antipathy was not limited to those involved in the London team. Rather, reflecting on the traditionally inclined nature of the party bureaucracy, G. D. H. Cole observed an organization with a tendency for internal mistrust of, and outward hostility towards, professional help (Cole 1948: 124).

Conclusions

The business of modern political communications appears to be an inherently Machiavellian activity. Yet many of the methods and controversies associated with a contemporary exponent such as Peter Mandelson can be identified in the earlier pioneering approach of his grandfather and fellow Labour partisan Herbert Morrison. Both saw the need to cultivate journalists at a time when their party colleagues saw the profession with little but contempt. Reflecting this interest, the two men supervised the augmentation of press and public relations departments in those organizations that came under their respective spheres of influence. Indeed, during the formative part of their careers, both spent several years working in the dominant media of their time. Morrison's background was newspapers whilst Mandelson served as a television producer on a current affairs programme. Neither was bound up with the journalistic priority of delivering copy as much as making sure the overall output was effective. Such skills were far from commonplace within the Labour movement.

In their formative work the two political organizers developed reputations for providing selected journalists with good, informative stories and interesting features. Unlike his grandfather, Mandelson embarked on his political career at a time when, to paraphrase McLuhan, the 'medium' was increasingly becoming the 'message'. With the packaging of Thatcher, journalists and broadcasters became more self-conscious about their role as arbiters and deciders of political success and failure. By asserting his control over Labour communications strategy, Mandelson was well placed to benefit from the increased mediation of his party and politics in general.

Unusually for an inter-war Labour politician, Morrison showed concern with winning the support of middle-class voters. Similarly, in his role Mandelson proved himself a strong advocate of polling research, a source which proved influential in re-orienting the Kinnock and then the Blair-led Labour parties towards so-called 'Middle England'. In pursuing their electoral goals, both co-ordinated the setting-up of committees to advise the party on how to market itself. The two groups drew in specialist help from the leading London advertising agencies. The results of their efforts, that is Labour's 1937 London local and 1987 general election campaigns, showed a remarkable similarity in that they sought to personalize the party through strong promotion of the leader. The two campaigns were acclaimed as successes. They were also hugely expensive.

Ultimately the strategic activities of both men attracted considerable controversy. In a party like Labour the introduction of new communications methods was not always appreciated, particularly when it involved the promotion of those associated with the changes. For this reason, Morrison and Mandelson developed reputations for being manipulative politicians adept at building alliances with networks of largely unknown and unaccountable advisers. This created problems because, as Machiavelli would have understood, both became 'outsiders on the inside' with the ear of the prince/leader but with powerful rivals hostile to their continued success.

Notes

1   Taken from Gilbert, A. (trans.) (1989) *Machiavelli: The Chief Works and Others*, vol. 3, Durham, NC: Duke University Press, p. 1189.
2   Labour politicians reportedly the victims of negative press briefings included several prominent Shadow Cabinet members such as Bryan Gould, John Prescott and Michael Meacher. There was also trouble at party headquarters when, within months of becoming Director of Campaigns, Mandelson found himself engaged in a protracted dispute with one of his staff, press officer John Booth.
3   During the battle for the Hartlepool selection, rival nominee Stephen Jones' wife Kay made public complaints about the supposed underhand tactics of the Mandelson camp.
4   Morrison's interest in promoting the London authority was shared by another County Hall leader, Ken Livingstone, who fifty years on won acclaim for supervising a public relations and advertising campaign based around the theme 'Say No to No Say'. It was a strategy that proved successful in delaying the Thatcher government's plans to cancel local London elections as a precursor to the planned abolition of the authority in 1984. For more details see Channon, C. (ed.) (1989) 'The GLC's Anti "Paving Bill" Campaign: Advancing the Science of Political Issue Advertising', in *Twenty Advertising Case Histories*, London: Cassell.
5   Leslie had gained critical acclaim as the creator of the gas industry's 'Mr Therm' logo. Later, in the 1960s, he worked as adviser to government ministers such as Tony Benn. A wealthy businessman, Wansborough was introduced to Morrison by Hugh Dalton and stood as a parliamentary candidate for Woolwich West. Fraser worked alongside Leslie at LPE before becoming Director-General of the Independent Television Authority after the war (Donoghue and Jones 1973: 209).

References

Anderson, P. and Mann, N. (1997) *Safety First: the Making of New Labour*, London: Granta.

Bayley, S. (1998) *Labour Camp*, London: Batsford.

Casey, R. (1944) 'British Politics: Some Lessons in Campaign Propaganda', *Public Opinion Quarterly* Spring.

Cole, G. D. H. (1948) *A History of the Labour Party since 1914*, London: Routledge & Kegan Paul: 124.

'Mr Morrison calling London', *Daily Herald*, 25 February 1937.

Donoghue, B. and Jones, G. (1973) *Herbert Morrison: Portrait of a Politician*, London: Weidenfeld & Nicolson: 96.

Edelman, M. (1948) *Herbert Morrison*, London: Lincolns Prager: 24.

Franklin, R. and Larsen, G. (1994) 'Kingmaking in the Labour Leadership Contest', *British Journalism Review* 5 (4).

Gould, P. (1998) *The Unfinished Revolution: how the Modernisers Saved the Labour Party*, London: Little Brown.

Heffernan, R. and Marqusee, M. (1992) *Defeat from the Jaws of Victory: Inside Kinnock's Labour Party*, London: Verso.

Hughes, C. and Wintour, P. (1990) *Labour Rebuilt: the New Model Party*, London: Fourth Estate.

Jones, G. W. (1972) 'Political Leadership in London: How Herbert Morrison Governed London, 1934–1940', *Local Government Studies* June: 1–11.

Jones, N. (1995) *Soundbites and Spin Doctors*, London: Cassell.

'Design and Modern Taste', *Labour Organiser*, 1937, no. 193.

Labour Party NEC Minutes, 23 January 1950.

Machiavelli, N.(1997) *The Prince*, London: Wordsworth Classic Edition.

MacIntyre, D. (1999) *Mandelson*, London: Harper Collins. (See also Routledge 1999: it is significant that Blair is the only other current Cabinet member to have had his life chronicled twice.)

Madge, C. (1945) *Pilot Guide to the General Election*, London: Pilot: 24–5.

McSmith, A. (1996) 'The Myth of Peter Mandelson', in *Faces of Labour*, London: Verso. (This interesting book gives sketches of several party figures: the devotion of a whole chapter to Mandelson underlines his influence within the organization.)

Morgan, K. O. (1992) *Labour People*, Oxford: Oxford University Press: 178, 182. (The antipathy between Philips and Morrison perhaps explains why the latter's Fabian Socialist Propaganda Committee launched in 1941 was marginal to the strategic formulations of the party. That said, the Committee did itself suffer from being too unwieldy. Morrison did nevertheless emerge to play a role, chairing the campaign committee prior to the 1945 general election. (See Gorman, J. (1996) 'The Labour Party's Election Posters in 1945', *Labour History Review* 61 (3) 299–308.) In government he continued to take an interest in presentation and became a keen proponent of the new Central Office of Information: see Rose, R. (1967) *Influencing Voters*, London: Faber & Faber: 61.)

Morrison, H. (1920) 'On the fighting of a Municipal Election', in *The Labour Party Handbook of Local Government*, London: George Allen & Unwin: 201.

—— (1921) *The Citizen's Charter*, London: Labour Party.

—— (1923) 'Can Labour win London without the Middle Classes?', in *Labour Organiser*, no. 34.

—— (1945) 'Labour Must Capture the East Lewishams', in *Labour Organiser*, no. 278.

—— (1960) *An Autobiography*, London: Odhams: 285.

Routledge, P. (1999) *Mandy*, London: Simon & Schuster. (See also MacIntyre 1999: it is significant that Blair is the only other current Cabinet member to have had his life chronicled twice.)

Shaw, E. (1994) *The Labour Party since 1979: Crisis and Transformation*, London: Routledge.

—— (1995) *The Labour Party since 1945*, Oxford: Blackwell.

Stewart, M. (1974) *Protest or Power*, London: George Allen & Unwin: 48.

Wring, D. (1996) 'From Mass Propaganda to Political Marketing: the Development of Labour Party Election Campaigning', in Rallings, C. *et al.* (eds) *British Parties and Elections Yearbook 1995*, London: Frank Cass.

—— (1997)'The Professionalisation of Political Campaigning: the Case of "Very Old" Labour in Britain', paper to the Images of Politics Conference, Amsterdam, September.

—— (1998) 'The Media and Intra-Party Democracy in Britain: "New" Labour and the Clause Four Debate', *Democratization* 5 (2).

3

Management

HENCE YOU HAVE AS ENEMIES ALL THOSE
YOU HAVE DAMAGED IN TAKING POSSES-
SION OF THAT PRINCEDOM, AND YOU
CANNOT RETAIN AS FRIENDS THOSE WHO
PUT YOU THERE, SINCE YOU CANNOT
GIVE THEM SUCH SATISFACTION AS THEY
LOOKED FORWARD TO, AND SINCE YOU
CANNOT USE STRONG MEDICINES
AGAINST THEM BECAUSE YOU ARE
INDEBTED TO THEM.

THE PRINCE[1]

8   Renaissance realpolitik for modern management

Alistair McAlpine

Machiavelli was if nothing else a politician. He understood politics and, after his death, the publication of *The Prince* changed politics in such a way that politics would never be the same again. My career has been both in politics and in business for 15 years when treasurer of the Conservative Party, at the nexus of both these arts. Arts indeed they truly are, for Machiavelli regarded politics with much the same enthusiasm that his colleagues in Renaissance Florence regarded paintings and sculptures. His approach to politics and its conduct was as painstaking as the approach of the great painters and sculptors, his contemporaries, to their art. Machiavelli refined the art of government to a point where it was no longer a job, rather a scientific occupation based on the experience of history, changed and adapted to apply to the lives of his contemporaries.

His work *The Prince* is without doubt a work of art. The almost perfect book and, because this book is a work of art, it has stood the test of time – as relevant to politics today as it was the year it was written and, as I have tried to show in *The New Machiavelli* (McAlpine 1997), as relevant today to business as to politics. This is despite the fact that politics and business are different arts, as different as sculpture is from painting. Machiavelli claimed to have studied the ancients and used their actions and reactions to justify the conclusion that he reaches in *The Prince*. In fact, I believe that Machiavelli studied those around him, discovering human instincts and describing those instincts with telling truthfulness. The actions of the ancients Machiavelli merely preyed on in order to justify his previous conclusions.

My first brush with Machiavelli was in the writing of a small book the same length as *The Prince*, started in 1980 and finished in 1991. In that year I had just retired from politics in time to witness the treachery that brought Margaret Thatcher down. No longer an official of her party I should, I suppose, have taken an objective view of this event, if it is possible to take an objective view of treachery. Two thoughts raced through my mind in those days: the first, that Margaret Thatcher had been less than well served by her servants; the second, that the supreme servant Machiavelli, not being princely, was badly placed to advise princes. He would have been better placed to advise servants who, it seemed in those days, were badly in need of some advice. It was in this mood that I completed *The Servant*.

Margaret Thatcher had been the subject of treacherous attacks often enough; in 1980 members of her cabinet made a puerile attempt to overthrow her. It was in that year that I began to write *The Servant*. After this treachery, the stage was set for a fight in the Machiavellian tradition. My anger in those days arose from the sheer injustice of that attack on Margaret Thatcher. That anger was the first and the last that I felt while active in politics. Anger has no place in politics or boxing, anger only causes a thoughtless attack. My book *The Servant*, written in anger, was reworked and the anger tempered by myself in 1991. When it was published by Faber & Faber, I wrote the following dedication: 'To the most magnificent Baroness Thatcher of Kesteven, Prime Minister of Great Britain 1979–1990, from one of her many Servants, who believes she could have been better served'. That dedication, I modelled on the dedication in Machiavelli's great work *The Prince*. In fact, I used the style of Machiavelli's writing, and *The Prince* as my model, for the whole of *The Servant*.

There was, however, one important difference between the approach to politics of *The Prince* and that of *The Servant*. *The Servant* is a work that tries to instruct servants how best to help a Prince carry out his idea. Machiavelli's *The Prince*, some people believe, was an application for a job – others, a cruel joke. In the foreword to *The Servant*, I wrote the following: 'When he wrote *The Prince*, Machiavelli was presenting himself for a job. Of all the activities of idle men, politics can be the most exciting and those like Machiavelli left stranded by its tides will always try to return.' (McAlpine 1991). Likewise, it is the same for those who have tasted success in business. Joke or job application, Machiavelli would have given his eye teeth to get back into politics. This desire to stay forever in his chosen profession is in common with the older generation of successful businessmen.

Machiavelli believed that, through his knowledge of history, he could show a Prince how to conduct himself. How to apply techniques learned from historical events to his advantage. But history is a fallible guide and it is curious that a man seeking employment from a successful Prince should presume to advise him on his conduct. For many years I have reflected on Machiavelli's work, *The Prince*, reconfirming my conclusion that, far from advice to a Prince, Machiavelli had identified irrefutable truths about the human character – his book *The Prince* was merely the flesh around the skeleton of these truths.

Nowhere in the entire work does Machiavelli predict the downfall of a state or ruler or even a contemporary general. Unlike Nostradamus and many others who predict dire events, even the end of the world, Machiavelli confines himself entirely to an understanding of the circumstances of mankind. He is right, of course, for it does not matter whether you are engaged in ruling a nation, fighting a war or running a business, the first principle to understand is the importance of human nature. Humans come in all shapes and sizes and so it is with their natural intelligence. Machiavelli understood this and he also understood how people behaved in the myriad of different circumstances in which they found themselves. Machiavelli, like all of us, was a fallible human being, beset with conceit, pride and all the other aspects of our diverse characters. His ideas appeared original not because they had not been thought of before – indeed, many cunning and successful men and women must surely have taken into account human failings when planning the downfall of their enemies. Machiavelli's fame comes from the fact that he dared publish a work pointing out the inherent defects in the character of mankind.

Machiavelli's ideas about human nature can be applied to any subject, indeed a New York publisher once suggested that I write a work applying them to sex. (I believe, however, that someone has since written such a book.) My next attempt, after *The Servant*, at getting to the root of Machiavelli's masterpiece was to use his thoughts in applying them to the conducting of business. Not that I record it as an original idea, for Anthony Jay had already written the excellent *Management and Machiavelli* (Jay 1967).

All my life, I have been a business man, when not working as a building contractor, buying and selling, looking for opportunities to make a profit. My life has been an untidy mélange of politics and business: working in a family business, I came across the absorbing phenomenon of family politics; working on building sites, I visited trade union politics and the craft of persuading people to carry out tasks for which they had no inclination. As treasurer of the Conservative Party, I came across the nexus of politics and business; retired from that role, I am now a voyeur in the business of the politics practised by those no longer in the political arena, the politics of history. How history is modelled as clay to portray the image that the craftsman requires.

The Prince is in fact a guide as to how men have behaved, not a work predicting how they will behave. Despite Machiavelli's reputation for evil thoughts – T. B. Macaulay (1827) wrote of Machiavelli, 'out of his surname they have coined an epithet for a knave and out of his Christian name a synonym for the Devil' – there is no evidence to suggest that Machiavelli was himself an evil man. However, he clearly understood the capacity for evil that lurks in all of us. The point is not that Machiavelli advocated evil-doing, rather that he accepted that all human activity, and especially politics, will to some degree involve evil-doing. Having acknowledged that evil is unavoidable, Machiavelli tries to show his Prince how to recognize it for what it is and how to use it to his own advantage. In fact, he had a rather casual attitude towards evil and its consequences. His dying words expressed the view that he did not care about going to hell, in fact he preferred to go there as he would then be in the company of Popes, Princes and other grand people. This might lead one to believe that he preferred the company of Princes regardless of their morality or, more likely, that he continued his lifelong fight against corruption into his dying moments.

In my book *The New Machiavelli: Renaissance Realpolitik for Modern Managers*, I have taken the lessons Machiavelli preached, added some insights gained in the course of my own perambulations through life and applied them to the activity of conducting business. This is more appropriate than might seem to be the case for, as will become clear to those who work with international corporations, there is a striking similarity between the behaviour of the city states of fifteenth-century Italy and that of the great corporations of the last half of the twentieth century. Into this work, amongst Machiavelli's precepts and my own observation, I have worked an apologue using characters who can be found in all businesses. The amiable employer, a person who longs to be liked, the able lieutenant, a person of honour and undoubted ability, but with one failing – the fear of accepting the ultimate responsibility – and, finally, the obliging employee, a person of some talent but with a distinctly limited ability, who while useful is also cunning and greedy. These players illustrate the drama of a life in business with all its attendant honour and dishonour, courage and cowardice, wisdom and folly. In the book, I hope that I have provided a guide for the reader, a safe path through the complicated world of business. This book will, I hope, equip him or her with the insights into human nature which are needed to survive in the jungle of greed and treachery that is commerce. Indeed, not only to survive, but to prosper and to prosper with honour in what, when honourably conducted, is perhaps the most exciting and rewarding of all pursuits open to mankind.

In the book, I have tried to show the same joy in business that Machiavelli showed in politics – with all the elements of failure and success, courage and cowardice that you find in *The Prince*. The treachery is here, the plots, the plans, and above all a sense of fear. It must be remembered that Machiavelli, if his work *The Prince* was a job application, did not get the job. I suspect that Machiavelli knew full well that success does not come from handbooks. Certainly, I believe that you cannot succeed by reading a book on success, not least for the very reason that the criterion for success varies from person to person. One person's success may well be another's abject failure. Your own personal success is something hidden deep inside you and it may take many years for you to totally understand the mystery of what constitutes your personal success, in the same way that it took politians centuries to fully under-stand the power of Machiavelli's reasoning. Indeed, you may never know the nature of that personal success. How often is the millionaire as unfulfilled as the pauper? How sad is the person perceived as happy by friends and relatives? Our lives are a mixture of emotions, our souls filled with both good and evil. In *The New Machiavelli* I try to demonstrate that it is the circumstance that dictates how much of the good or how much of the evil from our secret characters is uncovered in our striving for what we once believed to be success.

In both *The Prince* and *The New Machiavelli*, the need to focus your energies is shown. The need to press on, once a particular course has been embarked upon. In the case of both books, the need to be ruthless is stressed. Neither book, however, promises success. If you follow Machiavelli's precepts in *The Prince* you will likely rule; you will, however, be following the ideas of those who have apparently succeeded or apparently failed.

Machiavelli produced a remarkable work of art in his book *The Prince* – small, neat and almost perfect. Because it is a work of art, its words can be applied in that form to other subjects: I have chosen to use them in the context of business, to mock conventional wisdom in order to encourage individualism and imagination. The order of the chapters in *The Prince* has been changed in *The New Machiavelli* to roughly fit a business career. The last chapter in the Everyman Library edition of *The Prince*, chapter xxvi, *An Exhortation to Liberate Italy from the Barbarians*, has been omitted. The last chapter in *The New Machiavelli* is entitled 'Creating One's Own Luck'. Its inspiration comes from Machiavelli's words: 'How much fortune can influence human affairs, and how she should be resisted' (Machiavelli 1995).

Nowhere in the entire text *of The Prince* is the difference between the age of Machiavelli and that of today so well demonstrated as in his words on luck, and I quote:

> For my part I consider that it is better to be adventurous than cautious because fortune is a woman and if you wish to keep her under, it is necessary to beat her and ill use her; and it is seen that she allows herself to be mastered by the adventurous rather than by those who go to work coldly. She is therefore, always woman – like a lover of young men, because they are less cautious, more violent and with more audacity command her.
>
> (Machiavelli 1995)

How expert Machiavelli was in the matter of women, I do not know. Despite, however, the fact his advice is definitely flawed in the idea that the female sex responds well to a beating, the thrust of Machiavelli's words is still relevant today. Still at the heart of the advice which should be given to the one who would prosper in business, is an exhortation to show courage, honour, energy, ability, perseverance and above all total dedication, for these are the ingredients of success and, taken together, they are the alchemy that allows success to become a possibility. They do not, however, guarantee success.

The student of success at this juncture will surely say, 'And what of luck? What part does luck play in commercial success?' The whole point of Machiavelli's Prince is to find a scientific way to success. Success should not be left in the hands of luck. The individual, if he or she believes in the power of luck, should spend their time on the racetrack or in the casino, where those who have similar beliefs tend to spend their time. Ask any gambler and you will be told that success is due to an expertise with mathematics or prior knowledge, or both of these combined to form the skill that the gambler believes to be his trade. The unluckiest gambler is the gambler who appears to have luck at his first attempt – all that gambler's winnings will be returned. In words taken from *The New Machiavelli* (McAlpine 1997): ' ... as for luck, approach both luck and God with caution. The former is even with the best of efforts uncertain, while the latter demonstrates quite regularly the certainty only of death.' Oscar Wilde got luck about right when he said: ' ... success is entirely due to luck, ask any failure'. Frederick the Great was of the view that the older one gets the more convinced one becomes that ' ... his majesty king luck does three quarters of the business of this miserable world'. Machiavelli takes a middle course: 'I hold it to be true that fortune is the arbiter of one half of our actions.' A famous golfer remarked that the more he practised, the luckier he got.

So there you have it, there is no certainty as to the nature of luck, for it is in fact as Oscar Wilde suggests, 'success is entirely due to luck, ask any failure'. In reality luck is merely how we excuse failure. However, events in the examples of success and failure used by Machiavelli in *The Prince* all could be explained by luck. In as much as luck cannot be relied upon to deliver success, handbooks on corporate management are no more use in this respect than luck.

While it is possible to teach the parameters of the law and to describe the technicalities of accounting, *The New Machiavelli* shows that the sum of these crafts, however, does not add up to a skill in commerce. To be successful materially in business needs an instinct, a similar but different instinct to that displayed by talented gardeners who can grow any flower or plant almost anywhere – called, for lack of a rational explanation, green fingers – or, for that matter, the way a person talented with animals is able to persuade them to breed and then to prosper where others fail. Business is about organizing people so that they behave in a motivated and orderly fashion. Running a business is about leadership, and here I will describe several principles of leadership.

The first is loyalty. It is of utmost priority when you are assessing those you employ, particularly those that are closest to you. Loyalty, however, commands loyalty – it not only must be given, it must be seen to be given. It means concern for others in sickness and health, in good and bad times. It is essential to recognize those who are disloyal only when circumstances force them to be disloyal or whether disloyalty is a part of their character. For such people are the most destructive that you will encounter. Then, of course, comes trust which is based on integrity in all our actions. Do not expect those you employ to put their trust in you if you do not trust them. After that, fairness. An employer needs to be scrupulously fair. Criticisms should be objective, based on facts – not on hearsay and rumour and other people's opinions, people who have their own agenda. Then, ability: if you appoint or promote those to a level above their ability, do not expect them to inform you if they cannot make the grade and, above all, do not blame them for your mistakes. Finally, behaviour: there must be respect at all times. If you respect others they will respect you. Abusive language, aggressive behaviour, drunkenness, disloyalty, refusal to carry out company policy or to co-operate with others is totally unacceptable.

Do not be tempted to change old friends for new, no matter how clever the new ones appear to be, and never allow newcomers to persuade you to act against your better judgement and, in particular, persuade you to turn against those who have given you their loyalty. Never shirk from your responsibilities or fail to express your appreciation and gratitude to others and never be afraid to make firm and unpopular decisions and, above all, be your own person. These are simple rules worth following quite as much in one's private life as in the context of one's business. These principles are the backbone of *The New Machiavelli*. Do not imagine, however, that these are the only principles of leadership or, for that matter, that you can just pick up this list of principles and by applying them become a leader. Leadership is a much deeper and more profound art. One that cannot be practised by taking a few rules from a book and attempting to follow them. At best these principles are reassurance for those who already practise them. A checklist for those who have the art of leadership in their souls.

In chapter 2 of *The New Machiavelli*, I describe the attributes necessary for starting a business; again, these cannot be learned. Here Machiavelli's advice is to the point:

> ... he should follow the example of the prudent archers who, when the target they want to hit seems too far away, bear in mind their bows' capability and set their aim considerably higher than the intended target, with the intention, not of shooting above it but of reaching it with the help of the high trajectory.
>
> (Machiavelli 1995)

My own great-grandfather – a man who started life aged 14 in the coal mines and, by the time he was in his mid-twenties, as a builder employed over a thousand workers – had a similar guide to life: 'aim to jump over the moon and you may jump over the rooftops'. A man supremely ignorant of the existence of Machiavelli, he had come to the same simple conclusion. To own your own business you must want to own your own business. The aspiring proprietor should ask him or herself two questions: what do I regard as success? Then, why do I want success? Indeed, in order to succeed one needs first to analyse success. If the answer to these questions is that you require security and independence then beware, for proprietors seldom enjoy security and, as for independence, the role of a successful proprietor must be entwined with the existence of the company. *The Prince* is littered with examples that illustrate this statement. If it is wealth that you seek and through wealth position, always remember that position can be achieved without wealth; furthermore, business success is about total commitment and in this commitment lies the danger that the aspiring proprietor will damage both health and family.

In business, at first glance success appears to be the making of a large sum of money. Money however is only a crude guide much used today in order to judge success. Study any of the lists that are published showing the apparent relative wealth of 100, 1,000 or perhaps even 10,000 individuals in Britain, or for that matter the world. The aspect that such lists all have in common is the ability to distort the situation that each of those listed find themselves in. Success is an immensely personal emotion. It is entirely possible to be judged a failure by these crude indices, yet be regarded as an outstanding success by your peers; equally it is entirely possible to be judged a rip-roaring success by your peers, yet feel yourself to be a miserable failure. Success is a thing of the mind. How you achieve success is a matter of morality and, in time, the mind will judge its own morality, in much the same way that we look at the snapshots of a family album and memories return.

The desire to trade, however, is an instinct. It is either in you or not. To start a successful business you need to have a compelling desire to start that business. The vast majority of people do not run businesses, neither do they aspire to commercial success. As a consequence the one who aspires to run a business has a responsibility to those who do not have such ambitions. First, this responsibility is specific to those who help you achieve your success, employees and customers. Second, this responsibility is to others in general, those who live in your village, town, country and, finally, the world. Without realizing this responsibility and at least attempting to fulfil this responsibility, the fine wine of success will turn to the ashes of greed and selfishness in your mouth. Your success will crumble even as it reaches its high point; where your commercial activities continue to prosper without honour, your spirit will become increasingly uneasy.

Never fear failure, indeed failure can often lead to the greatest of triumphs. Machiavelli's work *The Prince* is a fine example of this. Rejected in his lifetime, published 15 years after his death, it is now regarded as one of the world's truly great books. Similarly, the paintings of Van Gogh, a painter who failed to sell a single picture during his lifetime, now hold the world record for the highest price ever paid for a work of art. Failure can be for the individual quite as sweet as success; such a failure, however, must be an honest failure, failure that comes despite the fact that you have tried with honesty and energy to succeed. When people speak of success and failure, tales of failure are always so much more interesting than those of success. Beware, however, of telling tales of past failures, for people on the whole dislike failure; they, in their superstitious way, believe that failure is much the same as 'the flu', that failure is a disease that can be passed from one to another. Equally, they flock to success largely because they believe that success begets success and there is profit to be had from an association with apparent success.

In truth, you will neither fail nor succeed by an association with either failure or success. Your success is entirely in your own hands to shape into a form that you believe to be congenial to your own morals and principles. No person is responsible to another for failure or success. In *The New Machiavelli*, I advise that an aspiring business person should always take advice from a failure, for the single reason that a failure knows, if that person is honest, why they have failed. Study insolvency, take a clock apart to know how it works, take a business apart to know how it works.

At no point in *The New Machiavelli* do I dismiss the idea that business skills can be taught, only the notion that they can be taught to anyone. By applying the principles of a political tract to the conduct of business, I have tried to show the nonsense of the notion that a handbook of any kind, however brilliant, should be taken as a rule book for success. In undertakings that are of a totally different nature, the techniques applied need to be different. Business and politics are totally different; in *The New Machiavelli* that difference is described thus:

... both business and the practice of politics are trades, but different trades. Business is like the game of billiards: you set up your shot having considered many possibilities. Politics is like tennis: you react and turn your opponent's shot against them. In business you're far less dependent on the skill, or the lack of it, of your opponent. No set of rules will be satisfactory, for if those rules work from a business point of view, they are unlikely to work from a moral point of view.

(McAlpine 1997)

In *The New Machiavelli*, I have tried to show that success without honour is worthless, that deceit is the currency of failure. Honour and morality are two of the touchstones of success: without these two, success is a poor thing. People, however, being individuals and each thinking in their own way and coming to their own conclusion, may well decide to convince themselves that there is no need for honour, morality or charity. It is important to realize that such an attitude is possible and never to rely upon a person behaving with either morality, charity or honour, just because that is how you would behave in similar circumstances. There is, however, a reluctance among most people to admit that this fact is true, as true today as it was in an age where Machiavelli first floated the notion that the evil in mankind should be recognized for what it is and used to the advantage of the one who is able to recognize this evil. Even today, nearly five hundred years later, we are still reluctant to accept this aspect of human nature, for to do so leaves one open to the charge of cynicism, when in fact all you show when you take these possibilities into account is that you are realistic about the human condition.

Machiavelli, however, showed no fear of such an accusation and with both of my books, *The Servant* and *The New Machiavelli*, I have followed in his tradition, trying as best I can to expose the reality of life rather than obscuring such reality with tidy phrases. *The Prince, The Servant* and *The New Machiavelli* are not books that promise solutions, rather they offer, each in their own way, only advice to assist those well on the track to self-fulfilment and, in the case of my books, mock those who would rely on handbooks to provide success for them. In the case of *The New Machiavelli*, there is also advice for those who fail: first, let no bitterness enter your life from missed opportunities or adverse luck; consider very carefully the mistakes that you have made and why you have made them, but waste no time on success that you have never had.

Sir Francis Bacon in 1605 wrote, 'we are much beholden to Machiavelli and others that write what men do and not what they ought to do.' Today, however, such a statement would be regarded as highly cynical. The fashion among reporters in the latter part of the twentieth century has been to write what they believe the actions of a person to be, regardless of whether that person has actually behaved in that way. Meanwhile, there are whole areas of social behaviour that are not reported at all, because we as a society are terrified to speak their names. When we look at a person we assess their character by the standards of our own characters. The dark sides of our characters are hidden, so we hide the dark side of the characters that we try to assess, fearful that – by admitting the dark side of another's character – we may be forced to accept the dark side of our own character. It is this denial of another's character defects, out of self-interest, that leads to trouble in any exchange with another person, whether that exchange be political, social, legal or commercial.

In *The New Machiavelli*, the chapter dealing with the establishment is a parallel of chapter xi in *The Prince*, 'Concerning ecclesiastical principalities'. Machiavelli attacked what he perceived as a corrupt Church. My attack on the establishment is an attack on a corrupting and weakening force that has been present in the social and commercial life of Britain for the whole of the twentieth century. This attack should not be misunderstood; it is not an attack on any particular establishment, it is an attack on all establishments, not just an attack designed to replace one establishment with another. Not just to replace the landowners of the first half of the twentieth century with the merchant bankers of the second half, or for that matter to replace the merchant bankers with pop stars and footballers in the last two years of the century. Nor do I argue to replace the solid and dull monarchy of the twentieth century with a set of saints and populists in the twenty-first. Britain has been undergoing a dramatic change in the last quarter of the twentieth century, a time during which I have been involved in politics and when the great debate has been about Europe.

Europe has been the overwhelming political issue and my writings should be seen in that context. The idea that, if all the European nations joined as one, then life will be easy, that there is not a problem that cannot be solved by a system. That bureaucrats really do know best, that each state needs to be a nanny to its people, and that Europe is the greatest nanny of them all. That a politician in Brussels can legislate to cover every eventuality. No, the instincts expressed in my writing are the very reverse of all this. Each human is a sovereign being different from all other humans and likely to behave in an unpredictable way that will confound those who try to categorize humans into behavioural groups. A new establishment of pop singers and footballers is no more attractive to me than an establishment of psychoanalysts and physiothera-pists. Establishments, major and minor, spring up in every walk of life, from breeding prize rabbits to the management of businesses. While I have shown that there is no dishonour in failure, nor inherent honour in success, I do not believe that failure should become institutionalized as is the case in a society where establishments flourish. While at first they help these undertakings, in the end establishments debilitate them, as the Church in Machiavelli's day debili-tated the states of Italy.

From chapter to chapter in *The New Machiavelli* I have used Machiavelli's ideas as a sounding board – for my ideas and the ideas of others well-versed in business management. When you have developed a power structure in your business, do not disrupt that structure by the use of consultants or temporary staff. Students of *The Prince* will have observed that Machiavelli does not think well of Mercenaries. On the financing of businesses, bankruptcy is the spur to capitalists and profit is capitalism's reward. Without the spur and the reward, capitalism cannot truly function and commerce dies. Anyone who doubts the lack of a banker's ability to understand another man's business, has only to observe that the greatest bargains are those businesses bought from bankers. Anyone who doubts the ability of those who work in a business to know its true value, has only to observe the great profits made by businesses recently purchased by those who work in them. Refinancing a business and rearranging its debt is critical. Consider debt as an army advancing forward in an even line. Some of your soldiers will fall, so there must be replacements available to fill those gaps. Debt must be dealt with in an organized manner. Debt must be addressed; to wait for inflation, further take-overs or chance to deal with debt is a sure road to bankruptcy.

On the use of craftiness in business, Machiavelli writes:

> ... everyone understands how laudable it is for a Prince to keep his word and live with integrity and not cunning. Nonetheless experiences show that nowadays those princes who accomplish great things have had little respect for keeping their word and have known how to confuse men's minds with cunning. In the end they have overcome those who preferred honesty.
>
> (Machiavelli 1995)

These words have a ring of truth about them. While these words should be taken into account when dealing with others, they should not, however, be a guide to how you should deal in business. The person who lies to achieve his or her ends will in truth be found out and such achievements exposed as frauds.

Those who are already powerful may well get away with the lies or at least believe that have got away with those lies. In truth, however, liars only invite the lies of others and there is no honour in their success and their failure is held in contempt by all. Through lies, these people will create great enemies; people do not care to be deceived, nor do they care to be tricked. The lies of tricksters will fester in the minds of their victims. Should the trickster prosper by deceit and one day become powerful, then the trickster will become the victim of those to whom the lies have been told. At the moment of the trickster's greatest triumph the victor will expose the trickster as a fraud. Do not forget that the ones who would rise by the use of lies live with those lies, always waiting for another to use those same lies to pull them down.

Machiavelli, in the quote that I have chosen here, writes not of liars or their lies; rather he refers to craftiness and the dangers of dealing with a crafty individual. There is a great difference between the use of craft or even cunning and the use of straightforward lies. When you dismiss an employee, always do this in such a way that the dismissed employees feel that they have been promoted. Find them a better job or merely tell them that they are too good for your organization. 'On the avoidance of contempt' from *The Prince* becomes 'public relations', 'why the princes of Italy have lost their states' becomes 'why businesses fail'. 'How a Prince should act in order to gain reputation', 'the advantages and dangers of fame', and so it goes on. The weaknesses and strengths of humans are pointed out, greed, deceit, vanity, the power of jealousy, the dangers of revenge, dishonesty, flattery and intrigue. Public relations men, who are in reality hired gossips, swindlers, cowards, and heroes – they are all there. They struggle for success expressed in terms of money, when they should struggle for success expressed in terms of soul. In *The New Machiavelli* it is pointed out that

> ... in whatever dire straits a person engaging in business may find themselves, such a person must always strive to retain their self respect, as that self respect will be their salvation during hard times; you should take care not to part with your self respect, cheaply on your rise in business. For the time will come when your self respect is of incredible value and without self respect you will be entirely lost.

(McAlpine 1997)

There is no bank statement or stockbroker's report on a person's investments that prints out that person's greatest asset, there is no training manual or business school that teaches the dangers that this asset self-respect may be lost. Machiavelli, in his book *The Prince*, however, teaches 'for a man to act entirely up to his professions of virtue soon meets with what destroys him among so much that is evil.' Words that Mr Blair and Mr Cook might have noted when they declared their intentions to have an ethical foreign policy for Britain. The difference of approach between Machiavelli and McAlpine is that, while we are both acutely aware of the dark side of all human characters, he is a realist while I am, still, a romantic. Machiavelli offers advice in order to help a person achieve a demonstrable and finite success. I, for my part, am doubtful about the reality of such a success being an acceptable condition unless it is achieved with honour and maintained with morality and charity. As for those who will give business a try – balancing courage and fear while letting instincts run free, engaging in the most exciting and exacting of races, striving for the exhilaration of success, risking the despair of failure – *The New Machiavelli* offers these words: 'In the end, whether or not your business prospers or fails is all a matter of how you behave and the decisions that you take, it is up to you. The secret of success, if there is such a single and singular secret, is the determination to succeed and not the determination to avoid failure.'

Note

1   Taken from Gilbert, A. (trans.) (1989) *Machiavelli: The Chief Works and Others*, vol. 1, Durham, NC: Duke University Press, p 13.

References

Jay, A. (1967) *Management and Machiavelli*, London: Hodder & Stoughton.
Macaulay, T. B. (1827) 'Essay on Machiavelli', *Edinburgh Review* March.

Machiavelli, N. (1995) *The Prince*, ed. G. Bull, London: Penguin.
McAlpine, A. (1991) *The Servant*, London: Faber & Faber.
—— (1997) *The New Machiavelli*, London: Aurum.

THIS LEADS TO A DEBATE: IS IT BETTER TO
BE LOVED THAN FEARED, OR THE
REVERSE? THE ANSWER IS THAT IT IS
DESIRABLE TO BE BOTH, BUT BECAUSE IT
IS DIFFICULT TO JOIN THEM TOGETHER
IT IS MUCH SAFER FOR A PRINCE TO BE
FEARED THAN LOVED, IF HE IS TO FAIL IN
ONE OF THE TWO.

THE PRINCE[1]

9 From the dark to the light

Ranges of the real skills of management

Brian Stone and Jayne Pashley

Introduction

The generic skills currently developed among business undergraduates at the Manchester Metropolitan University (MMU) are group working, interpersonal skills, leadership, problem solving and the like. While these are unquestionably relevant and useful in their management careers, they follow a tradition which does not seem to have changed over at least fifteen years. The question arises whether there are relevant skills frequently used in management, which are not presently considered for teaching at university level. If this is so, then university course designers should research them, discover them, know about them – and should design them into courses.

For relevance, they must therefore consider, at least, all the business skills which practising managers use at work, the foundations of which can be laid at university.

This paper aims to stimulate serious debate by going to what may seem to be extremes. Its hypothesis is that there are 'real' skills frequently used by practising managers which seem too unconventional, or even too unethical, to teach on university courses. It will build a list of these 'real' skills and will develop the idea that each skill category contains within it a range of managerial skills from the laudable, via the acceptable, through to those frankly to be described as disreputable – from the 'light' skills to the 'dark', as it were.

While detailed research among practising managers on the frequency or otherwise of 'real' skills usage will eventually be necessary, a first step is to compose and refine the list and the definitions. The taxonomy, a sample of which appears here, is a result of exploratory research among fledgling managers both as to definition and, with their judgement, as to usage.

What follows results from a series of conversations between a tutor in business studies and a graduate of three years' employment. It might have been reasonable to suppose that the graduate would have taken a consistently realistic, cynical view and the tutor a constant idealistic, conventional one. But that would impugn some of the idealism of youth, and belie the experiential scars of business academics with eclectic careers behind them ....

Management skills

It could be helpful to contrast the management skills managers actually use, as opposed to 'what industry wants'. There are grounds for cynicism about the latter: it would not be difficult to encounter many in industry who have not the faintest idea what they want in the way of skills in its graduates; nor can they define the terms they use when they make pontifical statements about it; nor indeed can they clearly and unequivocally define what 'skills' are.[2]

Business lecturers live in the hope that they teach something useful, but they remain aware that there is a fair amount of real-world experience which contrasts with the theory. More often than not, that theory is purist or normative, but it contrasts with observation and might fail to alert the student to the rather more sinister facts of the real world of work. And as Machiavelli points out, 'It is necessary for a prince wishing to hold his own to know how to do wrong, and to make use of it, or not, according to necessity' (Machiavelli 1985: ch. xv).

Tutors will deny, however, that they are idealistically remote from reality. In fact, confronting reality is a deliberate and constant policy and they do believe that 'all armed prophets have conquered, and the unarmed ones have been destroyed' (ibid.: ch. vi). One of the authors had a group of recent undergraduates who re-visited Belbin (1981), under his explicit encouragement: the theme is that Belbin's group roles may be what a group *needs*, but the students looked at what a group usually *has*. Belbin suggests that groups need the TW, the CH, the SH, the CW, the PL, the RI, the ME and the CF.[3] However, on their frequent group projects the students observed that what they get is the BL, the SU, the CP, and the FO, among others.

The BL is the 'Backend Loader': the person who leaves it all to the last minute and then comes through, usually causing extreme palpitations for Belbin's CF (Completer/Finisher). The SU is the 'Sucker-Up', who does little actual work on the student project but is in constant contact with the tutor to report progress; the CP is the 'Cherry-Picker' who will do the plum sections of the project, the parts which are either interesting or easy, or both; and the FO is the 'Fizzler Out', who is enormously energetic at the start but who then completely disappears to spend energy on personal non-group work. Additionally, most groups would recognize the RP, the 'Rubbish Producer', who earnestly works very hard to produce material which is so incompetent or illiterate that it cannot possibly be used in the finished assignment.

But this is more than a scholarly satirical sideshow: certainly tutors might want to discuss, at least, the likely projected typical behaviour of role-takers observed in project work over the years, so as to warn the group of the problems they may encounter. And they are indeed pledged to prepare students as best they can for the vicissitudes of employment.

That principle should – and often does – extend itself to teaching, which ranges in attitude in the most professional from the idealistic to the cynical; a pragmatic approach, matching that of final-years who suffer slings and arrows on industrial placement and who subsequently take a range of attitudes to the appropriateness of theory, as the present authors have discussed before (Stone and Pashley 1997).

A final-year option on the MMU BSc. (Hons) Business includes Public Relations and, often enough in final-year group projects in other subjects, students discuss at the idealistic end ethical principles of PR. This unquestionably prepares them at work for engendering positive spin; but it also braces them to recognize the straightforward lies which people often enough use to put a beneficial light on their shortcomings or mistakes, the darker aspect of 'handling the truth'.

Dark skills

This piece will now go on to develop that idea, a set of thoughts developing from many years of commercial experience and discussed with prominent industrialists, namely, the 'dark skills of management'. Bluntly, very early in managerial experience people meet managers who are patently skilled liars, gender-manipulators, self-promoters, backstabbers, and the like. If these skills have any effect on the career it is frequently enough a positive one, depending on the level of skill.

If for the sake of argument this regrettably cynical assertion is accepted, and if management course designers are genuine in their desire to prepare students for a real and pragmatic world, this would have course design implications. Perhaps students should find on the first year of a business degree such subjects as 'Backstabbing I', or later on 'Advanced Gender Manipulation', or 'Lying III'. This would prepare them with needed skills which would certainly advance careers.

However, academics would have two categories of problem here: one, the ethical difficulty of claiming in the university prospectus that such courses are offered, as core, one presumes; or rather, the difficulty of putting any positive spin on subjects with names as honest as those suggested. Then, second, there would be the difficulty which will already have occurred to any who wonder about the factual basis of some of the foregoing cynicism: that of conducting respectable social research: which respondents will admit to using, developing and being proficient in the dark skills?

It was intimated earlier that this matter had been discussed over the years with practising industrialists. One of the more eminent of these commercial contacts came up with exactly these problems, and suggested that perhaps both can be solved with the idea of a 'dark-to-light' continuum.[4]

Take first the matter of handling the truth. In *The Prince* (Machiavelli 1985), chapter xviii, it is averred that 'it is necessary to be a great pretender and dissembler; and men are so simple and so subject to present necessities, that he who seeks to deceive will always find someone who will allow himself to be deceived'. This was alluded to earlier, contrasting positive truth spin at the light end with lying at the dark. If these are classified under a generic and neutral head, say, truth handling, this is the result:

'Light' usage	Skill	'Dark' usage
Using skilled judgement to discern when to tell the whole truth, or to refrain from disseminating truthful information, on the basis of advantage to the section, division, organization, society.	Truth handling	Deliberately disseminating untruths, or failing to disseminate truths/the whole truth, for personal or organizational advantage, with good judgement of the likelihood of exposure.

It would be much easier to ask executives if they use the skill of truth handling, ask for critical incidents to illustrate its use by them at the light end, then ask if they have *observed* a dark use, and research the frequency and importance, in their view, of the whole range of truth-handling skill.

But does that solve any ethical problem of the offering? In some ways, it does because, should a course offer truth- or information-handling skills, it might set out to develop the light end of the range at university, and then warn students to guard – and defend themselves – against the dark-end usage. Students, like everyone else, need to reduce cognitive dissonance (Festinger 1957), the more urgently and traumatically if they emerge from university with only the light side as preparation, and less so if prepared for the dark.

Self-defence

This leads to consideration of another generic skill: defending oneself against attack. In most managerial occupations there are people who would be comfortable with causing career damage to rivals, and perhaps business courses should provide the equipment for effective reaction. Managers might consider it important to possess the facility to be able to hit people very hard just after recognizing that they have been attacked, to the extent of actually causing their opponents damage in return. In fact, causing the opponent slightly more damage than that intended by them might even be seen as aesthetically satisfying.

That would be the dark side – but equally important is the need to investigate and ameliorate the deeper roots and cause of the antagonism in the first place. Some would describe that as a (neo-)feminine approach, which perhaps need not be explored here (but refer to Hofstede 1991); but in the longer run it might be considered managerially effective. The table would extend itself, then, like this:

'Light' usage	Skill	'Dark' usage
Promptly spotting antagonistic moves against oneself and taking timely action to minimize damage to oneself for the overall benefit of section, division, organization; and taking action to solve the underlying problem where the antagonism is personal.	Self-defence	Counterblow: promptly spotting antagonistic moves and taking timely action or antagonistic counter-action to minimize damage to oneself and/or maximize damage to opponent.

The positive version of the self-defence skill is the idea of destructive self-promotion. The link is 'dropping people in it', an eclectic set of skills that qualifies for inclusion under both heads. Essentially the skill is manipulating self-image to let people know how wonderful the defender is, without any particular regard to the facts, but ensuring that they are seen to be *comparatively* excellent, that is, better than others. Stephen Potter (1952) defined being one-up as seeing to it that the other fellow was one-down.[5]

But then there is also plagiarism. Even defining it is convention-dependent: on the one hand tutors want students to quote authors, but only see it as illegitimate if they do not follow the conventions of citation. Straightforward plagiarism without acknowledgement is popular and extensive in business and perhaps courses should, while preventing academic plagiarism, be simultaneously inculcating the skills of business plagiarism. Examples are, even if anecdotally, legion of managers having to put up with colleagues, especially superiors, commandeering original ideas and selling them as their own, and having been helpless to do anything about it.

It was the experience of a contemporary of one of the authors of this piece, newly appointed after graduating, who proposed a well planned project which he was not allowed to progress because of the lack of foresight of his manager. He confided in a new work colleague, who promptly remodelled the project and used it to secure an extension of her own employment contract. When challenged, the self-promoter claimed that she was completely justified in that (a) her re-modelling made the original radically different, and *in any case* – authors' italics – (b) only with her experience could the project work. Rather than rock the boat, the manager agreed the stolen project could commence.

However, surely the drive to be acknowledged for achievements is legitimate as a motivation – where the achievements are one's own. Now 'Fortune, like a woman, is friendly to the young, because they show her less respect, they are more daring and command her with audacity' (Machiavelli 1985: ch. xxv). Many people after graduation go on travel/working vacations or gap years. They are usually young and have negligible experience. But it is self-promotion which gets them jobs in a variety of industries. This includes marketing what little work they have done as well as possible and at all opportunities: 'hotel and catering operations' (bar work and waitressing), 'responsible managerial work' (as 19-year-olds on placement), 'management consultancy experience' (on student projects), 'publishing' (their assignments), 'extensive IT skills' (well, Word 6.0) – after all, if you don't ask, you don't get. They are indeed motivated and quickly learn the ropes, and therefore no one or no business usually suffers: they gain willing, able workers.

It may therefore be averred that self-promotion is an essential requirement for success providing nobody is damaged, and the table-entry looks like this:

'Light' usage	Skill	'Dark' usage
Being able to ensure that one's genuine achievements are fairly acknowledged; being able to draw them skilfully but unobtrusively to the attention of influentials; being able to claim credit for all that is one's own work. Being able correctly to place oneself in location or time to benefit from credit for one's work or ability.	Self-promotion	Causing one's achievement, skills or technical abilities to be known to influentials, to the cost of rivals for position. Directly or indirectly causing negative facts/the drawbacks/ mistakes of rivals to be known to influentials, to the cost of rivals, for self-promotion ('Dropping In It'). Claiming the work/ideas of others as one's own (plagiarism).

Gender handling

The matter of masculine/feminine was raised briefly, earlier. Clearly there are managerial skills deployed in working with people of the opposite sex, or indeed the same sex. Exploiting gender differences is something which it is not difficult to encounter and observe in typical managerial situations. Indeed, the Prince was exhorted to recognize fortune to be woman and consider it necessary to keep her down, to beat her and to struggle with her. The more enlightened (males *and females*) have, of course, found new, different and effective ways of wrestling with the wily opposite sex.

The abuse of a real or perceived power is much documented in the increasing number of sexual harassment cases. However, here the reference is made to a subtler manipulation of personal characteristics (while understanding that there is a more global matter of exploiting individuals regardless of gender: when it was suggested to one student on a research project that she must respond to requirements that she interview without discrimination, she commented that 'an idiot is an idiot no matter what sex, colour or creed … ').

A graduate contemporary of one of the authors has a sales team manager who, driven as he is by his masters to maximize sales from his team (and his own bonus), uses an advanced skill of playing off members of his team against one another. Here it would be possible to invent a new category of meta-skills to include this, or it might be included elsewhere. Here, however, his use of gender is the relevant aspect.

He goes to his female sales people and tells guarded stories in which he would never be openly discriminatory, but will say enough to raise doubts and discomfort in their minds. On one occasion he was heard to say to a married woman with children: 'Cameron has been putting in a lot of extra hours recently, really makes a difference to the team. We're fortunate to have such flexible people, aren't we?' What he actually meant was 'Cameron is going to get the promotion this year because he can work late nights and weekends and you, with your kids, cannot'. His intention was to drive her harder, to make her put in longer hours and accept more onerous duties and trips – for the greater benefit of the sales figures.

He is not sexist, it seems: the same manager will exhort his male staff to improved performance by talking about the qualities of his hard-working female staff who always get their paper-work in on time, understand their difficult clients and bring a sense of harmony to the office. It would be invidious to describe this as other than skilled, whatever other judgements might also apply. There is at least no discrimination on the grounds of sexuality, but only some question as to the ethics of manipulation. Again, then, should business courses not be teaching this expertise and facility? Could not the case be made for developing students in their capability of making the optimum use of available resources? In the centre column of the table, the generic skill is in dealing with people effectively on the basis of their gender; and there is an associated entry in the light column.

It really should be accepted that (a) there are old-fashioned 'masculine-feminine' stereotypes, (b) both men and women retain some belief in them and (c) people exploit supposed stereotypical qualities and prejudices. But there are also neo-stereotypes, most of them positive: women are supposed to communicate and empathize, men are action-oriented and solution-driven. There is merit in developing at least skills of flattering men/women with those images, and using the resultant self-identifications to develop relationships and improve organizational performance towards any targets. In group work at the MMU the tutors always balance the sexes, on the brutally crude basis that the young women will bring a sense of assiduity and the young men a pragmatic logic to the end result. The table now has this increment:

'Light' usage	*Skill*	*'Dark' usage*
Having sufficient sensitivity and understanding of gender identity to be able to understand, allay disadvantages of, and make the most of, perceived gender-based qualities or characteristics, both personal and interpersonal.	Gender handling	The ability to cause people to behave in desired manners by manipulating their characteristics or relationships in gender terms (male–male, female–female, male–female, female–male) for personal advantage.

The skill of bull

The next area for consideration is skills in 'bull',[6] by which is meant making the exaggerated most of a tiny amount of knowledge. Potter (1952) was cited earlier: here is his description of a (specifically) student skill: 'to "edinburgh" implies a spreading, a dissemination of despondency among other persons working for an examination by an appearance of solid knowledge, of calmness in the face of an approaching crisis, and a desire to help ...'; as, for example, in the experience of both authors when a couple of final-year students came up with the idea of ringing everyone else on the course, late at night, to lend a 'few words of wisdom' before each impending final exam, not just for a joke but in an attempt to reduce averages. Eventually, in fact, they realized that they themselves were losing too much sleep and they abandoned the campaign.

There is, of course, the potential for dark-skill combination, for example, bull-plus-in-grouping: many readers may recall, in their youth, attending conferences where the delegates might have been closed ranks of 'colleagues' long-established in the field. The majority talk up not only what they do, but also the obstacles that they have faced and the hard time anyone would face with little or irrelevant experience. Fortunately, one's political skills (some indeed developed at university) permit the discount of much of the prediction of gloom. It is, though, 'unnecessary for a Prince to have all the good qualities I have enumerated, but it is very necessary to appear to have them' (Machiavelli 1985: ch. xviii).

There is the nice side to that, too, of course. To be widely read or cultured permits a manager to contribute to a wide range of business topics and mix business socially with a range of colleagues. In many advanced-level behavioural subjects on business courses, tutors enjoy seeing students range from Shakespeare to Star Trek, from Freud to French cuisine, from Marx to motorbikes. It adds richness and aids communication and relationships. Indeed many would love to advance this sort of education, as perhaps the Oxbridge masters of earlier years are reputed to have done. So this is proposed:

'Light' usage	Skill	'Dark' usage
Polymath abilities: knowing something about any topic likely to be raised either professionally or personally in business life, and being able to express that knowledge more or less competently.	Expressions of knowledge	Bull: more or less successfully deceiving others into thinking that one knows more about the topic in hand than one does.

Networks

There is another skill closely associated with the above, namely, being able to include or exclude people from networks, for one's own personal advantage. This connects with the last point also in that it is a weapon that men have been accused of wielding to the detriment of women – who have been catching up – for a long time. It is not difficult to find examples of the pain of in-grouping (and out-grouping). At the top end of banking, for example, there is perceived to be a public-school mafia, while in the dealing room you need a strong regional accent, preferably Greater London. Those who work for a bank are often asked by unfamiliar colleagues 'Are you a banker?' by which the interlocutor *only* means 'Have you worked in a bank since leaving school, and specifically in domestic branch banking?' The enquiry is usually not pure, but openly flavoured with discrimination: a negative reply would confirm the asker's impression that the asked is an outsider, a dilettante and a fly-by-night, which *simple facts* the asker would invariably make plain to the asked, and to his listening cronies.

In many business circles there are masonic-style in-groups: the old school, the right university, acceptable club membership. Should business tutors teach our largely comprehensive-school, and totally new-university, students how to appear to have a different background? On the other hand, they could be taught their own form of exclusivity; and they could certainly learn some simple mechanical clerical techniques, such as judiciously leaving people's names off circulation lists.

Then again one can show the ethical benefits of networking. Both authors have more or less been involved in the set-up and running of a student part-time employment service. They have been instrumental in convincing many doubting minds as to why they should lend their support. This included influentials in bodies as diverse as the academic community, student union officials, local business and commercial collective organizations, and individual employers.

Getting the backing of credible contacts at the head of their particular field provided the service with a high profile, and inroads to information, which were needed to quickly set up a service to alleviate the financial hardship of students. Operating within a small community meant that one contact could be used not only to elicit information, but also to provide the names of other potential contacts. Being able to introduce oneself to a contact with a referral from another figure in the community provides a head start in building that relationship.

Machiavelli claims: 'and since he had allies ... that depended upon him, he was able to construct whatever building he wished on such a foundation'; which, he says, required great effort to acquire and little to maintain (Machiavelli 1985: ch. vi); and now this:

'Light' usage	*Skill*	*'Dark' usage*
Skilled collection of and use of a network of influential personal and business contacts, their abilities and command of resources, for personal or organizational ends, to the benefit and mutual support of all.	In-grouping and networking	Skilled collection of and use of a network of influential personal and business contacts, their abilities and command of resources, for personal ends, without regard for the needs of other members. The deliberate exclusion of people, to their disadvantage.

Politics

It must also surely be important to show prospective managers how to handle politics. Already on their final year on the MMU business sandwich degree, students are asked to comment and reflect, realistically, on the vicissitudes of their industrial placement and are encouraged to tell the truth as they see it. And, in a Business Consultancy unit, students are confronted with a real-world, imperfect problem-solving situation which often enough requires very skilful personal and interpersonal manoeuvre.

But do we need to go further? In an advanced organizational behaviour unit, the same students have a couple of seminars using the metaphor of organizations as political system, tracing the lines of the eponymous chapter in Morgan's book (1997). Those taking that option explore the varying balance adopted in different organizations between *power, authority, influence, rights, limitations, privileges, resources, objectives* and *obligations*. The study is scholarly enough to concentrate on theory and observation, but it is admittedly normative to an extent, in that from the ivory tower one can discuss the attempt to maintain balance, to sustain *status quo* and to correct instability. And it is an option, not a core subject.

In this context, however, course designers might also include, either as core or as elective, something along the lines of a series of seminars in, say, the Practicalities of Office Politics, or Organizational Self-Defence classes; or Situational Management; and at this point, for the first time, tutors might dare to suggest Machiavelli as a recommended author for *business* students, rather than just those interested in politics or history. In most people's 'political' experience they will have found that only after gaining an awareness of the political make-up of an organization, with all its coalitions and power bases, can any real progress be made. A move in the wrong direction at the wrong time can send one three steps back, or at best simply get one nowhere.

A graduate acquaintance of the authors has found it expedient to manipulate power bases to maintain her performance and that of her section despite a poor immediate superior: she weaves a convoluted path in order to bypass her immediate manager to have her schemes agreed by her director, whilst managing to balance the retention of reasonable day-to-day relations with the immediate boss – who, by the way, derives benefit from the efficient working of his section. Only after a period of hitting brick walls was she driven to such measures and found the tactic worked. This would therefore seem to be a necessary management skill and might not training, even at university level, be conceivable as legitimate? And the table-entry is shown opposite.

In all, then, we might be nearer to a course design that Machiavelli himself would have approved of, though there is the opportunity and stimulus and, without question, the need to engage in rich empirical work on these skills enumerated herewith, among others.

There remains a sort of meta-ethical problem. Academics would still be wary of overtly offering the dark side of the skills, for reasons, in that they may – no,

'Light' usage	Skill	'Dark' usage
Being able to use and balance objectives, power, rights, responsibilities, relationships and resources for the benefit of the organization and of oneself, in that order, having regard for the beneficial effect on others.	Political manoeuvre	Being able to manipulate and balance, power, rights, responsibilities, relationships and resources for the benefit of oneself and the organization, in that order, with little/no regard for the effect on others.

they do – see it as their public duty to elevate a rolling new generation of ethical managers; although, sadly, it could be suspected that there may be a healthy prospective market for a vocationally skill-based BSc. (Hons) in Disreputable Business Practice. Meanwhile, the least they can do is ensure that the health warnings are apparent on the packages of the light skills as taught on present business degrees. The balance must be struck: as tutors balance between warning freshers about the dangers of the big city, stopping short of frightening them, so they need to inculcate the light skills but have dialogue about the dark … which leaves them in the position of the discoverers of nuclear power, who want it used for the production of domestic energy, but will not take responsibility for the fact of the design and production of weapons of mass destruction.

But then,

> A Prince must know how to make good use of the nature of the beast, he should choose…the fox and the lion; for the lion cannot defend itself from traps and the fox cannot protect itself from the wolves. It is therefore necessary to be a fox in order to recognise the traps and a lion in order to frighten the wolves.
>
> (Machiavelli 1985: ch. xviii)

And employers of business graduates know that they are at least reasonably well educated in the ways of the business world: the last word from chapter xviii, 'He who has known best how to employ the fox has succeeded best … '.

Notes

1 Taken from Gilbert, A. (trans.) (1989) *Machiavelli: The Chief Works and Others*, vol. 1, Durham, NC: Duke University Press, p. 62.
2 See Hirsch (1989):

> Most organizations appear to respond to the complexity of defining good management by going for a mixture of characteristics of various kinds. They usually span aspects of the persons themselves (personality, intellect, attitudes or motivation) as well as things that the person can do (skills and competences). They sometimes also include measures of job-related knowl-

edge (qualifications, past experience, etc.). Achievement (in terms of overall performance) is also taken as a proxy for 'skills' ....

3 Belbin's original model suggested that successful groups needed to contain someone taking each of the eight following roles: the Team Worker, the Chair, the Shaper, the Company Worker, the Plant/Innovator, the Resource Investigator, the Monitor/ Evaluator and the Completer/Finisher. Later versions included a ninth, the Specialist.
4 Here tribute is to be paid to Lord Stone of Blackheath, Managing Director of Marks and Spencer plc, in conversation with whom the idea of a black–white range arose.
5 But not in the south ....
6 The reader is asked to pardon the euphemism, if not the expression.

References

Belbin, R. M. (1981) *Management Teams*, London: Heinemann.
Festinger, L. (1957) *A Theory of Cognitive Dissonance*, New York: Harper & Row.
Hirsh, W. (1989) 'Defining Managerial Skills', *IMS Report* 185, Sussex University.
Hofstede, G. (1991) *Cultures and Organisations*, London: McGraw Hill.
Machiavelli, N. (1985) *The Prince*, trans. G. Bull, London: Penguin.
Morgan, G. (1997) *Images of Organisation*, London: Sage, 2nd edn.
Potter, S. (1952) *One-Upmanship*, London: Rupert Hart-Davis Ltd.
Stone, B. W. and Pashley, J. (1997) 'The Application of Theory to Practice in Student Group Business Projects', *Capability* 3 (1), April.

I BELIEVE THAT I SHOULD BE ABLE TO PUT
A LITTLE MONEY ASIDE AFTER THIS TRIP,
ONCE I RETURN TO FLORENCE, I SHOULD
LIKE TO PUT IT INTO SOME SMALL BUSI-
NESS. I THOUGHT ABOUT GOING IN FOR
RAISING CHICKENS, BUT I NEED TO FIND
AN AGENT TO RUN IT FOR ME.

LETTER TO LUIGI GUICCIARDINI,
7 DECEMBER 1509[1]

10 Corporate governance
Real power, Cecil King and Machiavelli

Ken Simmonds

In May 1968, the entire board of International Publishing Corporation (IPC) voted to remove their absent chairman, Cecil King, from the board. Ever since, clauses in company articles that permit a board to remove one of its board members have been called Cecil King clauses. These clauses are becoming the rule rather than the exception. Many companies have even adopted variations that permit less than board unanimity in approving a vote for removal. Given that Cecil King clauses gained their name from removal of a chairman, why have so many chairmen allowed them to be put before their own shareholders for adoption?

The answer to this question probably lies in the fact that the adoption of a Cecil King clause can produce exactly the opposite outcome to chairman removal. It can provide an effective tool for a chairman or chief executive to gain power over a board and retain tenure well beyond the time justified by the performance of the corporation over which they preside.

This paper looks at the role of Cecil King clauses in building power over corporate boards and how tenure is retained through exercising that power. It also looks at the ways in which shareholder interest can be protected by limiting the tenure of those presiding over under-performing corporations. There are strong cultural norms that press for retirement or removal of under-performers. Most find these impossible to oppose. But Machiavelli tells us to expect and prepare for the most selfish behaviour. He would recommend absolute legal limits to tenure for all directors. He would also argue strongly that, given their potential for misuse, Cecil King clauses should be legally prohibited.

Consolidating power at the top

The consolidation of power by a chairman or a chief executive is a well-established art. Whoever gains power first then moves to control the selection and terms of engagement of the other, and of all other, directors. Each director's future within the corporation is then in the hands of that power holder. One outspoken word against the power holder by an executive director and the executive's appointment is brought to an abrupt end. Usually the terms of an executive director's appointment will provide that termination of the executive post also entails an end to their board appointment. Any executive director's position is thus very weak when it comes to boardroom opposition to the power holder.

Non-executive directors may have no stronger position. In the first place they are likely to have been personally chosen by the power holder and to have no interest in challenging their patron's performance. Had they posed any potential threat, their appointment would have been vetoed by the power holder. Astute power holders may simply choose trusted friends (Mace 1971). One British study, by ProNed, claimed that 60 per cent of chairmen made their last non-executive appointment 'through personal connections, without making an objective appraisal of the skills and experience required' (Edgecliffe-Johnson 1994). Research into the composition of US boards also concluded that the longer chief executives were in power, the more difficult it became for share-holders to add new outside directors to monitor them. (Hermalin and Weisbach 1988: 605).

For non-executive directors who have no friendship loyalty, their main role as an executive director in another corporation may be another impediment to action against a power holder. They may fear the consequences that any 'revolu-tionary' action they take may lead to within their own firm. If they are the power holder there, they will probably not wish to give any demonstration of how board revolution might be fomented. Yet, even if they are not the power holder, they might be all too aware that their own superior would not look kindly on a subordinate moving against the power holder in another corpora-tion. Justice Arthur J. Goldberg of the United States Supreme Court expressed the view in no uncertain terms that this possibility should prohibit non-executive directorships for those who are executive directors elsewhere:

> It is ... my view that management officials of corporations in active service should not serve on the boards of companies other than their own. I say this on elementary conflict-of-interest grounds.
>
> The management of corporation A, which serves on the board of direc-tors of corporation B, is not very likely to take up cudgels against the decision of the managers of corporation B. That is quite understandable because they will instinctively feel that it would be inappropriate to do so because they are both management people.
>
> The normal inclination – again, quite understandable – is for outside management people who are sitting on a board to support the manage-ment of the corporation.
>
> (Goldberg 1977)

This leaves the truly independent non-executive members of a board. The incentive to speak out against a non-performing power holder is not great even for this rare breed. Any indication of opposition during the first term of a typical three-year appointment, normally renewed only once, could lead to the disappearance of any support for a second term from anywhere on the board.

The non-executive director considering opposition to a power holder must know that support would be difficult to raise. On many boards, the majority will be executive directors. Their support against somebody with clear power over salaries and dismissal is not something a non-executive director could count on. Why indeed should any executive director risk directorship and career to back a non-executive director whose chance of successful opposition is so slim?

Independent non-executive directors are necessarily very much on their own. They must find the bulk of their support from outside the board if they wish to depose a power holder.

Cecil King clauses: threat or protection?

The existence of a Cecil King clause does not give an independent director much help in deposing a non-performing power holder. How can the support of executive directors be gained unless the power holder publicly shows weakness? Before Cecil King's dismissal by his board, he had clearly discredited himself in front of his entire top management team.

In February 1968, the top management of IPC met in London for a conference captioned IPC '73. The conference programme was designed to review the performance of the past five years and to plot the path for the next five. IPC had been formed only in 1963 out of the Daily Mirror Group of which Cecil King had been chairman since 1951. After a profits peak in 1966, however, IPC profits and share price had fallen steeply. In a manner that was typical of his behaviour, King deigned to attend the three-day conference for only one evening. Rapidly and without expression, he read a speech prepared by assistants on the state of the economy and the state of IPC, then consented to answer questions. As one of the staff responsible for taping the conference describes it:

> It was painfully apparent to everyone listening that, whatever his past planning had been like, his thinking for the future was restricted to the intuitive feeling that the only growth opportunity in publishing was provided by books, and that in no circumstances could IPC ever be taken over.

The outside chairman gave his impressions of the conference the following day:

> He started favourably, until he reached Wednesday evening when the 'old man' came along. He stopped. He apologised, explaining that in America the term 'old man' in this context meant no disrespect, but was merely the colloquial term for the boss. 'So', he restarted, 'along came this old, old man … '. The laughter was at first tentative, then prolonged. King's spell had been broken.

(Cleverley 1971: 225)

Within a week the deputy chairman and managing director had commissioned a consulting study on future strategy and board structure. The coup came in May.

Cecil King clauses, however, contain little threat for a power holder who does not publicly invite attack from other directors, as did Cecil King. In fact, for a power holder it is the post of chairman or chief executive that is harder to defend, not the post of director. Public corporations rarely have any special clauses in their articles relating to appointment or removal of a chairman or chief executive. Neither post has a statutory protection. A board that loses confidence in its chairman or chief executive may vote either out of office by a simple majority. Without a Cecil King clause they could be voted off the board only by the shareholders, but a board voting them out of the office of chairman or chief executive would have broken their power position anyway.

The security of power holders' tenure does not stem from the absence of a Cecil King clause that could be used remove them. It stems from their ability to keep individual directors or small groups from attacking them, because of the likelihood and severity of their reaction. In this respect, a Cecil King clause can be a powerful tool available to the power holder.

A Cecil King clause provides the power holder with power over an independent non-executive director. Any non-executive who indicates opposition without the support to carry it through to deposing the power holder can be asked quietly to resign, with the threat that otherwise the power holder would deliver enough votes to ignominiously vote the director off the board – for boardroom incompatibility or some similar non-specific allegation.

It is not surprising that there are few recorded cases of Cecil King clauses being used in this way. Confronted with defeat before a campaign has really begun, most non-executive directors would tender their resignation and move on without any blemish recorded against their performance. The victorious power holder, moreover, would have a vested interest in an amicable resignation. There would be little value in publicizing any rift, lest the cause of the disagreement focused poorly on the power holder.

The only evidence that can be advanced concerning the use of Cecil King clauses as threats is a statement made to the author by Sir John Hoskyns when chairman of EMAP. He claimed to have found such a clause very helpful several times in corporations of which he had been chairman.

The protection that a Cecil King clause offers a power holder is even greater if it permits less than board unanimity in removing a director. No member of a coalition of two or three non-executive directors could be threatened by a clause that required the votes of all directors other than the one against whom the motion for removal was directed. A clause requiring only a 75 per cent majority of the board, however, could be implemented by the votes of 9 directors out of a board of 12.

The lower the percentage of the board votes required for removing a director, the larger the minority that a power holder can afford to override. The power holder could simply utilize the Cecil King power sequentially against a minority group, eliminating them one by one. Instead of the Cecil King clause being used to protect the corporation against one troublesome director, it then becomes an extremely powerful method of eradicating dissent on the board and preventing the emergence of a dissenting coalition.

The adoption of Cecil King clauses

Apart from four provisions rarely used concerning insanity, bankruptcy, legal bans or continuous absence, the Companies Act gives shareholders the sole power to remove a director before the term of appointment expires. All Cecil King clauses giving boards the power to remove directors have been knowingly adopted as changes to their Articles of Association by the companies which adopt them. Quite often these changes have been suggested by company solicitors who from time to time will be consulted about updating Articles. Most company solicitors have a standard set of current wordings for Articles against which they will check the companies' old Articles and suggest changes. Certain firms of solicitors have standard sets of Articles containing Cecil King clauses. The reasons given by solicitors for the clause will probably be that it will be useful in the event of a 'renegade' director emerging and avoid the time delays and bother of explanation if removal has to be put to a shareholder vote.

While solicitors may instigate consideration of a Cecil King clause, it is the power holder who will approve the clause before the recommended changes in the Articles are put first to the board and then to the shareholders in the Annual General Meeting. In this process, the board itself is really the only point at which a Cecil King clause approved by the power holder can be effectively questioned, but a Board majority is all that is required and most power holders can deliver that very easily. Once approved by the Board, the proposed new Articles that may be many pages long will be placed before shareholders in such a way that any significant objection or debate is extremely difficult and rejection of a single change most unlikely. In any case, the circle will very likely be closed by the recommendations for the new Articles being described to shareholders as 'recommended by the company solicitors'. The illusion is created of a standard legal process. The reality is that the shareholders are being asked to vote from themselves, to the power holder, a powerful weapon to control the board membership and extend the power holder's security of tenure.

The wording 'recommended by the company solicitors' was precisely that used by EMAP plc to add its Cecil King clause. Two non-executive directors, Mr Joe Cooke and the author of this paper, opposed changes in the EMAP Articles that removed a requirement for 5 non-executive directors and added a Cecil King clause providing for removal of a director by a 75 per cent majority of the board.

Although dissent by the two directors was included in the notice to shareholders of the Annual General Meeting, they did not circulate shareholders directly. The chairman of the EMAP board, however, did approach major institutional shareholders for their support. In particular, he approached the Association of British Insurers (ABI) whose investment committee had been very active in advocating more shareholder-oriented corporate governance. Strangely, however, they had in 1990 advocated the inclusion of Cecil King clauses in company Articles (ABI 1990), although without detailed explanation as to why. The ABI included as members Prudential, Standard Life, Commercial Union, Clerical Medical and Eagle Star.

In correspondence with the ABI not disclosed to other shareholders of EMAP, the EMAP chairman entered into a commitment that EMAP would consult with the ABI if its board should wish to reduce the number of non-executives below numbers indicated in the Cadbury Guidelines. The net effect of the changes recommended in the Articles was to take from shareholders generally any right to express their views on removal of a director, but to give an unpublished commitment to some shareholders that they might have a prior say in any such removal. An added twist was that ABI members, including the Prudential in particular, had themselves adopted Cecil King clauses. To speak out against the EMAP move would be to castigate corporate governance of their own institutions.

Nevertheless, upon receipt of the EMAP chairman's commitment the ABI investment committee recommended support of the EMAP Article changes. The changes were defeated by those attending the shareholders' meeting but carried by proxy votes.

By entering into this sort of arrangement 'off the record', the ABI forfeited its right to take a moral leadership in corporate governance. The question still remains as to whether the ABI recognized the dangers of Cecil King clauses and backed off because of their members' own vulnerability, or whether the ABI failed to understand what Cecil King clauses could lead to.

There is no comprehensive list of which public corporations now have Cecil King clauses in their Articles. A December 1996 study by PIRC of the top 129 UK companies by market capitalization, however, showed 62 per cent to have some type of Cecil King clause with 15 per cent permitting removal of a director with less than unanimity (table 10.1). If this pattern holds for all corporations listed on the London Stock Exchange, already 15 per cent of UK corporations make it difficult for a minority coalition of two directors to hold out against the rest of a board that may be dominated by one power holder.

When should a power holder be deposed?

However difficult it may be to remove a power holder, directors have a responsibility to do so if it is in the interests of the corporation. Above all, the board has a responsibility to maximize shareholder value, subject to meeting the requirements of the societies in which the corporation operates. A board will have failed in its task if shareholder value has decreased, or if the increase in shareholder value has been clearly less than others could have achieved. In such a case, the person who has held the power position and presided over the poor performance should either move on or be removed.

Several large US corporations finally confronted the overwhelming evidence

Table 10.1   Prevalence of Cecil King clauses (129 largest UK corporations by
capitalization December 1996*)

	Number of corporations	%
Have Cecil King clauses		
Board approval required by:		
– All directors	74	58.0
– 20% of all directors	2	1.5
– 80% of remaining directors	1	0.8
– 75% of all directors	8	6.3
– 75% of remaining directors	3	2.3
– 50% of all directors	3	2.3
No Cecil King clause	38	28.8
	129	*100.0*

Source: PIRC Intelligence (10 (11) December 1996)

*excludes British Energy plc

of poor performance and removed chairmen in the early 1990s. These included
John Akers of IBM, Paul Lego of Westinghouse Electric, James Robinson of
American Express, James Kettelson of Tenneco, Robert Stempel of General
Motors, Rod Canion of Compaq Computers and Kenneth Olsen of Digital
Equipment (McCarroll 1993: 44–5). Publication of ratings of the 'best' and the
'worst' boards has further increased the pressure on under-performers (Byrne
1996).

Another case for the power holder moving on can be made when younger
executives have shown that they can out-perform the power holder in creating
shareholder value. And there is an absolute case for removal of chairmen or
chief executives who themselves remove 'young turks' because they represent a
threat to their power holder position. Executives who can add significant shareholder value are rare and firms that dispose of such internal talent may find it
impossible to replace the full value lost.

Frequent references to movement of talented managers in analysts' assess-
ments of public corporations show that shareholders do place value on new
blood coming through. Future top management has a value. For example,
when Mr David Arculus, the EMAP plc managing director, announced that he
would join United News and Media plc following the highly publicized EMAP
board dispute in 1996, EMAP value dropped around £250 million and United
News and Media gained £250 million in the one day.

Finally, idiosyncratic actions can lead to an *ad hominem* case for the departure of a chairman or chief executive. The recent case of disparaging comments
about club supporters by both the chairman and chief executive of Newcastle
United Football Club was an example of individuals clearly out of step with the
rest of the organization.

Limited-term appointments versus removal for under-performance

Reliance upon power holders being removed for under-performance is widely perceived as fraught with difficulties. Measurements of shareholder value added are complex and many exogenous factors may affect performance. Even when it is quite clear that a power holder has presided over under-performance, however, the difficulties of breaching their power still exist. A protracted battle could hurt shareholder value even more.

One way around the problems is to make limited-term appointments. Writing on the difficulties of deposing a chairman, Sir Adrian Cadbury had this to say:

> Perhaps all that can usefully be said on the possible need to replace a chairman is that it reinforces the argument for limited terms of office and that if it has to be done, let it be done speedily.
>
> (Cadbury 1995: 167)

Limited-term appointments have their own set of problems, however. If they were to be limited by statutory authority, it would mean that outstanding performers might have to depart too soon. Young stars could look ahead to a short tenure only. Short-termism might be encouraged. Without statutory authority, the strong power holder would be able to engineer an extension of tenure even given under-performance. In fact, a renewed fixed term might hold off any further attempt to depose the power holder for the duration of that term.

Why not rely on market forces for tenure?

Whenever corporate governance concerns point towards regulation, the issue arises of unnecessary and possibly inefficient interference with an efficient market. Why should it not be left to the market to settle the tenure of top management? If other management could do better, then they pay the shareholders a higher value than the shareholders would have achieved with current management holding to its tenure.

Power to retain tenure is of course ultimately limited by the market. The shareholders can extract value by selling to a bidder hostile to management. Nevertheless, management in power can do a great deal to forestall market operation. They can reject merger and take-over offers and engineer complex defences.

How far a board will go to defend itself against an activating shareholder is illustrated by the epic proxy battle won by the board of the Union Bank of Switzerland (UBS) in 1976. A group of rich private clients, led by Mr Martin Ebner who headed the private BZ Bank, had bought large quantities of UBS registered shares each with five times the voting power of a bearer share. They planned to vote in a new board and unlock the hidden value within the under-performing UBS. The UBS board responded by calling a shareholders' meeting to convert registered shares into bearer shares, requiring a 66.67 per cent majority to carry the proposal. They finally emerged the victors with 66.8 per cent of the votes, but only by an ingenious method of buying registered shares on a forward-dated basis from one of the challengers at a significantly higher back-dated price. The seller was guaranteed a 13 per cent profit because the price of the registered shares had fallen. At the same time, the seller retained the voting rights on the day of the vote and could exercise them to support the board. If the sale had not been forward-dated, the bank would have owned its own shares and been unable to exercise the votes (Rodger 1995).

Where shares are widely held, it may be virtually impossible for shareholders to do anything but wait for a hostile take-over that breaks through management defences. Shareholder value would have to fall well below reasonable expecta-tions before dispersed shareholders would initiate any action themselves. Shareholder initiation is extremely cumbersome and costly. There is no statu-tory provision for shareholder costs to be reimbursed, yet to obtain the 15 per cent shareholder backing required to give notice of a motion to change a board may require a lot of organization.

Market intervention from outside may be slow to appear; appear only after significant failure in producing the shareholder value that is possible, and yet still be thwarted by management. Nevertheless, action initiated by shareholders is unlikely to come before a hostile attempt at take-over from outside.

There is another compelling reason why the market is not the answer. With a take-over or merger, the existing shareholders get only part of the value the new management will produce from the position they acquire. Buyers expect some of the value, otherwise few would pursue a bid. Why should existing share-holders not ensure that internal executives who could do as well as outsiders were given the power to do so – and hence keep all of the shareholder value produced?

Machiavelli on the tenure of power positions

While Niccolò Machiavelli knew nothing of limited liability corporations and their governance, he did know about city governance. And he did have very definite observations about extending tenure to a powerful leader. In fact, he attributed the dissolution of the Roman republic to just two things: the strug-gles over agrarian laws and prolongation of military commands (Machiavelli 1977: 215).

Machiavelli recognized clearly the temptation to extend tenure to prolong good performance. He cites Lucius Quintus Cincinnatus as an outstanding example of wisdom in rejecting extended tenure. The plebeians had extended the command of the tribunes. Not to appear weaker, the Senate decided to prolong Lucius Quintus' consulate. He refused to accept the decision, claiming that bad examples should be eliminated, not compounded by even worse examples. Despite his warning, prolongation of magistracies became a practice and, following that, so did the prolongation of military commands.

The first for whom a military command was extended was Publilius Philo. Feeling that Publilius had victory within his grasp as he came to the end of his consulate, the senate did not send his successor to the field of war at Palaeopolis. Instead they made him proconsul. Machiavelli points out that, although this action was carried out in the public interest, it ultimately enslaved Rome. The more the Romans went abroad with their armies, the more it seemed that extensions were necessary and the more they were used. As a result, fewer experienced military command and reputation became restricted to a few. Furthermore, when a citizen had commanded an army for a lengthy period of time, he gained its support and made it his personal supporter. The army forgot the senate and recognized him as leader. In due course Sulla, Marius and Caesar were able to find soldiers to follow them against the public interest. Caesar was ultimately able to seize Rome.

Cecil King and cultural limits to power

Corporate governance discussions focus primarily on regulations and laws for the limitation of tenure and the power of removal. So did Machiavelli. He clearly favoured laws: 'hunger and poverty make men industrious and laws make them good' and 'when good custom is lacking the law is immediately necessary' (Machiavelli 1977: 28). This attitude stemmed from his stated belief that 'men never do good except out of necessity' (ibid.: 28). He believed that private interest would eventually predominate. Yet Machiavelli praised Lucius Quintus Cincinnatus for his wisdom in rejecting extended tenure on the grounds that there was a greater social benefit involved. His praise implies another belief that, in determining tenure of social office, social interest should be the prime consideration. Social interest should override the interest of the individual whatever the individual's legal position on further occupancy.

If Machiavelli could perceive social benefit and how personal interests conflicted with it, so could others. Given that they did, surely some social sanctions must have emerged to prevent the pursuit of personal interest over public interest for very long. Perhaps his belief in law stopped Machiavelli looking for the social sanctions that did in fact exist.

Applying such a search to today's corporate governance, we do indeed find that social sanctions emerge to pressure power holders to give up their tenure if they do not perform. Only in very extreme cases will these pressures be beaten off by the failing individual.

Cleverley, who was a participant along with the author throughout the Cecil King affair, analysed the whole process in anthropological terms. He claimed that society retained the age-old myth of the fisher king and applied it to corporate governance. In the world of top executives and their powers, we structure myths of heroes, gods and semi-gods. The myth is built up around the business leader who ascends from his back garage to build a huge organization and acquire demi-god status and supernatural powers. Inconvenient contrary facts are either ignored or magnified as a series of trials in the path of the hero as he climbs towards divinity. Ultimately he ascends into heaven and takes a place in the mythology of business in the past. Or he incurs the wrath of the gods for challenging their omnipotent power and is reduced to dust and his supernatural powers broken forever. The omnipotent market will not be transgressed.

Fortune, Forbes and *Management Today* build and propagate these myths every month. As the performance changes for a corporation so does the myth about the power holder. He stands for the business and for its relative success or failure. If the king is not virile and potent, the firm is laid waste. If the firm is laid waste, the king is not virile and potent. The leader of a successful firm, whatever his real age, is young at heart, decisive, forceful and foresighted. The leader of a poorly performing firm is staid, conservative, long-serving and risk-avoiding.

To view a myth maker at work, look at the issue of *Fortune* dated 27 April 1998. There appears an article on Hank Greenberg, 73-year-old chairman of American International Group (AIG). The heading sets the stage for the myth building: 'AIG: Aggressive. Inscrutable. Greenberg.' We learn that he is the chairman of 'giant' insurer AIG. He 'feels good' and is 'widely and enthusiastically admired for his management abilities'. AIG performed because 'It had Hank Greenberg …. Who in the face of everything awesome about the assignment kept turning out earnings gains. In the 31 years he has been running AIG, earnings per share have dropped in only one year'. Later, you would not be surprised to read: 'This man, you should understand, can be charming. But he is also tough, demanding, impatient, focused, tireless, tenacious, and just about every other adjective in the Thesaurus that suggests drive and determination' (Loomis 1988: 76–8).

Here is the myth as Cleverley depicts it, referring cleverly to a king who could be Cecil King:

> Once upon a time there was a king. In his youth he had been a mighty warrior and a wise ruler. His kingdom had grown and prospered. His people had been rich and proud. But he had grown old, and his courtiers and barons had grown grey alongside him. As a result, his kingdom had fallen into desolation and neighbouring kings had stolen parts of it for themselves.
>
> Nevertheless, as yet his lands were wide. Many people believed them to be still fertile. They believed that only the king's dotage caused its barrenness. And so, one day, there arrived at the king's court a message from a great magician, who had used his secret powers to build himself a kingdom out of nothing. The message demanded that the old king gave up his realm or be prepared to do battle for it.
>
> The old king and his courtiers knew their powers were declining. The contemptuous demand was, however, too much for their dignity to accept. They prepared themselves for battle, but their hearts were low. Although

they knew that their people loved the old king for what he had given them in the past, they also knew that most of them were sorely tempted by the magician's promises of riches.

Then one day a young prince rode up to the king's castle. He was richly dressed and powerful. He came from a faraway land where his father had also been a king. When his father died, the prince had ascended to the throne, pacified his kingdom, and restored its fortunes. But he had made a vow to seek out new lands and new riches, and to build for himself an empire that men everywhere would know and respect and fear, as they had the emperors of old. He offered the old king a treaty: he would do battle against the magician in his stead, but in return he must be given half the kingdom and the stewardship of the rest. As the prince was young and strong, and as he had fought many battles which had made him famous around the world, the old king agreed.

When the day of battle came, the young prince was loved by all who saw him, by gods as well as men, and this magic was too powerful for the sorcerer-king who left the field uttering dire warnings. But from that day forward his magic powers deserted him, and before the year was past he even lost his own kingdom. The prince however took over the stewardship of the old king's realm, made it prosper, and conquered other countries as he pursued his dream of empire.

(Cleverley 1971: 215–6)

So Cecil King had become an 'old, old man'. There was a need for a new king. No market action was needed. The prince arrived and the cycle repeated. Two years later Don Ryder took over at IPC from a 'failing' Hugh Cudlipp, who had proved to be a weak prince. The myths began again. Cleverley (1971) gives examples of the press descriptions of Ryder at the time:

The Guardian: 'firmly in the saddle'
Daily Telegraph: 'intensely ambitious'
The Sunday Times: 'archetypal hard-faced, hard-playing, hard-working, uncompromising professional'
The Observer: 'active, ruthless, straightforward, a real businessman'
Evening Standard: 'strenuous eighteen-hour working day'

Conclusion

Under-performing power holders must survive four tests if they wish to continue their tenure. The first to confront them will be the myth writers and propagators who re-adjust the power holder's own myth based on the 'truth' of under-performance. Their threat will grow stronger over time as the myth is expanded to include failure as an acknowledged fact. Spin doctors will be little help.

The second test comes with the confrontation of the market jackals attracted to under-performance by the myths and the opportunity to switch wealth away from shareholders. The third test comes from recalcitrant shareholders somewhat reluctant to exercise governance power and unable to give their champions, the non-executive directors, enough magic to overcome the power holder.

The final test is the law – if indeed we follow Machiavelli's still pertinent observations and set fixed terms for all directors. This would prevent under-performing power holders from extending their tenure. Shareholder benefit would almost certainly outweigh any short-term costs from regular departure of successful top executives. Without statutory fixed terms for all directors, however, Cecil King clauses remain as potentially very costly to the shareholders who voted for them. Any benefit from directors being able to remove a 'renegade' director quickly is minimal. The costs of reinforcing under-performing power holders, on the other hand, are high. Machiavelli would tell us to use the law to forbid Cecil King clauses altogether. With such clauses gone, independent directors representing shareholder interests will be that much more able to stop executive directors pursuing their own interests at the expense of shareholders.

What would Machiavelli himself say about our recent corporate governance review? He would say that arguments for self-regulation and less regulation are against the public interest and motivated by those who wish to hold positions they have already attained. Our own mythology of business would tell us that a corporate governance review which under-performs must of course be written by old, old men without strength, power or vitality.

Note

1   Taken from Atkinson, J. B. and Sices, D. (trans and eds) (1996) *Machiavelli and His Friends: Their Personal Correspondence*, Dekalb, IL: Northern Illinois University Press, p. 191.

References

Association of British Insurers (1990) 'The Role and Duties of Directors – A Discussion Paper', London: ABI.

Byrne, J. A., 'The Best and Worst Boards', *Business Week*, 25 November 1996, pp. 82–106.

Cadbury, Sir Adrian (1995) *The Company Chairman*, Hemel Hempstead: Director Books.

Cleverley, Graham (1971) *Managers and Magic*, London: Longman Group.

Edgecliffe-Johnson, A., 'Old Boys Haunting the Boardrooms', *Daily Telegraph*, London, 30 October 1994.

Goldberg, Justice A. J. (1997) 'Some Observations in the Effectiveness of Outside Directors', *Subcommittee on Citizens and Shareholders Rights and Remedies*, Washington: US Senate.

Hermalin, B. E. and Weisbach, M. S. (1988) 'The determinants of Board Composition', *RAND Journal of Economics* 19 (4) Winter: 589–606.

Loomis, C. J., 'AIG: Aggressive. Inscrutable. Greenberg.', *Fortune*, 27 April 1988, pp. 76–8.

Mace, M. (1971) *Directors: Myth and Reality*, Boston, MA: Harvard Business School Press.

Machiavelli, N. (1977) *Discourses on Livy*, trans. J.C. and P. Bondanella, Oxford: Oxford University Press.

McCarroll, T., 'Board Games', *Time*, 8 February 1993, pp. 44–5.

Rodger, I., 'Ebner Client Adds New Twist to UBS Saga', *Financial Times*, 2 January 1995.

4
Political management

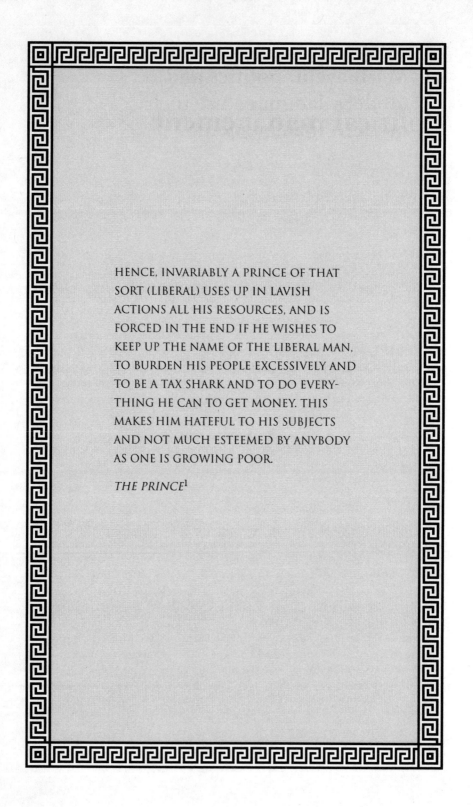

HENCE, INVARIABLY A PRINCE OF THAT
SORT (LIBERAL) USES UP IN LAVISH
ACTIONS ALL HIS RESOURCES, AND IS
FORCED IN THE END IF HE WISHES TO
KEEP UP THE NAME OF THE LIBERAL MAN,
TO BURDEN HIS PEOPLE EXCESSIVELY AND
TO BE A TAX SHARK AND TO DO EVERY-
THING HE CAN TO GET MONEY. THIS
MAKES HIM HATEFUL TO HIS SUBJECTS
AND NOT MUCH ESTEEMED BY ANYBODY
AS ONE IS GROWING POOR.

THE PRINCE[1]

11 Machiavelli, politics and modern language use in modern management

Terry Berrow

What I wish to examine in this short chapter is the use – and, I regret, the abuse – of Niccolò Machiavelli's work (notably) in modern management writings. In such writings, he is depicted as a modern 'spin doctor', dealing in 'issues management', or 'power politics' in organizations. In addition, I wish to look at the related notion of using the term 'political' in new ways, which completely discounts the definition used for two thousand years or more, and using – and abusing – language in a way that can stultify academic debate. In this latter area, one specific example will be provided, but, as readers will appreciate, this 'borrowing' from the academic discipline of Politics and other Social Sciences could be elaborated upon more fully. Finally, a few comments will be made about the use of language in general, and how this affects academic debate.

It is now almost five hundred years since Machiavelli (1469–1527) wrote his famous political tract, *The Prince*, which is now part of every Political Theory syllabus at learned universities. This little book has been equally extolled and reviled by successive generations. Indeed, *The Prince* was in the first edition of the Papal Index of Prohibited Books, being seen as 'diabolical', an enemy of liberality, introducing evil into politics, and was thus ultimately anti-Christian. To admirers of this terse little book, it is seen as merely a primer in politics, introducing realism instead of medieval idealism and claptrap. As one political observer notes: 'all he did was to explain the reality of politics' (McAlpine 1997). What is often forgotten, or indeed never learned, however, is that Machiavelli also wrote his *Discourses*, which examines much of the same subject matter as *The Prince* and much more!

There is no doubting the central importance of Machiavelli as a political theorist in a long and distinguished lineage of writings about the nature of the state. In the western tradition, the starting place for this writing about the political process is often seen as the Greek City State, with giants such as Plato, Aristotle and later the Roman writers. Machiavelli was particularly impressed by this latter pre-Christian group, who are extensively quoted in his writings. In short, although he was writing about, and for the good of, contemporary Florence, he looked back to the pagan period.

Machiavelli's *The Prince* is epigrammatic and rightly quoted in political

circles, when one is looking at how to take power and to maintain it in a political system. Indeed, that was Machiavelli's purpose. One must remember that
he was just 29 when he became the Second Republican Secretary, responsible
for foreign affairs, in the unstable city of Florence. He was in the post between
1498–1512. Savonarola had been burned to death in 1498 and political
violence was common. When the Medici were returned to power in 1513,
Machiavelli lost his exalted position, and was implicated in a plot against them,
for which he was severely tortured. For the rest of his life he wanted to be back
in office, and he wrote *The Prince* as an aid to new rulers, notably the Medici.

His main role model for *The Prince* was the Duke of Valentino, Cesaré
Borgia, who personified the naked ideal of power. Machiavelli particularly
alluded to Borgia's resolve, determination and single-minded ruthlessness. He
admired the way that Borgia mercilessly slaughtered a group of mercenaries
who dared to plot against him, and poured scorn upon the notion of friendship
in politics. Lying, for reasons of state, was equally acceptable.

In short, a ruler should not be bound by traditional ethical norms, and 'it is
much safer for a Prince to be feared than loved' (Machiavelli 1970).

The advice is quite clear – a Prince should be concerned only with power and
the rules that lead to success in political actions. This has been termed 'power
politics' by some, 'realpolitik' by others.

He is principally concerned with gaining power and maintaining it in an
entity called the state.

To Machiavelli, the prevailing conditions of city-state political life demanded
ruthlessness. In particular, if states had become 'corrupted', they could only be
restored by a great man, a Prince. This thesis relied on human nature being
constant, and looking to the pagan past for inspiration. His method is intuitive
rather than logical and he bases his conclusions about how princes should
govern not on abstract considerations, but on the writings of those he admired
from the past, and contemporary circumstances. His written style is pared down
to a minimum and very direct. He hoped to influence a man of greatness and
once more be placed back into the heart of city-state politics.

Machiavelli's amoral approach earned him opprobrium from a variety of
sources, including Cardinal Pole, who in the 1640s referred to him as 'Old
Nick'. The respected historian, Macaulay, joined the vilification process.

From the above, it is clear that Machiavelli in *The Prince* had written a political tract of his times, rather than a discursive, dianoetic work, which is found in
The Discourses. As he is reputed to have said: 'It should be welcome to a prince,
especially a new prince'.

Undoubtedly Machiavelli's writing and method have been seen as breaking
new ground in the art of government, as George Bull (see Machiavelli: 1970)
so perceptively states.

So, to bring us back to our central theme, Machiavelli was a political writer
with a capacity to shock. His pithy observations have been used in the political
sphere for the past five hundred years. But is that all?

Of course not. Machiavelli has been used in the management studies arena, as some guru on management principles in such areas as 'change', 'power', 'politics' or some such 'buzz' word (or should that now be 'sound bite'?).

It is quite common in management books about strategy and organizational behaviour to see references to Machiavelli (almost always *The Prince*) and what strategies to follow in certain business situations. In effect, Machiavelli is seen as a guide to action.

One writer thus states:

> *The Prince* is the 16th Century equivalent of Dale Carnegie's *How to Make Friends and Influence People.*
>
> (Crainer 1994)

The same critic thinks Machiavelli's insights 'are as appropriate to many of today's managers and organisations as they were nearly 500 years ago'. Indeed, on 'managing change' in modern business life, Machiavelli is just one more management guru, amongst many others (Crainer 1994).

Within this context, top modern executives are seen as 'natural rulers', into whose hands the organization can be entrusted. The parallel is drawn between Machiavelli and the modern manager and a direct intellectual lineage is drawn between *The Prince* and modern management techniques.

But is this an accurate reflection? Is it fair to see Machiavelli as a top fifteenth-century management consultant? The writer thinks that the links are tenuous at most in some areas and quite erroneous in others. Quite clearly, Machiavelli is dealing with an entity, the city state, whose existence and continuity demands organizational, structured approaches. Is one really suggesting that the modern managing director/chief executive is a Cesare Borgia? Is the political state the same as a business organization? Machiavelli would have had difficulty with this notion.

The business organization is of course subsumed within the state and far less important. Likewise, when Machiavelli, in his writings, talks of killing political enemies, it is not a metaphor, but a practical solution to the problem of opposition and a lesson to others. His advice to 'devastate them' (i.e. enemies) is equally uncompromising and *not* figurative.

Machiavelli's advice is *not* harmless rhetoric, nor colourful metaphors, but spoken in earnest. In one section, 'Principalities after Conquest', he provides the following advice: 'Whoever becomes the master of a city accustomed to freedom and does not destroy it, may expect to be destroyed himself' (Machiavelli 1970).

Admiringly, he speaks of Cesare Borgia's timing: 'Cesare waited for his opportunity; then, one morning Remirro's body was found cut in two pieces on the piazza at Cesena with a block of wood and a bloody knife beside it' (ibid.: chapter on 'Acquisitions and the help of fortune'). This is clearly no advice that a modern manager could use.

Another piece of advice based on observing Borgia was, 'by destroying all the families of the rulers he had despoiled .... He killed as many of the rulers he had despoiled as he could reach, and very few escaped'. But, as already mentioned, Borgia (the Duke of Valentino) was Machiavelli's ideal role model:

> I cannot possibly censure him. Rather I think I have been right in putting him forward as an example for all those who have acquired power through good fortune and the arms of others.
>
> (Machiavelli 1970)

Why then is Machiavelli so often quoted in management and business areas? The first reason is that he is so eminently quotable. The aphorisms offer wonderful 'sound bites' to today's management 'spin doctors' and after all they are not meant to be taken literally, are they? It is seen as simply a little black comedy. This is particularly true as most people will not have read *The Prince*, let alone his longer *Discourses*. Furthermore, little will be known of Machiavelli's contemporary life. In short, Machiavelli is more often cited than actually read! Read him in his entirety and see how relevant he is to modern political life.

But please do not expect a latter-day Tom Peters to spring from the page with the latest business rhetoric. Look at, for example, the political life of Margaret Thatcher and see the relevance of *The Prince*. But note that, even in this highly relevant area, 1980s/1990s Britain is *not* fifteenth-century Florence.

Another reason, I suspect, why Machiavelli is quoted so often is because of his notoriety and the gravitas that five hundred years of history provides. Because modern management theory does not have this ancestry, it may be seen as lacking passion, somewhat mundane and an intellectual upstart. Machiavelli thus provides the necessary intellectual pedigree to the mongrel, management studies. It also provides a 'hero' to quote at apt moments.

If Machiavelli is 'borrowed', why not other political theorists? After all, they are also concerned with the state, the organization of power and change. Why not use Aristotle, Plato, de Tocqueville, Locke, Hobbes, Bentham, Marx? Or indeed many more. After all, they cover much the same ground as Machiavelli. The reader may decide to undertake this exercise and will quickly realize that some other theorists can be used equally effectively to bolster this intellectual lineage.

It is quite specious to use Machiavelli as a modern management consultant and intellectually dishonest to plunder his writings for quotable aphorisms, which can be, and often are, taken out of context. If serious academic study was paid to Machiavelli, *The Discourses* would be quoted far more, because Machiavelli did *not* favour the principality as a form of government; he favoured the republic. But *The Prince* is so much shorter! And de Tocqueville *et al.* are so much longer and thus considered far less quotable. Machiavelli's true genius is seen in political science and 'borrowing' his talents for aspects of management science is invariably erroneous.

Using Machiavelli's talents in a relevant area should be applauded, but so often the linkages are at best tenuous and trite. This approach can also be seen in the 'borrowing' of 'politics' as a term in management studies.

For two thousand years the western tradition of politics has been about resolving disputes and has sometimes been alluded to as 'the art of the possible'. It has always been associated with various forms of government. From the time of Aristotle, politics arises in organized states

> ... which recognise themselves to be an aggregate of many members, *not* a single tribe, religion, interest or tradition. Politics arises from accepting the fact of the simultaneous existence of different groups, hence different interests and different traditions, within a territorial unit under a common rule.
>
> (Crick 1962)

As Aristotle pointed out, politics is *one* possible solution to the problems of order and, in many countries, is not the most usual method. If one pursues a 'political' order, then groups are recognized as being different and provided with a sense of legality and a means to articulate their differences (ibid.).

Politics is thus highly functional, creating order, reconciling differences in states, and is, as Aristotle called it, 'the master science'. It is a quite specific term, which is often abused. Like Machiavelli, 'politics' has been taken up by management studies and used in an incorrect way. Henry Mintzberg's *Politics and the Political Organisation* (1991) typifies this approach, but there are many more examples that could be cited. He thus states: 'Conflict, and politics that go along with it have become not just acceptable but fashionable ones'. Mintzberg uses the term 'politics' in relation to organizations. This was certainly never intended by ancient political writers and often Professor Mintzberg is quite simply talking about 'power struggles' in a very small (by comparison with the state) organization.

> They (organisations) may help to create politics, but their internal behaviour is *not* political simply because their individual function is quite different from the state itself. And, unlike the state, they have no acknowledged legal right to use force if all else fails.
>
> (Crick 1962)

The organization depicted as a microcosm of the wider political macrocosm is simply reductionist and, when taken to its logical conclusion, is absurd. The business organization is not a complex construct like the state. It is the state that provides the order in which business organizations exist – they are subordinate parts of that order.

According to Mintzberg's neologism of politics we get a new definition:

> The system of politics in contrast, reflects power that is technically illegitimate (or perhaps more accurately, alegitimate) in the means it uses, and sometimes also in the ends it promotes. In other words, political power in the organisation (unlike government) is not formally authorised, widely accepted or officially certified. The result is that political activity is usually

divisive and conflictive, pitting individuals or groups against the more legitimate systems of influence, and when those systems are weak, against each
other.

(Mintzberg 1991)

He continues this reinterpretation of two thousand years of tradition by the
following:

What characterises the organisation dominated by politics is a lack of the
forms of order found in conventional organisations. In other words, the
organisation is best described in terms of power, not structure, and that
power is exercised in ways not legitimate in conventional organisations.

(ibid.)

Thus, conflict and 'political activity' in organizations are synonymous. 'Politics'
is thus dismissed:

Little space need be devoted to the dysfunctional influence of politics in
organisations. Politics is divisive and costly, it burns up energies that could
instead go into the operations. It can also lead to kinds of aberrations.
Politics is often used to sustain outmoded systems of power and sometimes
to introduce new areas that are not justified. Politics can also paralyse any
organisation to the point where its effective functioning comes to a halt
and nobody benefits. The purpose of an organisation, after all, is to
produce goods and services, not to provide an arena in which people can
fight with one another.

(ibid.)

The author quotes at length in order that Mintzberg's 'politics' can be clearly
seen.

But what is wrong with changing the meaning of politics? Initially, one can
only ask why one would want to change a term that has been in specific use for
several thousand years. At the very least it is confusing. Furthermore, there is a
hint of academics using the legitimacy of a term, rather than being original
enough to devise a new one, specifically relevant to the observed phenomenon.
Thus, if conflict is endemic to organizations, so be it! But why not call it 'power
struggles', poor 'interpersonal relations', 'poor communication' or any other
appropriately coined expression, rather than 'politics'? Surely, in the new millennium, we have enough wit to articulate discord in a business organization.

Equally, why, if one needed so desperately to call something 'politics' in an
organization, did not one use it as a positive, functional force, creating harmony
and order? Why use it in this antithetical way? Used in the positive way, it is
only half wrong!

Again, we come back to managerial sciences and their lack of intellectual
pedigree. It is palpably specious to use 'politics' in the sense that Professor

Mintzberg and others use it. It is even more ironic when one sees a grudging appreciation of 'politics' to correct deficiencies in an organization: ' ... the system of politics, whose means are (by *definition*) illegitimate, can sometimes be used to pursue ends that are in fact legitimate ... ' (1991). Whose *definition* is this?

The sad part of the misuse of Machiavelli, and the abuse of 'politics', is that it need not have been so! George Orwell, for example, encapsulates this area of language abuse in much of his writings, both implicitly by example and explicitly in various articles. Modern management writers could take Orwell's (1957) words to heart. He says that language 'becomes ugly and inaccurate because our thoughts are foolish, but the slovenliness of our language makes it easier for us to have foolish thoughts'.

View the above in context of the earlier material covered. For Orwell, language consisted increasingly of phrases tacked together with words *not* chosen for their meaning. Fifty years on, this seems as relevant as ever. Orwell suggests that, in this process, thought corrupts language and vice versa. Thus, 'politics' is just one example. Orwell's advice on this matter is so simple, and yet so profound: 'Let the meaning choose the word and not the other way about'. In addition, simplification of language is important, as is the need *not* to suffer from an inferiority complex over the standing of one's subject.

This chapter started by looking at the political writer Machiavelli and the narrow use of his works by modern management writers. It followed by looking at the way that 'politics' has also been 'borrowed' (or abused?) and calls for a more simple and honest use of language in these academic areas. It is not the author's intention to promulgate this or that theory, or to be an academic whinge. It is simply a call for writers in the area of management studies to look very carefully at the social context of writers from five hundred years ago and to be fully aware that what those writers stated, they *did* mean. Furthermore, to think very carefully about using existing and accepted terminology in new ways that adds nothing to its usage, and indeed, can detract from it.

To those who are interested in Machiavelli my advice is to read *him* – not other people's interpretation of *him*. Judge for yourselves the relevance of Machiavelli to business tactics, as opposed to the real Political World. And remember if you have the time, also read *The Discourses* as well as *The Prince*.

Surprisingly, Benito Mussolini in his *Preludio al Principe* put this viewpoint most clearly:

> I wanted to put the fewest possible intermediaries, old and new, Italian or foreign, between Machiavelli and myself, so as not to spoil the impact of direct contact between his teaching and my actual life.
>
> (Mussolini 1924)

To statesmen, Machiavelli is, and always will be, highly relevant. To modern business strategy, this writer feels that Machiavalli is over-used and often irrelevant in such areas as 'change', 'power', 'politics'.

Finally, if one is quoting fifteenth-century writers, or indeed 'borrowing' from other disciplines, one should be at great pains to be clear about precisely what one is attempting to say, and not take the easy option.

Note

1   Taken from Gilbert, A. (trans.) (1989) *Machiavelli: The Chief Works and Others*, vol. 1, Durham, NC: Duke University Press, p. 59.

References

Crick, B. (1962) *In Defence of Politics*, Harmondsworth: Pelican Books. (Especially chapter 1, 'The nature of political rule'.)

Crainer, S., (1994) *Financial Times*, 'On Machiavelli', 19 December.

De Wit, B. and Meyer, R. (1998) *Strategy: Process, Content and Context*, Minneapolis, MN: West Publishing.

Jay, A. (1964) *Machiavelli and Management*, San Diego, CA: Pfeiffer Press, revised paperback edition, 1994.

Johnson, G. and Scholes, K. (1999) *Exploring Corporate Strategy*, London: Prentice-Hall Europe, 5th edn.

Lynch, G. (1997) *Corporate Strategy*, London: Pitman.

Machiavelli, N. (1970) *The Prince*, trans. G. Bull, London: The Folio Society. (There are other translations, but this author thinks this to be the best available.)

—— (1990) *The Discourses*, Foreword by Bernard Crick, London: Penguin.

McAlpine, A. (1997) *The New Machiavelli*, London: Aurum.

Mintzberg, H. (1991) 'Politics and the Political Organisation', in *The Strategy Process*, Hertfordshire: Prentice-Hall.

Mussolini, B. (1924) *Preludio al Principe*, quoted in Machiavelli (1970).

Orwell, G. (1957) *Inside the whale and other essays*, London: Penguin. (Especially chapter 11, 'Politics and the English language'.)

Strauss, L. (1958) *Thoughts on Machiavelli*, Chicago, IL: Chicago University Press.

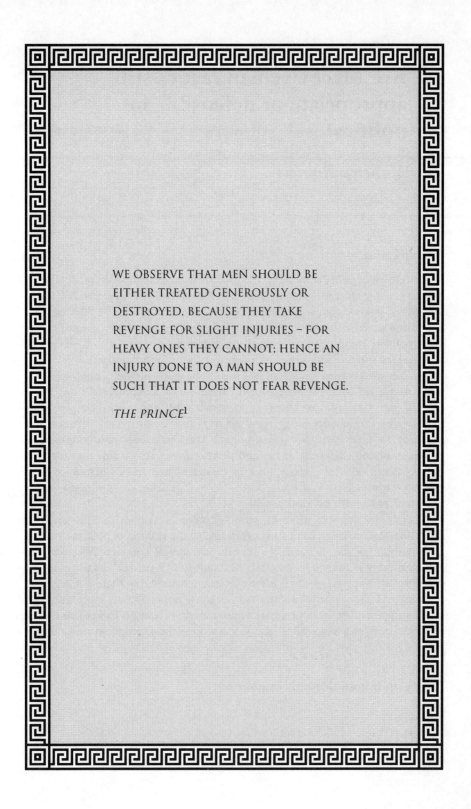

WE OBSERVE THAT MEN SHOULD BE
EITHER TREATED GENEROUSLY OR
DESTROYED, BECAUSE THEY TAKE
REVENGE FOR SLIGHT INJURIES – FOR
HEAVY ONES THEY CANNOT; HENCE AN
INJURY DONE TO A MAN SHOULD BE
SUCH THAT IT DOES NOT FEAR REVENGE.

THE PRINCE[1]

12 Are Machiavellian tactics still appropriate or defensible in politics?

Maureen Ramsay

Introduction

In the history of political thought, the case for immoral behaviour of all kinds is nowhere more forcibly stated than by Machiavelli in *The Prince*. Here, Machiavelli is associated with the doctrine of moral expediency and deviousness in political actions; the divorce of politics and private morality; the justification of all political means, even the most unscrupulous, on grounds of reasons of state and the use of fraud, force, coercion and deceit for political ends.

Machiavelli has been castigated as a man inspired by the devil, as an immoral writer and a deliberate teacher of evil. 'Machiavelli' and 'Machiavellian' have entered the language as terms of reproach and dishonour. Despite this, Machiavelli's arguments have been echoed and endorsed by writers and statesmen from his own time to the present day. Machiavelli's enduring contribution to political thought, policy and practice is the remarkably resilient idea that politics involves or even requires the transcendence or the violation of ordinary moral principles; that fraud, force, lies and violence are justified because they are necessary for political success.

All subsequent justifications for immoral means in politics are concerned to show that Machiavellian tactics are a response to the realities of political life and a recognition of the element of necessity in political conduct. All stress the incompatibility between the demands of traditional or private morality and the requirements of power politics. All justifications assume that there is something different and special about politics that makes it impossible to apply the same moral standards that are appropriate in private life; that in politics the end justifies the means; that consequentialist calculation is the appropriate reasoning in politics.

Justifying immoral means in politics

Machiavelli

For Machiavelli, immoral means were justified when they were necessary to achieve good political consequences. Machiavelli's arguments were supposedly based on a realistic assessment of human nature and the political situation. The realities of the human and political condition dictate behaviour which by conventional standards would be considered wrong or unjust. This is because politics poses questions for which conventional morality is inappropriate. In times of necessity the Prince must be unconstrained by normal ethical ideals and adopt methods which, though they are contrary to those ideals, lead to beneficial consequences.

Political morality frequently demands that the Prince must act immorally – he must learn how not to be good. It is not just because of the special nature of the political situation that there is a rift between moral and political behaviour. Machiavelli's view of human beings as natural egoists with a lust for domination and glory led him to see history as an arena of conflict, treachery and violence and to see politics as the struggle for power. The result was inter-state aggression and domestic turmoil. The roots of this conflict were psychologically located in the nature of human beings. The solution was social and political. In order to acquire and hold on to power, ensure self-preservation, create order, stability and general prosperity, an ethic of consequences must be the statesman's ethic. Conventional or private morality is inappropriate to the political domain when its practice defeats political goals. Given the state of the world and the nature of human beings, immoral actions are necessary and what is politically valuable depends on prudential calculation.

Political realists

One way of legitimizing the Machiavellian idea that the end justifies the means in politics, common in exegesis of *The Prince* and in realist texts, is to argue, following Croce (1925), that politics is an autonomous realm of power, free from the ethical constraints and limitations of the moral realm. It is a separate sphere beyond good and evil. This implies that in politics moral considerations, impulses and principles are irrelevant. Means–end calculations are relevant and appropriate in politics, because politics is rightly concerned with furthering the interests of the state. Chabod (1958) claimed that Machiavelli 'swept aside every criteria of action not suggested by the concept of raison d'état'. Raison d'état refers to what a statesman must do, what it is logical and rational to do in order to preserve the health and strength of the state. The necessity of furthering the interests of the state justifies fraud, force, lies and violence. The ends of politics dictate not the morality, but the rationality of the means.

Though the term raison d'état is now seldom used and the doctrine rarely defended in its original form, its spirit continues to the present day in the terminology of the problem of power, power politics and the power state. It is seen in utilitarian calculations regarding the best interests of states, in the idea of the rationality of the politics of interests and in the political realism or realpolitik that dominates international relations theory. Political realists, like apologists for raison d'état, assume that the struggle for survival and security, power and dominance by sovereign and self-seeking states characterizes and propels international politics. The very structure of international society creates situations of irreducible conflict. According to realists, statesmen think and act in the national interest defined as the preservation of security or the struggle for power. In their relationships with other states, they must at times pursue courses of action that would be legally or morally wrong if applied to domestic politics or to private individuals. Political realists see their elevation of national interests over ethical ideals as being amoral rather than immoral. In this they are part of a continuous tradition which understood Machiavelli to be saying that politics is beyond or above morality.

An objective science of politics

Other commentators see in Machiavelli's advice not an immoral or amoral doctrine, but an ethically neutral technical imperative of the form 'if you want to achieve x, do y'. The ends themselves are not justified as rational or good, the means to achieve them are neither praised nor blamed. They are advocated only as necessary to achieve the end in question. On this view, Machiavellianism as a method is both ethically neutral and politically uncommitted (Renaudet 1942, Olschki 1945, Cassirer 1946). Because this technical imperative can apply to a variety of political actors, princes, tyrants, republicans or democrats, Machiavellianism can be described as an applied science that informs political actors about what they must do, if they want to achieve their ends, whether these be liberatory, revolutionary, democratic, nationalistic or despotic.

It is this reading of Machiavelli which has allowed modern management writers to appropriate Machiavelli. They claim that his advice and strategies can be transferred from the context in which he applied them, to the problems of managing large corporations in the twentieth century and to parallel roles and situations in contemporary business contexts (Jay 1967, Calhoon 1969, Buskirk 1974, Shea 1988, McAlpine 1992, 1997). According to Jay, Machiavelli's message is simply, 'if political success is what you want, this seems the most effective way to achieve it' (1967: 33). Because Machiavellianism is a method of scientific enquiry, it can be applied in non-political contexts to arrive at a set of strategies for achieving objectives in any large organization. Jay, like those who claim that Machiavellianism is a value-free science of politics, implies that moral questions in business are not only irrelevant, but illegitimate. He complains:

> The trouble is that too much writing on management has been concerned not to examine it, but to attack or defend it; and not on the legitimate ground of whether it has been successful or unsuccessful …. The only helpful way to examine organisations and their management is as something neither moral nor immoral, but simply a phenomenon.
>
> (Jay 1967: 33)

Utilitarians

Others have understood the Machiavellian relationship between means and ends in a different way. From a utilitarian or consequentialist perspective, morality is not irrelevant to politics. Utilitarians judge actions by the good consequences they promote, so that prudential calculation is not just rationally required, it is also morally justified. Political imperatives are part of morality. There is a specific morality appropriate to practical politics that is different from a morality of absolute principle. The difference is not a contrast between expediency and principle, the amoral, immoral and the moral, but a contrast between one type of morality and another. The morality appropriate to political life is not based on abstract ideals, but is a utilitarian or consequentialist morality whereby actions are judged according to the good consequences they promote. On this view politics is not divorced from ethics. Politically necessary actions decided by prudent evaluation of the political consequences to which they are likely to lead, are themselves overwhelming moral considerations.

The case for consequentialism in political life rests on the claim that it would sometimes be wrong for politicians to refuse on moral grounds to disregard ethical norms and standards that are adhered to outside politics. It would be irresponsible to act out of pure motives of individual conscience or in accordance with moral principles if doing so is contrary to the general welfare of society, the national interests or the common good. In practical politics it is necessary to adopt a consequentialist ethic when ends that are judged to be good cannot be achieved without recourse to means which, if judged according to the principles of alternative moral traditions, would be impermissible. Adherence to moral principles in these circumstances would make the end unrealizable. If the aim is to maximize good consequences, then justifiable political means exclude no class of actions as wrong in themselves independently of the good consequences that result. All other moral considerations are subordinate to this. Consequentialism, then, morally sanctions actions normally classed as immoral or unjust because the use of fraud, force, lies and violence can have beneficial political consequences and this is what counts morally.

'Dirty hands' arguments

Recent philosophical writing on morality and politics does not promote the view that morality ought not to apply to politics or endorse the consequentialist view that there are no moral problems as long as good ends are achieved (see Walzer 1973, Williams 1978, Hampshire 1978, Nagel 1978). They acknowledge that competing moral principles are not so easily jettisoned and moral conflicts not so easily smoothed away.

The politician who breaks a moral rule in order to achieve a good end is both justified and at the same time guilty of a moral crime. Despite the good consequences of immoral acts, there is a 'moral remainder', an 'uncancelled moral disagreeableness', a moral cost involved (Williams 1978: 62). The paradox of actions which are morally justifiable, but despite this morally wrong, is characterized as the dilemma of 'dirty hands'. Walzer in his discussion of this paradox, explains that 'a particular act of government may be exactly the right thing to do in utilitarian terms and yet leave the man who does it guilty of a moral wrong' (Walzer 1973: 161).

Although these writers acknowledge the moral costs involved in adopting Machiavellian tactics, they conclude that consequentialist calculation is neces- sary in politics, that immoral acts are inevitable and on the whole justified. Walzer concludes that politicians cannot do good in politics unless they are prepared to use the necessary means for 'no one succeeds in politics without getting their hands dirty' (Walzer 1973: 164). Williams takes a similar view:

> ... it is a predictable and probable hazard of public life that there will be these situations in which something morally disagreeable is clearly required. To refuse on moral grounds ever to do anything of that sort is more than likely to mean that we cannot even pursue the moral ends of politics.
>
> (Williams 1978: 62)

Nagel and Hampshire both agree that political ends justify the use of immoral means warranting coercive, manipulative and obstructive methods that would be prohibited in private life.

The distinction between public and private morality

To show what is unique about the political sphere that licenses Machiavellian tactics, these writers make a sharp distinction between the public and the private and claim that politics deserves special treatment as an area outside of or within morality. The following contrasts between the public and private supposedly justify making concessions to the immoral behaviour of politicians.

1 The moral dilemmas associated with the necessity to lie, manipulate, betray, cheat, steal and kill arise more frequently in public life and in the execution of public policies than they do in private life. Violence and force are always a prospect in politics and in the normal run of things do not occur in private life.
2 Political actors are responsible for policies which have greater and more enduring consequences that affect the lives and well-being of a greater number of people than the actions of private individuals.
3 In modern democratic politics, actors in political life are representatives of and accountable to the people. They have obligations and duties attached to their representative roles which require them to serve the interests of, and explain and justify their policies to, those they represent. Therefore politicians' actions ought to be assessed in a different way. Their representa- tive role permits or requires them to use immoral means for the sake of those they represent.

These considerations supposedly lead towards consequentialist morality in politics and the justifiable employment of means that in private life would be prohibited. However, some of the considerations that make political activity different from private activity provide good reasons for avoiding the use of immoral means rather than for thinking that they are justified. Even if it is the case that moral conflict arises more frequently in politics than in personal relations, immoral means are not obviously justified by reference to the frequency of moral dilemmas or to the possibility of the use or threat of violence or force which is constantly present in political life. If it is true that danger is ever present and that conflict is more frequent in politics, then this could be all the more reason for adhering to moral principles rather than a justification for overriding them. The frequency of moral conflict and the greater possibility of violence and force does not automatically license fewer moral restraints or legitimate methods excluded for private individuals. The greater prevalence of lies, violence and force cannot on its own justify the general habit of performing such deeds or even for thinking that they are always necessary. Similarly, though political decisions may have more important and far-reaching consequences that affect larger numbers of people than personal decisions, this might lead us to suppose that political actors and policy makers should be more cautious and more reluctant to employ immoral means or to depart from moral standards than actors in private life.

Nor does it follow that the politician's representative role justifies a bias towards consequentialism. The claim that, in a modern democratic society, public officials are representatives of the people and accountable to them and it is this which justifies assessing actions on consequentialist grounds raises special problems for the use of democratic dirty hands. In this respect, the most difficult means to justify are those which involve concealment, deceit, secrecy and manipulation. If politicians deceive their citizens, these acts by virtue of their secrecy and public ignorance of them cannot meet the criteria of accountability because they cannot be made public. Citizens cannot support or oppose government actions and decisions and this contradicts the basic principles of democratic society based on consent and representation. The justification of lies and deceit on consequentialist grounds seems to violate democratic principles, rather than being compatible with the politician's role in modern democratic societies. The politician's representative role would seem to prohibit the use of such means, rather than endorse them. The alleged differences between the public and the private sphere do not show that consequentialist justification is appropriate to political activity or that politics is above, beyond or exempt from the moral order.

Problems with Machiavellian tactics

Just ends

In some senses it is puzzling why Machiavellian tactics and means–end calculation are thought to be appropriate to and license immoral actions in the political sphere. Machiavellian tactics are especially difficult to justify in politics precisely because consequentialist calculations themselves provide restrictions on their use. In consequentialist calculation, the justification for immoral means must in the first instance depend on judgements about the worth or value of the ends they achieve. Political officials, political realists and those who concede to their claims typically justify lies, fraud, force and violence for reasons of state, when the national interest – or its analogue, the public interest – is to be protected and promoted. But there is widespread disagreement on what the national or the public interest is and how much value should be attached to it.

The concept of the national interest has no generally accepted meaning and is subject to different and controversial interpretations (Nincic 1992: ch. 6). There is no consensus on how the public interest ought to be defined, how it should be measured or on who should decide how it is to be determined (see Schubert 1962 and Sorauf 1957, 1962 for an examination of the various meanings attributed to the term). In theory, there may not be a difficulty on agreeing on ends which constitute a just cause, which are in the national or public interest, such as the preservation of law and order, national security, democracy, freedom, peace and economic prosperity. In practice, though, the scope of these ends can be so widely interpreted that almost any policy could come within their boundaries and any means be said to serve them. The ambiguity and vagueness of these concepts weakens their value as analytic and justificatory tools for assessing the morality of a particular policy.

Just means

In practice it is difficult to establish a generally accepted political end which would legitimize or excuse acts of power politics. This difficulty would seem to make consequentialist justification particularly problematic in politics. But, even if a just cause could be found, the type of means used to achieve a good political end would have to satisfy other criteria to be justified on consequentialist grounds. These criteria involve the efficacy and proportionality of the means. On straightforward consequentialist criteria, immoral means would have to be the only alternative to achieving the good end, the harm incurred must not outweigh the good to be attained and there must be a reasonable chance of success in achieving this end through these means. If justifiable means must satisfy these criteria, then it would seem that even fewer immoral means could be legitimate in politics. Fraud, force, lies and violence are rarely the only alternatives in politics, the overall harm caused by them frequently outweighs the good intended and their use often has counterproductive effects.

Fraud, secrecy and deception have unacceptable costs in terms of the toll they take on the democratic principles of accountability, participation, consent and representation. The habitual use of these means can corrupt and spread with long-term consequences contrary to the public interests. When deceptions are uncovered, the resulting distrust of politicians undermines confidence in the political system generally and with it the ability of politicians to pursue policy objectives effectively. The use of force and violence to achieve political ends is rarely the only or the best alternative, because diplomatic channels have not been exhausted and because each state's national interests depend on continuing good relations between states. Moreover, the use of force or violence may rebound, lead to retaliation by opponents and endanger peace and self-preservation. In situations of political conflict the practical difficulty of accurately predicting long term consequences – and the efficacy of the means to meet them – are magnified, because judgements about the probable effects of conflict are hard to make and often matters of serious disagreement.

In politics, as opposed to private life, these familiar problems with means–end calculation are intensified, because of the added likelihood of distorted judgements, discrimination, ideological bias, error and self-deception involved in politicians' judgements about the necessity, appropriateness and utility of the means they use to further national or public interests. As a result, they may overestimate the benefits to be gained or overlook alternative solutions to the problem. Of course, if immoral means are counterproductive or unsuccessful, if they create more harm than good, then political consequentialism would not endorse them. Utilitarian considerations themselves provide restrictions on fraud, force, lies and violence for technical, instrumental reasons. What this discussion shows, though, is that, even if we accept immoral means in politics are justified on consequentialist grounds, this very acceptance rules out much immoral behaviour in both foreign and domestic affairs.

Contextualizing the problem

The assumption that immoral behaviour of all kinds is necessary in politics and that a consequentialist justification can be given takes place within a theoretical background which seems to presuppose a Machiavellian view of the world. This automatically excludes consideration of alternatives to Machiavellian techniques to achieve political ends, and does not sufficiently distinguish the political situations in which the need for dirty hands occurs.

The masculinist context

Feminists challenge the Machiavellian view of the world and the enduring notion that it is impossible to apply, in politics, the same standards that are appropriate to the private sphere. They question the very legitimacy of the distinction between the private and the public spheres of action and so the belief that there are different standards of morality appropriate to each. They argue that the personal is relevant and related to the public, in the sense that practices traditionally associated with women's domestic and caring role provide a fund of values that could inform, inspire and regulate political life. If politics were informed by 'maternal' virtues, by a female 'ethic of care', then the public and the private would not be governed by different standards of judgement, but political morality would be constructed by and connected to private virtue

(Ruddick 1980, 1990, Gilligan 1982, Held 1984, Noddings 1984, Tronto 1993).

The above analysis leads feminists to argue that the divorce of political from private morality advocated by Machiavelli, and by those who have internalized his legacy, is inextricably linked to male values, assumptions and modes of reasoning. Like Machiavelli, subsequent realists understand power as domination and suppose that politics is about gaining and maintaining power through force or strength. They emphasize the violence and force that are ever-present possibilities in public life, and reduce what it is rational to do in politics to strategies of control and coercion, fraud and force. This male ethos pervades the discourse of action, conflict, conquest and domination in *The Prince*. It is seen in Machiavelli's admiration for the masculine qualities displayed in bold, belligerent, resolute and effective actions and in his negative ranking of the stereotypical female values of peace and co-operation (Gunsberg 1995: 125, 128).

Feminists argue that the picture Machiavelli and political realists give of human nature is informed by assumptions that are stereotypically male. Machiavelli thought that human beings in general were fickle, eager for gain, domination and power, who always judge actions by their results. For Machiavelli, the need for dirty hands was part of the human, as well as the political condition. Political realism is underpinned by a conception of human beings as competing individuals, each concerned to further their own interests. Their relations with others in the public sphere are characterized by suspicion, anticipation of the threat of force or violence, and instrumental calculation. For modern advocates of realpolitik, Machiavelli is relevant to the contemporary world because his principles are rooted in an unchanging human nature. They assume that, because human nature is the same, Machiavelli's strategies can be applied not just to the ruling of the state, but to the problems of managing large organizations (see for example Jay 1967: 21 and McAlpine, ch. 8 of this volume). Jay argues that modern corporations can be compared to city states because they are impelled by the same human emotions of greed and fear and pride, or self-interest, competitiveness and a desire for security (p. 23).

According to feminists, though, these are over-simple generalizations about human beings, which obscure their differences and complexities. In particular, the emphasis on self-interest and competition does not take account of female motivation derived from their experience of altruism, nurturing, empathy and mutual support. The discourse of conflict, conquest and prudential calculation denies the reality of human interdependence and the importance of care, reciprocity and co-operation in human relationships. Emphasis on the rationality and necessity of means–end calculation and evaluating actions from an impersonal view devaluates female ways of thinking and reasoning which are intuitive and responsive to particular needs in particular situations. The consequence of these denials is the subordination of female values; the impossibility of a politics not reducible to the power of coercion; the exclusion of alternative solutions to conflict and the elimination of space for a non-instrumental morality.

Feminists suggest that female values, imperatives and modes of reasoning associated with mothering and care could radically transform our understanding of politics and its characteristic modes of reasoning. Hartsock (1984) argues that women's experience of caretaking contradicts the masculinist conception of power as domination, because caretaking takes place within a perspective that posits not conflict, but connection and mutuality. Ruddick (1980, 1990) links maternal thinking and the life-preserving values implicit in the practice of mothering to peace politics and non-violent conflict resolution. Mansbridge (1996) identifies women's interpersonal sensitivity, active listening skills, emotional empathy and understanding of the needs of others as crucial for settling conflicts through mutual persuasion. The values associated with women's caretaking role may enrich and improve political discussion and open up the possibility of a transformative political practice. From carers' knowledge of human need and interdependence, from their ability to respond creatively and imaginatively to political problems, solutions may be derived, different from those of the strategic political realists.

Feminist discussion attempts to show that the Machiavellian problem occurs within a theoretical framework and a political context that presupposes and endorses male characteristics, values and norms. Because these are not universal, feminist analyses cast doubt on the reduction of politics to the struggle for power and domination and the acceptance of amoral statecraft. They challenge the view that conflict is endemic and the appropriateness of a political morality that embodies male views of human nature and rationality. In doing so, they challenge the assumption that violence, fraud and force are necessary in politics and that means–end calculation is the rational and realistic response to political problems. They suggest that political morality could be informed by the virtues of the private and understand politics itself as potentially virtuous.

The democratic context

It is not just feminists who challenge the Machiavellian view of the world and who suggest alternatives to Machiavellian tactics. There is an implicit challenge within a liberal democratic world view which suggests a way out of the realist intrinsic and the potential for norms of behaviour to counter realist values. It is to be remembered that the need to transgress moral norms originally arose in a Machiavellian world where relations between states were anarchic, inherently conflictual and characterized by the struggle for power. In the context of lawlessness, where there was no check on power, where states must rely on their own resources to protect their interests, morality was thought to be justifiably overridden in relations between sovereign states to protect their national or strategic interests. Within this paradigm, arguments for the practical necessity of immoral action, for the breaking of promises, for lies and violence can seem compelling. It is easy to see how they are thought to be inevitable and how alternative solutions to conflict are ruled out.

Justifications for lies and violence as rational and realistic responses to political problems are less compelling, though, when applied to political contexts which do not conform to the realist model. Notions of practical necessity and raison d'état are inappropriately applied in the context of relations between and within liberal democratic states. That is in the context, not of competing hostile states, but of shared understandings and of complex interaction and interdependence between states. Here, it could be supposed that mutual recognition, legitimation and common standards should dictate norms of inter-state behaviour and give rise to generalized principles of conduct which constrain activity and preclude calculations about their own advantage. In these international contexts, the Machiavellian discourse of conflict, confrontation, conquest, domination and prudential calculation between states is more fittingly replaced by the discourse of interdependence, co-operation, collaboration, reciprocity and conciliation among states. Alternative solutions to lies and violence are opened up because they are implicit in the relationships between and within liberal democratic states, the principles which govern them and the values they share.

In domestic affairs, debates about political morality take place in our societies, in the context of a democratic, not an anarchic, political order. In both international and domestic affairs, the background situation is not necessarily or automatically characterized by conflict, suspicion, hostility, the anticipation of force and violence or domination and suppression. In these circumstances, claims that political ends necessitate immoral means are not so justifiable. The regulative ideals which acknowledge the interdependency of nations and which are supposed to preserve the balance of power between them would seem to undercut and replace arguments for the inevitability and necessity of fraud, force, lies and violence. Similarly, justifications for lies and deception within liberal democratic states can be undercut because these violate the democratic principles of accountability, participation, consent and representation. Fraud, force, secrecy and lies break the conditions on which power is checked by insulating governments from control and by enabling the powerful to maintain their monopoly of power. They violate the freedom from political power that is itself a condition for the existence of a democratic political order.

Arguments for the necessity, inevitability and justification of lies and deceit tend to ignore these different political contexts and the different power relations within them. Clarifying and distinguishing these contexts is important, because arguments for the inevitability and necessity for the use of immoral means may be more defensible in genuine Machiavellian contexts than they are in the context of dealings between and within liberal democratic states.

The management context

It is here that arguments for the relevance of Machiavellian strategies to modern management differ. I have argued that Machiavellian tactics are inappropriate to and outdated in the non-Machiavellian political context of relationships between and within liberal democratic states. But, modern business corporations are unlike modern states in two senses. First, they often operate without even the pretext of democratic control and public accountability; and second, they operate in a context that is, in some respects, decidedly Machiavellian. Management writers themselves compare large corporations to warring fifteenth-century city states; they, like Machiavelli, situate their problems in a world characterized by power struggles, intrigue, rivalry, conflict and competition. Perhaps it is not surprising, then, that they claim Machiavelli can provide guidance to today's managers to help them to achieve success and that they advocate the usefulness of Machiavellian tactics for 'surviving in the jungle of greed and treachery that is commerce' (McAlpine, ch. 8 of this volume). But however useful and successful these methods may be, Machiavellianism as a method cannot just be applied to a business context and still be a method that is defensible on Machiavellian grounds. The use of Machiavellian methods by today's managers may help them achieve their objectives, but these objectives are not Machiavelli's.

Machiavelli advocated ruthless strategies, not to secure and preserve power in a vacuum or to achieve success *per se*, but with specific purposes in mind. The point of power was to create and maintain a strong state to achieve a political good. This political good:

> consists of honour, glory, riches, liberty, justice and military security. It is the good of the whole community in which the individual finds his own good, and not the exclusive good of a class or a particular individual, even *The Prince*.
>
> (Parel 1972: 6)

If Machiavelli described the world as it is, unlike those who currently advocate his tactics, he did not accept it. The point was to change it for the better. He called for a regeneration of his own society and for a republican order where civic virtue, liberty, personal security and co-operation for the common good could be realized (Wood 1972).

Machiavelli is misappropriated when applied to managing institutions which are profit driven by private business and consumer individualism. Machiavelli denounced the pursuit of power by individuals or groups for private ends. He was a radical critic of the narrow self-interest, the commercialism, the idealization of prosperity and economic enterprise, and of the exploitation and corruption that he saw within his own city state, precisely because they undermined civic responsibility and co-operation for the public good. (For Machiavelli's criticisms of his own society see, *The Prince*, ch. xxvi, *Discourses* 1,

The Ass of Gold viii, *The Art of War* 1: viii, *History of Florence* I: xxxix, IV: xxxiii, VII: xxiii.)[2]

When modern management writers apply Machiavelli to the problems of management and marketing, they foreground the means necessary for success. In doing so, they forget the sense in which Machiavelli's use of necessity, means and ends, success and efficiency are applied to a different world, not to a parallel context; a world separated by a different ideological rationale, as well as by half a millennium. Management writers tend to sidestep the issue of the morality or immorality of the ends to be achieved by organizations and their management, when they claim the relevance of Machiavelli. But Machiavellian virtue, as the willingness and ability to do what needs to be done, Machiavellianism as a value-free political science applicable in any context, in the service of any end or purpose, is not to be found in Machiavelli. Those who claim the enduring validity of Machiavelli's ideas, and who see Machiavelli as a forerunner of contemporary marketing and management consultants, illegitimately detach his ideas from their setting. Machiavelli's advice becomes distorted when applied in dissimilar contexts and the use of Machiavelli's tactics in these contexts is not defensible, on Machiavellian grounds.

The 'real' context

Unlike management writers, political realists and consequentialists defend the tactics they advocate with reference to the morality and desirability of the ends to be achieved, even if these reasons of state, national and public interest defences are vague and open to diverse interpretations. But talk of political realism and political necessity disguises the fact that all too frequently politicians' tactics, like those of managers, cannot be justified with reference to a Machiavellian end or to any political good that he would have recognized. Just as Machiavellian means in business are not obviously explained or justified in relation to the public good, the pervasiveness of immoral actions in politics cannot wholly be explained or justified by the claims of realpolitik, the requirements of successful policy, still less by the desire to serve the national or public interest (see Cliffe and Ramsay 2000). Morally dirty decisions are often motivated by personal ambition; by the need to win and stay in power and to protect the interests of the policy makers. They can be variously explained by the need to defend the economic, social and political agendas of private groups and to conceal the effects of the influence of corporate, commercial or unelected sectional interests in policy making; by the need to avoid political embarrassment and exposure and to minimize public hostility and to avoid democratic accountability for actions and policies which are at odds with public beliefs and convictions. These means are not justified on consequentialist grounds, nor are they justified in a democracy, nor are they authentically Machiavellian in anything other than a degenerative sense.

Defending Machiavellian tactics in politics or advocating their usefulness for achieving management objectives blurs the context in which the need for immoral means arises by diverting attention from examining the kinds of political situations which supposedly render adherence to moral standards wrong, unreasonable or unrealistic. Political consequentialists obscure the fact that it is these conditions rather than the acts necessitated by them that should be subject to moral evaluation. Rather than accepting that immoral behaviour in politics is inevitable or that Machiavellian methods are essential for success in business, we should critically examine the kinds of situation that require dirty hands to be necessary. Examination of the contexts in which morality is overridden often reveals that in many instances the circumstances that supposedly justify these acts are themselves immoral, involve a violation of democratic values or are indefensible in terms of the public good.

But what is wrong and morally questionable is not simply the use of immoral means. What is wrong is the circumstances that called for the immoral means to be necessary. And it is these circumstances that require moral scrutiny and improvement. If modern Machiavellianism in business and politics is to be questioned, then the question must begin not with the efficacy or even the morality of Machiavellian tactics, but with the mutability and morality of the background circumstances which generate the need for Machiavelli's advice. Given this, perhaps it would be more realistic for political realists, for those who admire Machiavelli's pragmatism and for those who pride themselves on seeing the world as it is, to concentrate on transforming those aspects of social, economic and political life that need change in order to reduce the need for dirty hands in politics, rather than to focus on defending them as inevitable, necessary or justified.

Notes

1 Taken from Gilbert, A. (trans.) (1989) *Machiavelli: The Chief Works and Others*, vol. 1, Durham, NC: Duke University Press, p. 15.
2 Gilbert, A. (trans.) (1989) *Machiavelli: The Chief Works and Others*, vols 1–3, Durham, NC: Duke University Press.

References

Buskirk, R. H. (1974) *Modern Management and Machiavelli*, Battleboro, VT: The Book Press.
Calhoon, A. (1969) 'Niccolo Machiavelli and twentieth century administration', *Academy of Management Journal* June.
Cassirer, E. (1946) *The Myth of the State*, New Haven, CT: Yale University Press.
Chabod, F. (1958) *Machiavelli and the Renaissance*, Cambridge, MA: Harvard University Press.
Cliffe, L. and Ramsay, M. (2000) *Democracy and the Politics of Lying*, London: Macmillan.
Coady, C. A. J. (1991) 'Politics and the problem of dirty hands', in P. Singer (ed.) *A Companion to Ethics*, Oxford: Blackwell.
Croce, B. (1925) *Elementi di politica*, Bari: Laterza.
Gilligan, C. (1982) *In a Different Voice*, Cambridge, MA, and London: Harvard University Press.

Gunsberg, M. (1995) 'The end justifies the means: end-orientation and the discourses of power', in M. Coyle (ed.) *The Prince: New Interdisciplinary Essays*, Manchester: Manchester University Press.

Hampshire, S. (1978) 'Morality and pessimism', in S. Hampshire (ed.) *Public and Private Morality*, Cambridge: Cambridge University Press, pp. 1–22.

Hartsock, N. (1984) *Money, Sex and Power: Towards a Feminist Historical Materialism*, Boston, MA: Northeastern University Press.

Held, V. (1984) 'The obligations of mothers and fathers', in J. Trebilcot (ed.) *Mothering: Essays in Feminist Theory*, Totowa, NJ: Rowman & Littlefield.

Jay, A. (1967) *Management and Machiavelli*, London: Hodder & Stoughton.

Mansbridge, J. (1996) 'Reconstructing democracy', in N. J. Hirschmann and C. DiStefano (eds) *Revisioning the Political*, Boulder, CO and Oxford: Westview Press.

McAlpine, A. (1992) *The Servant: A New Machiavelli*, London: Faber & Faber.

—— (1997) *The New Machiavelli*, London: Aurum.

Meinecke, F. (1957) *Machiavellianism*, trans. Douglas Scott, London: Routledge.

Nagel, T. (1978) 'Ruthlessness in public life', in S. Hampshire (ed.) *Public and Private Morality*, Cambridge: Cambridge University Press.

Nincic, M. (1992) *Democracy and Foreign Policy: The Fallacy of Political Realism*, New York: Columbia University Press.

Noddings, N. (1984) *Caring: A Feminist Approach to Ethics and Moral Education*, Berkeley, CA: University of California Press.

Olschki, L. (1945) *Machiavelli the Scientist*, Berkeley, CA: University of California Press.

Parel, A. (1972) 'Machiavelli's method and his interpreters', in A. Parel (ed.) *The Political Calculus*, Toronto: University of Toronto Press.

Renaudet, A. (1942) *Machiavel: Étude d'histoire des doctrines politiques*, Paris: Gallimard.

Ruddick, S. (1980) 'Maternal Thinking', *Feminist Studies* 6 (1).

—— (1990) *Maternal Thinking: Towards a Politics of Peace*, London: Women's Press.

Schubert, G. (1962) 'Is there a public interest theory?', in C. J. Friedrich (ed.) *NOMOS V: The Public Interest*, New York: Atherton, pp. 162–76.

Sorauf, F. J. (1957) 'The public interest reconsidered', *Journal of Politics* XIX.

—— (1962) 'The conceptual muddle', in C. J. Friedrich (ed.) *NOMOS V: The Public Interest*, New York: Atherton, pp. 183–90.

Shea, M. (1988) *Influence: How to Make the System Work for You. A Handbook for the Modern Machiavelli*, London: Century.

Tronto, J. C. (1993) 'Beyond gender differences to an ethic of care' in L. M. Larrabee (ed.) *An Ethic of Care*, New York and London: Routledge.

Walzer, M. (1973) 'Political action and the problem of dirty hands', *Philosophy and Public Affairs* 2 (2).

Williams, B. (1978) 'Politics and morality' in S. Hampshire (ed.) *Public and Private Morality*, Cambridge: Cambridge University Press.

Wood, N. (1972) 'Machiavelli's humanism of action', in A. Parel (ed.) *The Political Calculus*, Toronto: University of Toronto Press.

IN FORMING AN OPINION ABOUT A
RULER'S BRAINS, THE FIRST THING IS TO
LOOK AT THE MEN HE HAS AROUND HIM,
FOR WHEN THEY ARE ADEQUATE AND
LOYAL HE CAN BE CONSIDERED PRUDENT,
BECAUSE HE RECOGNISES THOSE WHO
ARE COMPETENT AND KEEPS THEM LOYAL.
WHEN THEY ARE OTHERWISE, THE
PRINCE IS ALWAYS ESTEEMED LOW.

THE PRINCE[1]

13 Nicco and Charlie

A story of two political servants and of political management

Kevin Moloney

Spin doctors add to the amusement generated by democratic politics because they are highly visible members of the modern political servant class and are subject to much ridicule. Modern rulers need them in their attempt to manage the flow of persuasive communications crafted to gain public approval in a media-saturated liberal society. Our rulers employ spin doctors to lay off the risks to subordinates of being caught in possession of unpopular communications.

Niccolò Machiavelli, however, had a different style, dangerous for a democracy. He would not have admired spin doctors, the traceable, noisy, too visible voices of their masters. He would have disdained the tactics of Charlie Whelan, the only spin doctor to copy the tactics of Icarus and fly too close to *The Sun*. Nicco knew (and we know) that dangerous political servants are invisible ones who cannot be scrutinized and ridiculed. He would not have approved of journalists providing the scrutiny and the ridicule. But spin doctors have their passing uses: when these new variant folk-devils are named and shamed, it is one cheer for democracy.

Meet Nicco and Charlie

Machiavelli would not have been amused. He would have recognized other political servants when he met them but he would have been upset, some five hundred years after his accession to high political office in Florence, that standards had dropped. For him, these spinners do not serve the Prince well. They are not sly enough. They can be and are exposed by journalists, another class of political servants. They are scoffed at and laughed at publicly by those who watch the rulers, the citizens. And in these ways, rulers are diminished. For Nicco, the work of advancing the cause of Princes is always best done by sleight of hand.

Was Niccolò Machiavelli the first 'spinnozo'? Certainly not, for he was far too top drawer for that kind of semi-submerged and traceable influencing. He was, however, the first European modern to write a well known DIY textbook about how rhetoric and force can be combined to further the interests of political leaders. After xxvi short and easy-to-read chapters, it was clear that this was done without much principle, let or hindrance. He wrote too well for the sake of his reputation: few remember that this diplomat and civil servant was a patriot, a republican and against the clerical domination of his land. He thus argued five centuries ago – unconsciously – for modern democratic virtues: but his shortest book has determined his reputation – the sly one. He shocked the liberal conscience by revealing the inner workings of the political process: it is much nastier than its dignified, constitutional exterior suggested. He gave government its first health warning: politics damages your integrity because it breaks the connection with your ethics. Charlie Whelan, former spinner to his master, Chancellor of the Exchequer Gordon Brown, lasted less than two years in government and fell from grace because he became the story and not the background. Nicco would not have approved of celebrity status for political servants.

But Nicco and Charlie would have recognized enough of themselves in each other to commiserate. Whatever the rightness of their political beliefs, they will not be remembered for them. What they share is the below-stairs life of politics where rhetoric and force (either of arms, markets, public opinion or parliamentary majorities) are mixed together into persuasion to sell the policies of their masters upstairs. Exchange Prince for Chancellor and Chancellor for Prince and in that swap of masters we see Nicco and Charlie as two of a kind. Nicco and Charlie were not prime movers: they were servants. Read back copies of the Florentine *Sun* and it is clear that nobody took Nicco seriously on the reform of mercenary armies. Read the London *Sun* and it is clear that Charlie's gossip on Cabinet in-fighting was what was really wanted. The political servant is always denied public acclaim: his most likely fates are silent satisfaction and then rejection. Nicco was tortured in prison; Charlie was sacked and forced to write football columns.

Nicco and Charlie were Machiavellian, were brothers-in-slyness because they twist and turn everything to their masters' advantage while denying it. But despite this common heritage, variation abounds. Nicco was Very Old Machiavellian while Charlie was Very New. Nicco was a political servant in the age of absolute belief in God and the Divine Right of Princes. He sharpened his skills in times of elitism, ignorance and fear. For Charlie, the Zeitgeist was safer and marked by public access, the mass media and hostile editorial opinion. Nicco was a gent in an aristocrat's palazzo: Charlie was one of the lads in the Red Lion pub, Whitehall. Servants have their class systems too.

Nicco worked in a world of factions; Charlie operated in one of mass parties. Nicco talked and read in Latin and French: Charlie had a television in his office and talked estuary English into a mobile phone. One world talked in whispers to princely coteries: the other world briefs off the record to the mass media. One world was fashioned by the works of Plato, Aristotle, Cicero and the practice of the Sophists who were the first European political servant class. The other is fashioned by the thinking of Lippman, Laswell, Kotler, Grunig and the practices of the most modern political servant class: public relations people and marketeers in all their flourishing sub-sets of specialisms – spinning; polling;

focus group handling; political advertising; event management; makeovers, 'astroturf' lobbying (Scammell 1995, Franklin 1994, Harris and Lock 1996, Mayhew 1997 and Rosenbaum 1997).[2]

Nicco has put us on our guard: these new servants want to manage our politics. Shine more light on them and keep a weather eye open. Spinnozos? Spin doctors? How do they attempt to manage political communications? What strange, slang terms! Their sources are uncertain and are therefore occasions for waspish comment and pretty little phrase-making. Anyone can join in the etymological archaeology: many do; and few are complimentary. Clare Short MP coins 'people who live in the dark' and *The Observer* writes about 'the sultans of spin' (Rawnsley 1997). Ken Livingstone MP favours the return of the death penalty for spin doctoring: 'I have zero tolerance of spin doctors .... It degrades the democratic process. It's systematic lying' (*The Observer*, 6 April 1997). McSmith (1997: 299) writes of 'this political black art' which ' ... finally drifted across the Atlantic and into British political slang after the 1988 US presidential election ... '. *The Times* reports an age when only Eve span: 'In the old days, when the term 'spin-doctor' meant nothing more sinister than a Sadlers Wells physiotherapist ... ' (4 April 1997). Castle in *The Independent on Sunday* opines that the spin doctor 'is one of the more shadowy of modern heroes', a phrase derived perhaps from a time when Peter Mandelson was known as 'The Prince of Darkness' (28 December 1997).[3]

The wider electorate are none too impressed either. A Gallup Poll notes that 55 per cent of respondents had no idea of the term's meaning. Others replied: 'a doctor who goes around in circles'; 'something to do with homeopathy'; 'somebody who finds great difficulty telling the truth' (*The Independent on Sunday*, 28 December 1997). The phrase-making grows: 'think-spin' is reported by the weekend section of *The Independent on Sunday* (11 January 1998) as a policy-based quotation distinct from the more headline-attracting sound bite. In *The Guardian* Goldenburg and White reveal a 'spin patrol' to limit damage to the Foreign Secretary over the Royal Tour of India and Pakistan and 'spin pathology' to investigate why several and ambiguous interpretations of the Government's policy to join the Euro appeared in the media (17 October 1997). *The Daily Telegraph* confers the title 'grandfather of spin' on Michael Deaver, an aide to President Reagan (Peterborough column, 20 January 1998). Indeed, the slang appears to have become the short label stuck over the whole industry of public relations: Ewen's (1996) book *PR!* is subtitled a social history of spin. It is also spinning off into other walks of life, formally distant from politics. Note that English groundsmen who drained the grass in the new Paris stadium for the February 1998 rugby union match between France and England in the Five Nations Championship were praised as 'pitch spin doctors'. Indeed, one of Nicco's most fervent, modern admirers, Alistair McAlpine (1997), has written of PRs as 'twitchers of image'.

These easy, frequent references to spin suggest that spin doctors are a new, variant folk-devil; 'wicked' creatures in the vernacular sense of the word; persons to be half-admired, half-feared and wholly needed. They also suggest a wide, public awareness of a major structural feature of modern UK life – the pervasiveness of modern persuasive communications. These joshing references by journalists, competitive politicians and the public are important for the argument here: public ridicule is a form of control.

In plain English, what is spinning?

One explanation of the origins of the term comes from American baseball jargon of the 1980s when coaches trained pitchers on how to make the ball spin in mid-air in order to confuse the hitter. Hence the transferred meaning in politics of 'spinning' (first American and then British) is to give the words describing a policy, personality or event a favourable gloss in the hope that the mass media will use them.

But what does a spin doctor do? Two professional journalists (Jones 1995 and 1997; McSmith 1997) have written at length on the practice. Their witness establishes the semi-public nature of the spin doctors at work. The latter deals, at one remove from the public gaze, with political journalists, many of them lobby correspondents, whose professional task is to scrutinize the words and actions of government. This act of revelation by journalists can be extended to their sources, the spin doctors, especially where the journalists are not operating the normal lobby rules of non-attribution. Such disclosure is to be encouraged for public description and analysis is another form of control. McSmith (1997: 299) argues that spin doctors are 'a product of the age of instant communication' and they operate '... in the tiny space between when a political event takes place and when it is first reported to the wide public'. He adds: 'It is an axiom of political journalism that the public must be given more than the bare facts. Every event must be placed in a context.' There must be interpretation of the event in terms of policy and/or personality. (Nicco would have laughed at such a suggestion: it distracts from attention to The Prince.) The spin doctor wants to be first with interpretation, before even the journalist has decided his own.

McSmith gives examples of Peter Mandelson at work (ibid.: 299–302) – he who was the greatest spinning rival to Charlie; he who was the first modern UK spinner to make the social transition from the political below stairs to MP and Cabinet status; and he who was called Mandy. McSmith continues (ibid.: 302–3) with how important for spin doctors is knowing journalists and how knowledge of them can lead to their manipulation. It suggests a closeness between spin doctors and some journalists which raises questions about the practice of UK political journalism:

> There are senior journalists who by 1995 had relied on him [Mandelson] for the best part of ten years as their best source of information about internal [Labour] party affairs. He not only briefed efficiently, with a good grasp of how to present information in a way that conforms to contemporary views about what is or is not news; he provided a sort of after-briefing service. It was common, for example, for broadcasters to receive a morning

telephone call to tell them that a report written by A in newspaper X was interesting, accurate and worth following up, unlike the shoddily researched piece by B in a rival newspaper. What this implied, though the broadcaster might not know it, was that A had faithfully reproduced the content of a Mandelson briefing. Thus his clients would not only be given a well-sourced story to write but would have their reputations upheld among their peers.

(McSmith 1997: 302)

This alleged behaviour is manipulative: it is the private attribution of motives and performance of an other to a third party without the other knowing. It appears that some national political journalists allow themselves to over-rely on a single source for their news; that they do so over enough time for a patron/client relationship to develop; and that the relationship is characterized by the spin patron (in this case Mandelson) furthering his client journalists' interests and denigrating others' interests. McSmith was a political correspondent of the *Daily Mirror* when he wrote these words. They can be read as a critique of an unquantified number of UK national political journalists by one of their peer group. If such behaviour is widespread, they imply a pattern of unprofessional relationships between a dominant political operative and subordinated journalists.

Spun into dependency

Nicholas Jones (1995: 123) is another London-based political journalist who has written about this dependency culture. He notes that ' ... journalists are often desperate to speak to authoritative sources ... ' for interpretation; that they put themselves therefore into a subordinate position, and that ' ... a spin doctor cannot hope to operate successfully without first having established a coterie of trusted reporters and other contacts'. The implication is that journalists need spin doctors in the sense that a monopoly supplier of news means one source only on offer. McSmith (1997: 302) also picks up that Mandelson had early on ' ... assembled an idiosyncratic web of contacts in newspapers and broadcasting through which he channelled a flow of selected information by which he set out to alter the way political journalists perceived the party and its leader'.

Jones notes the influence of Mandelson in the 1997 General Election, for he ' ... was certainly the most influential of the leader's advisers', and that if ever, as Opposition Leader, Blair ' ... got involved in a disagreement with the news media, he relied on [Mandelson] to sort it out' (1995: 15). (In Blair, Nicco may also see something of a Medici.) Jones also notes that Mandelson would use his influence against party rivals for he had ' ... no hesitation in making use of his many contacts among political journalists to generate unfavourable coverage for anyone who sought to impede the path of Blair's supporters' (ibid.: 15).

Jones goes on to describe (ibid.: 273) a baleful power confronting himself and colleagues for he says that spin doctors ' ... have an ability to bamboozle broadcasters, journalists and their editors into downplaying or dropping stories which harmed Labour's image'. He also records (ibid.: 11) that Labour spin doctors were performing a quasi-investigative journalistic role when the Conservative Government was in power: 'As often as not it was a Labour propagandist rather than a diligent reporter who spotted an inconsistency or change in nuance in the government's position.' He amplifies this: 'Labour's spin doctors had the uncanniest knack of spotting ministerial gaffes which originally escaped that attention of the media and if there was a government slip-up to be exposed, Labour's timing was immaculate in revealing it at the optimum moment so as to block favourable publicity for the Conservatives' (ibid.: 273).

Labour also (ibid.: 272) went on to influence the news agenda with ' ... a non-stop supply of stories aimed at enticing the media away from an agenda which the government would have preferred them to follow'. Jones's witness confirms McSmith's: the patronage-through-information relationships; the dependency networks centred on spin doctors; their news-setting influence and their ability to upbraid, to compare unfavourably and so punish journalists.

Another witness of spinning at work is Draper (1997), but one who was not a journalist and who wrote from the Government's viewpoint. He offers a confirmation of spin doctor influence as seen from inside government. He describes how the Foreign Secretary Robin Cook was told by telephone at Heathrow airport by the Prime Minister's Press Secretary that the *News of the World* was going to carry the story of his affair with his secretary and that he had to decide whether to stay or leave his wife (who was with him) if the story was to be minimized. Cook returned the call to say that he chose his secretary. Draper comments (1997: 209): 'In a couple of hours, Labour's spin doctors succeeded in twisting the story from a potential farce into a tragedy that had already entered its final scene. It was media management at its best – and carried out from the best of reasons.'

This influence is more than technical news management: it is structural. Draper (ibid.: 218–19) later says that 'There is nothing new to the politics of spin, and it is not difficult to mount a defence of Mandelson's actions. He has simply been carrying out the Prime Minister's instructions ... .' Spin doctors are no doubt aware of their structural power. Draper recalls that Mandelson was once stung by a question from a BBC journalist about his role and replied with a jibe: 'Well, I'm sorry if you feel so inadequate that you have to have me write your scripts and fix your headlines.' Draper was chief adviser to Mandelson for four years.

Spinning: who is to blame?

There has been some attention paid to spin doctors by UK academics, but it is not substantial and is mostly anchored in a small but growing number of texts which see spin doctoring as a sub-set inside a larger phenomenon entitled 'political marketing'. This can be described as the transfer of business promotional skills to political campaigns. Scammell (1995: 4) writes of spin doctors 'skillfully elevating shiny image over substance' while Rosenbaum (1997: 91) notes they have ' ... to attach more importance to pushing interpretation than just facts'. He reminds us that spin doctors were 'press officers', 'information officers' and 'press secretaries' before the late 1980s and that in these guises they were part of modern political campaign teams whose appearance he dates in the UK to the mid-1950s. He notes that these operatives became more pro-active and aggressive in their dealings with the media over the period. But there is a lengthy history to these tensions and it was previously written up by Blumler and Gurevitch (1981), who categorized relationships between govern-ment spin doctors (a term they did not know) and journalists as being either like a contest or an exchange. The former characterized the media as watchdogs holding the government to account and the latter protrayed them in a market-like relationship of swapping information for publicity. They also remind the reader that language is a fashion in these matters: they do not write of 'sound bites'; rather 'golden phrases' (1981: 478).

So far, the argument is that exposing spin doctors at work is a chance for fashionable chatter and linguistic invention amongst the political class and for revengeful and scornful writing by some journalists: language is an expressive, political weapon in its own right. The argument, however, also has a structural aspect in that the treatment of spinning as humorous wordplay encourages questions about the nature of governmental persuasive communications. The exposure of governmental communications as a contest with winners and losers, a contest played out in semi-public and describable in a slang makes for a popular attention and awareness which is a civic good. It is a small plus for government-in-the-open via ridicule. The more journalists and quarrelsome politicians mock spin doctors; the more spin doctors snap querulously back; the better for informed, watchful, sceptical voters.

Nicco would not have liked this persiflage, for he would have known instinc-tively that public laughter and ridicule at the workings of official persuasion make it more difficult for the Prince to keep control over the governed. Humour reduces fear and deference and leads on to questions of why govern-ments in democracies persuade. How does persuasion stand between rationality and manipulation? Should journalists be watchdogs over powerful persuaders or passively trade publicity for information as in one of Blumler and Gurevitch's models?

Before attempting to answer, there is a prior question: why blame the poor servants? They are political operatives employed for their persuasive skills. It is, however, not these skills which make them distinctive because persuasiveness is a basic behavioural requirement of elected politicians: rather it is that spin doctors are in the service of elected politicians and are accountable to them and not to the broader public or electorate. Elections can call MPs, Ministers and their parties to account. Spin doctors are 'sheltered', so to speak, behind elected politicians and can be used by them to disguise the source of political communi-cations. Spin doctors are political servants with a licence to serve their masters and not the public. They are not accountable to the electorate and are used to camouflage the origins of governmental messages. This is offensive to accountable and transparent government for which a sine qua non is knowledge about the sources, intentionalities, flows, styles and destinations of political communications.

Spin control

Lack of this knowledge among the public/voters reduces the rationality of political debate. It is a basic assumption here that rationality and persuasion, as two modes for communicating about government, are in an uneasy relationship and that a democratic society should favour more rationality and less persuasion from politicians. To make rationality more potent in the creation of consent, it is essential to know who is transmitting political communications; to whom that transmitter is beholden; why there is a transmission and whether the transmitter is ready to be identified. It is a classic role of the media in a liberal, democratic society to scrutinize political communications in order to make these characteristics widely known. In receipt of the results, the public/voters can relate political communications to their own cognition maps and give them a free passage, or not, which is in line with their ideas. Without this exposure of the structure of political communications, it is hard to see how public policy can be decided in a way which is understood in a principally rational way. Without understanding based less on persuasion and more on rationality, there can be no informed consent to government.

Jones has argued that journalists need spin doctors for access to government news and he implies that this need creates dependency which leads to the manipulation of journalists. L'Etang (1996: 115) supports this thesis in another area of public policy, for she quotes journalists' opinion that they were manipulated by Greenpeace public relations people at the time of the Brent Spar contest in 1995. One conclusion from both these scenarios is that spin doctors will always be dominant in their relationship with journalists because of the latter's need for access.

This conclusion needs rebuttal for it gives the political servants too much influence, if not power. Moreover, it flies in the face of the proclaimed professional ethics of journalists as watchdogs in their Fourth Estate role and it runs counter to much modern evidence, for example *Washington Post* journalists in the Watergate scandal. Further, public choice theory offers the chance of conceiving the spin doctor–journalist relationship as a market one of exchanging publicity for information, where the currency for measuring the value of both is journalistic autonomy. This offers a model in which journalists can turn the terms of their trade with spin doctors to their advantage. It is a model of a competitive information/publicity market with downward pressure on costs to journalists' autonomy. Where there is a monopoly supplier of a good seeking high money prices, buyers can stop buying from the monopolist and seek alternative suppliers. In journalistic terms, the alternative sources are competing spin doctors; politicians within the government and/or outside it; and experts in interest and pressure groups. Journalists should use those sources which asked the lower price in terms of costs to their autonomy. (Here, Nicco would have laughed: for him alternative sources of information in a state would be a threat to the loyalty demanded by the Prince.)

It is not clear from the accounts of Jones and McSmith that journalists have vigorously sought these alternatives. They appear passive before new Labour spinners. Why was Mandelson not challenged with anti-Blair sources in the Labour Party? With more difficulty, perhaps, organized groups of journalists, such as the UK Parliamentary lobby, should withhold their need for government interpretation when it is priced in manipulative terms. Journalists should ask what is the benefit they are seeking from spin doctors. It is said to be access to politicians in order to explain motives behind words and action. Why not just report in the first instance and interpret later after shopping around in the information market for access on more equal, less humiliating terms? The restraining factors in any boycott of spin doctors are the involvement of all journalists and the agreement of their employing media organizations. Collective action of this kind would turn the strong 'pack' instinct of many journalists to a better behaviour than the demeaning one of submission to a news source. If, however, collective boycott is impractical, the public/electorate in a liberal democracy has to rely on the individualism of the maverick journalist for unspun political news. In the last resort, 'speaking truth unto power' is a matter of moral courage.

A second career for spinners

Nicco and Charlie. Very Old and Very New political servants. Separated by five hundred years of European politics. To believe in social progress, we have to conclude that there is little in common between the Italian Renaissance and our period. But perhaps career structures remain the same. The dispensability of servants led to internal exile for Nicco. This inevitability offered Charlie a new career as a writer.[4]

The chance to write memoirs comes to all political servants for they all eventually fail. They do so because they fall out with the gatekeepers in the media who block their access to readers and audiences; because their persuasive messages are heavily rejected by the public/voters; because they have to be sacrificed to save their principals; because their elected employers are voted out of office. Spin doctors' careers invariably end in tears.

Such an end is reassuring in a democracy for it reminds the public/voters who are more influential in the long run – themselves. What can they conclude about this fashionable political practice called spinning? First, they can understand it as a flattery of their ultimate influence, for spinning underlines the importance attached by politicans to staying aligned with majority public opinion. From this perspective, spin doctors are a regiment of tormentors raised to keep the media in line with a policy, a person, a party. Spin doctors and their political masters want journalists 'on message' precisely because they want the media to be messengers and the more passive, the better. Second, because journalists react to their spinning tormentors by ridicule, the public/voters are treated to a spectacle so enjoyable that they have appropriated parts of the script into their daily language. This linguistic appropriation suggests a leery, jokey tolerance of politicians and their ways. More ambivalently, this tolerance exists because spinning ways are the public's/voters' ways too. Is not spinning well known in their (our) daily lives? There it goes by another name: it is 'getting your way', 'sliding one past them', 'playing their game' at work and in dealings with the powerful and the official. I spin; you spin; he, she or it spins: the declension is a natural one. Third, the public/voters could conclude that the great national spectacle of political spinning played out in the public space before them is, ironically, a form of openness in government.

Machiavelli would not have approved of spin doctors for just this reason. For him, they fail the Prince because they can be observed (we hope) at their work of influence, persuasion and manipulation on His Behalf. We cannot approve of them either, but for better reasons. In our media-saturated society, we probably have to tolerate them but only if they are 'outed'. We should insist that political journalists do their duty by us as watchdogs in the contested marketplace of government communications. Once journalists do that duty by us, spin doctors are hidden persuaders exposed and that exposure makes for good slang, good gossip, good spectacle and more accountable politics.

Notes

1 Taken from Gilbert, A. (trans.) (1989) *Machiavelli: The Chief Works and Others*, vol. 1, Durham, NC: Duke University Press, p. 85.
2 The transfer of skills in the opposite direction of politics to marketing is rare and may have occurred only since the 1980s when markets became dangerous to those who seek to influence them.
3 In the same article, the noun 'spinners' is used: ' ... most spinners ... are invisible, the most effective messages are insidious ... ' (Castle 1997). These comments are disturbing for the argument here which wants its spin doctors where it can see them.
4 Charlie could open his own DIY book on politics with a personal view on chapter xxii of Nicco's: political masters are judged by the quality of their servants. Princes and Chancellors should remember that servants have ways of taking revenge.

References

Blumler, J. and Gurevitch, M. (1981) 'Politicans and the Press: An Essay in Role Relationships', in D. Nimmo and K. Sanders (eds) *Handbook of Political Communication* London: Sage.

Castle, S. (1997) 'The Things that Shaped our Year: the triumph of the spin doctor', *The Independent on Sunday*, 28 December, p. 9.

Draper, D. (1997) *Blair's Hundred Days*, London: Faber & Faber.

Ewen, S. (1996) *PR! A Social History of Spin*, New York: Basic Books.

Franklin, B. (1994) *Packaging Politics: political communications in Britain's media democracy*, London: Edward Arnold.

Goldenburg, S. and White, M. (1997) 'Fangs out for Mandelson: Blair Comes to Queen's Rescue', *The Guardian*, 17 October 1997, p. 1.

Harris, C. P. and Lock, A. (1996) 'Machiavellian Marketing: the Development of Corporate Lobbying in the UK', *Journal of Marketing Management* 12 (4): 313–28.

Jones, N. (1995) *Soundbites and Spin Doctors*, London: Cassells.

—— (1997) *How The General Election Was Won and Lost*, London: Indigo.

'Glossary of the 90s', *The Independent Weekend*, 11 January 1998, p. 75.

L'Etang, J. (1996) 'Public Relations and Rhetoric', in J. L'Etang and M. Pieczka (eds) *Critical Perspectives in Public Relations*, London: International Thomson Business Press.

Machiavelli, N. (1961) *The Prince*, trans. G. Bull, London: Penguin.

Mayhew, L. (1997) *The New Public: Professional Communications and the means of social influence*, Cambridge: Cambridge University Press.

McAlpine, A. (1997) *The New Machiavelli*, London: Aurum Press.

McSmith, A. (1997) *Faces of Labour: The Inside Story*, London: Verso.

'Tony is another Tory, says Ken', *The Observer*, 6 April 1997, p. 2.

'Burn out time for the political firefighters', *PR Week*, 6 February 1998, p. 7.

Peterborough column (1998) *The Daily Telegraph*, 20 January, p. 21.

Rawnsley, A., 'A year is a short time in politics', *The Observer*, 21 December 1997, p. 23.

Richards, P. (1998) *Be Your Own Spin Doctor*, Harrogate, Yorkshire: Take That Ltd.

Rosenbaum, M. (1997) *From Soapbox to Soundbite: party political campaigning in Britain since 1946*, London: Macmillan.

Scammell, M. (1995) *Designer Politics: how elections are won*, London: Macmillan.

Smith, T. and Young, A. (1996) *The Fixers: Crisis Management in British Politics*, Aldershot: Dartmouth Press.

'Fury of an inquisitor scorned', *The Times*, 4 April 1997, p. 20.

5
Machiavellian management thought in modern times

FURTHER, A PRINCE IS RESPECTED WHEN
HE IS A TRUE FRIEND AND TRUE ENEMY,
THAT IS, WHEN WITHOUT RESERVATION
HE TAKES HIS STAND AS AN ALLY OF ONE
PRINCE AGAINST ANOTHER.

THE PRINCE[1]

14 Machiavelli and Powell

Maximizing prophets

John Parkin

Machiavelli and Enoch Powell shared many things. Among them figure their relatively modest backgrounds – Powell senior was a schoolteacher, Bernardo Machiavelli a tax-lawyer – an enthusiastic army service, a talent if not a genius for poetic composition, long periods of political office and, to return to their youths, a classical education. This last is hardly surprising in a Renaissance Florentine, but it is easily forgotten that Powell was a Greek scholar of distinction both at school and then at Cambridge, being granted a chair in Sydney, Australia, just before the war and when aged but twenty-five. For neither man, I am sure, was ancient literature ultimately more than a hobby[2] – it was in enforced idleness that Machiavelli undertook his extensive analysis of Livy culminating in the *Discourses* – however their cast of mind is in both cases deeply marked by a training in rhetoric. The notorious 'rivers of blood' image from Powell's speech on immigration (April 1968) was in fact a quotation from Virgil (*Aeneid*: 6.87), whilst Machiavelli's equally famous fluvial metaphor – whereby the political world is construed as a struggle to build dikes and embankments to contain the river of *fortuna* – bears analogy with Terence and Ovid (Najemy 1993: 266–7).

What relevance has this to a modern political world to whose pragmatism and business orientation erudition and 'blood-curdling' displays of erudition may even be counter-productive (Brown 1995: ix)? In tacit reply to this (rhetorical) question, Margaret Thatcher proposed the diverting of educational funds towards the sciences as a means to promote national prosperity based on technocratic elites. Powell, far more traditional in his cultural perspectives, stood opposed to her line, supporting learning for its own sake (Heffer 1998: 887). Meanwhile the usefulness of the classical curriculum was a live issue in the Renaissance too, for when Machiavelli (1961: ch. xiv) in effect restricts the Prince's education to war, its organization and discipline, he is running, quite wittingly, against that school of contemporary opinion for which good education produced good moral grounding and therefore successful princely rule. However it is Machiavelli's task to describe a model prince, not to embody one: like Powell, he never rose above the middle ranks of political administration. Hence the learning he applied to his writing, described as a 'continuous reading of ancient matters' – *cose antique* (ibid.: Dedication), was part of the equipment which he offered his potential employers, plus an element in his own mode of self-expression, but it was never a prerequisite he imposed on the political leader.

Within their political careers they betrayed further similarities, including an almost obsessive interest in the issues, atmosphere and complexities of the political life. However, in terms of management and marketing it is worth recalling, first, their exceptional gifts as administrators. They shared an extraordinary talent for hard work, the close observation of facts, careful attention to detail and accurate reporting. Machiavelli's official and unofficial correspondence prove the vast range of responsibility conferred on him by the Soderini republic, which involved him not merely in diplomacy, negotiation and the drafting of reports, but also in projects of military leadership and even civil engineering, whilst, under Macmillan, Powell was first a Treasury minister of great acumen (he resigned with Thorneycroft in 1958, but remained an expert committee analyst of budgetary matters, praised in *The Observer* as 'the only MP (including the Chancellor of the Exchequer [Heathcoat Amory]) who understood the technicalities of the 1960 Finance Bill' – (Heffer 1998: 263), and then (from 1960–3) an avidly committed Minister of Health, whose policy initiatives remained valid for decades to come. One significant detail of strategy, moreover, is the way in which Powell fulfilled the key managerial principle of knowing the bedrock of his area of responsibility and so shortening his lines of communication: on his frequent visits to hospitals he insisted on meeting the staff *in situ*, for instance on wards and in sluice-rooms (Heffer 1998: 275), and with that minimum of formality which encourages the maximum value of spontaneous feedback. It is worth noting that Machiavelli too (1961: ch. xxiii) recommended that subordinates be encouraged to speak plainly and informally when briefing the ruler.

Second, their intellectual equipment, underpinned by the studies I have mentioned, provided a range of tools whereby they could catch and hold the attention of audiences and readerships, clarify issues (often to the predetermined advantage of their own case) and generate interest, notoriety and, in the end, whole concepts which, if not clearly defined, certainly subsumed many of the issues relevant to their own society and period: Machiavellism can be seen as implying something fundamental within the decline of medieval thought, while Powellism, as informing Thatcherism, foreshadowed (for better or for worse) deep structural changes in the economics and politics of contemporary Britain.

Experience and professionalism may be prerequisites for an influence of such proportions, but to create a consensus requires that ideas be marketed, something Powell ensured by an at times quite staggering rhythm of public speaking engagements. An assessment of his mode of address by David Watt is illuminating:

> He (sc. Powell) starts with some simple, essentially romantic idea such as patriotism or economic freedom, or Natural Man. On this basis a dry superstructure of logic is then raised. And finally this superstructure is adorned with irony, emotive allusion and adjectival embellishments. The embellishments catch the eye and the rationalisations satisfy the conscience

of some intelligent men. But what makes Mr Powell an important figure ... is the emotional attraction to many people of his own emotional assumptions.

(*The Times*, 7 March 1969)

Ever and again could the same patterns be discerned in passages from Machiavelli, but what are significant for immediate purposes are the marketing strategies implied by these and other techniques. Does not the sheer quotability of Powell underwrite the appeal of Powellism, and does not his reputation as a conviction politician sit ill with his exploitation of the media in a media democracy? In the preface to their marketing textbook, Kotler and Armstrong (1996: xiii) remind us that 'No politician can get the needed votes ... without developing and carrying out marketing plans', hence, while opposed to the televising of parliament, Powell still made sure that the press were given advance notice of speeches which Tory Central Office refused to distribute, and his dislike of the market-managing of party conferences did not prevent him hiring an advertising executive to run his own publicity machine. Is this not a tacit admission that in twentieth-century politics the mode of communication has replaced the Marxian principle of the mode of production as the key issue in the forming of attitudes (Masters 1996: 146)?

A metaphorical cast of mind – for both Powell and Machiavelli, Fortune was a lady[3] – this ability to clarify issues – according to Kavanagh (1995: 16–17) more a marketing strategy than a part of political discourse – the emphasizing of power words (e.g. *fortuna*, *virtù*, *nuovo*; Englishman, sovereignty, immigration) and the use of the KISS principle ('Keep it short and simple') can all be recognized within Powell's oratory and Machiavelli's writings. *The Prince*, after all, is a small book, whilst the *Discourses*, although comprising three lengthy volumes, are composed of relatively brief and clearly argued chapters, originating perhaps in the shared, exploratory interchanges of the discussion group, rather than in the mind of the isolated pedantic thinker.[4] Powell, meanwhile, preferred ever and again to publish compilations of his speeches rather than a comprehensive political thesis: in ancient Athens he would have been classed as a rhetorician, not a philosopher.

The point is that both were confronted by the task of marketing not only their ideas, but themselves: Machiavelli's republican past made him a political outcast when that republic foundered in 1512; Powell, too, is best remembered as a political outsider, though in his case this position is due more to repeated resignations on points of principle than to sackings or oustings. Granted the luxury of free time and an independent position, and intuiting the principle of 'seeing yourself as your own best resource' (Hart 1999: vi), both men, albeit from a position of weakness, employed influence, pressure, logic, reputation, style and force of argument as legitimate strategies within their self-promotion, for the greater good which underlay this process was (for them at least) of vast, even transcendental, import: the survival of the nation and culture into which they had been born.

Reality was a poor rival to this apparatus; as Powell argued to the Tory conference of 1968 (after falling out with Heath over the Birmingham immigration speech):

> Too often today people are ready to tell us: 'This is not possible, that is not possible.' I say: whatever the true interest of our country calls for is always possible. We have nothing to fear but our own doubts.

And doubt is dispelled as readily by Machiavelli when, in *The Prince*, his rhetorical imagination projects immediate success for the *principe nuovo*:

> Nor can I express with what love he will be received in all those provinces which have suffered from the foreign incursions: with what thirst for vengeance, with what persistent faith, with what piety, with what tears. What doors will be closed to him? What people will deny him obedience? What envy will stand against him? What Italian will refuse him loyalty?
>
> (Machiavelli 1961: ch. xxvi)

In fact Machiavelli's own lucid reasoning could have supplied a series of crushing answers to this series of rhetorical questions, beginning with the naming of the Pope, whose temporal power had frustrated Italian independence throughout the Middle Ages, as he himself was elsewhere to argue (Machiavelli 1975: Book 1, ch. 12).

So underlying, nay guaranteeing and justifying, their use of paradox, their political jeremiads, nay even their intellectual arrogance, one discerns as their ultimate metaphysic an extreme and over-riding patriotism. Both thinkers were convinced that their countries, the love of whom they stressed almost *ad nauseam*, faced the threat of political eclipse as a result of incursions from foreign lands. Powell always argued that he was not racist – citing his local work for coloured constituents as evidence – but, that issue apart, he also argued (here in an anonymous article) that 'the massive coloured immigration in the last decade … has inflicted social and political damage that will take decades to obliterate' (*The Times*, 2 April 1964), while in Machiavelli's case the language was more forthright – 'this foreign domination stinks in all our nostrils' (1961: ch. xxvi) – and the apprehensions better grounded: Florence, nay Italy, was to undergo centuries of foreign domination prior to the nineteenth-century Risorgimento to which he had looked forward in his own immediate future.

Meanwhile, in terms of metaphysical principle, their nationalistic sentiments outweighed all else, including perhaps their religion: after a long spell of Nietzschean atheism Powell reconverted to Christianity, but always emphasized the Anglican quality of his faith, while Machiavelli, probably no more than a conforming Catholic, preferred in his writings to praise Roman virtues and pagan ceremonials to the disadvantage of the politics of quiescence and passivity which had weakened Christendom.[5] More significantly still, they separated religious conviction from politics anyway, Powell for instance refusing to see the immigration issue as other than a political matter, and Machiavelli arguing trenchantly in *The Prince* that a virtuous man will be outmanoeuvred if, in the real world of conflicting interests and unscrupulous opponents, he practises virtue consistently:

> And many have imagined republics and kingdoms never seen or known in reality. For there is so great a discrepancy between how one lives and how one ought to live, that he who abandons actual practice for moral duty, is studying his own ruination rather than his own survival.
>
> (Machiavelli 1961: ch. xv)

The passage is often seen as the quintessence of Machiavellism and its distinction between moral values and the facts of political life surely encapsulates Machiavelli's main contribution to political philosophy. Moreover Powell, too, maintained a consistent distinction between his political and religious agendas, thus striking a refreshing attitude for those whose party leaders, for fear of losing votes, offer themselves to the camera while at prayer with their children, affect pious attitudes at funerals, nay even wed in the House of Commons chapel. Such a 'sugary, romantic, cosy religion' (Shepherd 1996: 499) Powell rejected, arguing that Christianity is relevant only to individual redemption, and specifically denying its pertinence to 'political action, social organisation, business ethics, or to any other practical choices that people have to make' (ibid.).

It remains moot how serious he was when declaring 'Often when I am kneeling down in church, I ... thank God, the Holy Ghost for the gift of capitalism' (Heffer 1998: 444). But the philosophical point here at issue could scarcely be deeper, at any rate for those thinkers who showered Machiavelli with opprobrium without choosing to consider him on his own terms, or for those of Powell's opponents who would force moral issues back onto the agenda, particularly concerning racism: Bishop Trevor Huddleston was to raise this question when debating with him in 1969. At the same time, if religion had retreated within Powell's political thinking to being either a matter of personal conscience or a gesture of patriotic loyalty, he certainly retained a sense of principle which cut right across personal advantage or the immediate return. If it is true that '"Just do it" ... has become the tacit standard of many in business, politics, law and everyday life' (Masters 1996: 1), this would scarcely fit with Powell's view, or, I believe, and despite superficial appearances, with Machiavelli's. Though applying their rhetoric to their experience and their reading so as to select, evaluate and manipulate facts, they always retained an awareness of metaphysical principles, even if these were in essence neither theological nor even moral. And I feel sure that, in the same way that Powell stood aside from Macmillan and Heath, Machiavelli would have claimed to be distinguished among the political servants of his day as being a man of conviction rather than of compromise, not to say of unscrupulous ambition.

Macmillan seems to have been loathed by Powell particularly for the way he manipulated the Tory succession in 1963, following which Enoch made another of his resignations, in that he refused to serve in the Home government. With Heath the difference was less principled than strategic, Heath putting Europe before Britain, Powell the reverse. However Powell rejected as a breach of promise the famous U-turn of 1972 whereby an election programme favouring monetarism reverted, in crisis, to an economics of interventionism. With Machiavelli, the key figure to consider is Cesare Borgia, the Papal commander whose political crimes remain legendary even today, and of whom Machiavelli's genuine opinion has been analysed to no clear conclusion. In *The Prince* (chapters vii and xvii especially) his moral guilt is acknowledged but dissolved in the greater goods of the order, trust and unity which he imposed and which were prerequisites for the resurgence of national pride which is the main purpose of Machiavelli's text, nay career.

Hence even if the Protean dissembler – be he the Italian courtier, the scheming trickster, even the wily Jesuit – has been seen as a key figure to emerge in Renaissance society (Agnew 1986: 76), neither Machiavelli nor Powell can be reduced to that type: many things he may have been, but Enoch was never a spin doctor. By contrast, both embrace a conviction politics, based on patriotism, and which lends an appealing clarity, not to say simplicity, to their thought: Powell was called 'lucid to the point of incomprehensibility' (*The Observer*, 29 January 1961). Moreover it barely needs repeating that Machiavelli was not simply the amoral pragmatist that one can find, if one looks for it, in certain of his writings, especially *The Prince*. In my view he looked beyond the extremely complex political realities facing him, and the practical proposals which he was forever devising in order to affect them, to greater goods which provided the impetus to his political motivation: the moral revival of *Italia*, the establishment of military power on the basis of citizen armies, the expulsion of foreign nations from the peninsula, the recrudescence of Roman *virtù* in an ideal Republic.

Ditto brother Enoch. If Machiavelli's rhetoric, nay his political life, was dedicated to the defence of Italy and/or Florence against the greater powers threatening it (France, Spain, the Holy Roman Empire, the Papacy), so Powell crusaded against the encroachments of Europe and America on the English nation and on British sovereignty. For him the race issue (like in fact the Irish issue) was merely a part of this campaign. He took it upon himself to defend an ethnic identity and a cultural tradition before they were destroyed by alien cultures and ultimately by a civil war which might come once his fellow-countrymen found the threat too great to be borne with tolerance and compromise. Referring to his political principles in a speech of 1963, he said, 'If you call this patriotism, so much the better; I would like to see the word in use again; we surely need the thing.'[6]

Yet, though one might argue that Powell's suggestion that the CIA were involved in Mountbatten's murder was absurd,[7] or that his insistence on the threat of racial violence simply served to make that violence more likely, he was far from reincarnating the insane jingoism of the 1930s fascists. He had no contact whatsoever with Mosley, nor directly with the National Front (Lewis

1979: 131). Arguably anti-black, he was entirely untainted with anti-Semitism. Furthermore, he never supported the building of an empire in Europe or anywhere else and, although committed at one time to the maintenance of a British presence in the East, he quickly abandoned that commitment, given the post-war experiences in India, Suez and Rhodesia, whereupon, unlike Heath, he came to oppose American (and British) involvement in Vietnam.

Speaking positively, his political and economic agendas merged in the perspective of Britain as a modernized, economically independent centre of commerce, trade and industrial production, protected by effective, independent (and non-nuclear) armed forces, untrammelled by superannuated ties to the Commonwealth, foreign aid payments of whatever kind, or irrelevant military incursions abroad (for instance in Iraq or Yugoslavia) and uncompromised by the ceding of sovereignty explicit in the treaties of Rome, Maastricht, the European courts, etc. Such a programme responded to the need to maintain an endogenous tradition of institutional and cultural identity which he loved to the point of spending years of spare time working on a history of the House of Lords (published in 1968) and cultivating the hobbies of fox-hunting and church visiting. It was a love about which he was unambiguous, see the 1963 speech quoted above.

It also facilitated a simplicity in his argumentation which, if not reducible to sound-bite politics, at least gave him a clear line compounding, for his opponents, anti-Europeanism, xenophobia and an uncompromising economic liberalism, which was Friedmanite *avant la lettre*,[8] and uniquely hostile to all State intervention, be it via nationalized industry, prices and incomes policy, or subsidized rents. These positions, and the arguments supporting them, Powell would pursue with the relentless logic to which we have alluded and often to the point of offending his specialist audiences: he had a tendency to lecture the Commons like an academic, rather than adopting the comparatively straightforward mode of discourse now customary there. However, while sharing Machiavelli's taste for a *ragione* which verged on dogmatism, he was still a parliamentarian of great charisma, particularly given that the logic gained its force and conviction from other sources, a point concerning which he was himself quite open.

Mutatis mutandis, the same might be said of Machiavellian discourse, and that less surprisingly in a period when the thinking of virtually every educated man was grounded in a rhetorical method which used classical stylistic patterns, detailed classical examples and general classical paradigms as the natural mode of political expression. In this connection Machiavelli could even be seen as exceptional, it having been opined long ago that here was the first philosopher since Aristotle to resurrect actual fact as the political thinker's real subject (for example, Dunning 1905). The point is arguable, and it may even have influenced others in the Renaissance of political theory – I am thinking of Jean Bodin (1966: ch. vi) – but at the same time *The Prince* itself is full of classical allusions, quotations and terminology, and might one not say that what can make it quite a difficult text for the modern reader, is in fact a concession to a contemporary reader, who would be expecting precisely this? For, in contrast with Powell, who would frequently recommend that politicians read history, Machiavelli grew up in a culture which regarded matters Roman and Greek as almost more politically compelling than an analysis of contemporary events (Gilbert 1965: Introduction) and in which one was encouraged to think that eloquence was power (Najemy 1993: 31).

Clearly at least two patterns are operative here: a structured analysis of fact (Watt's 'dry superstructure of logic') and a series of techniques intended to stimulate enthusiasm or anger on the basis of his nationalist principles (Watt's 'emotional assumptions'). The former may have gone beyond the comprehension of his popular audiences, as one of Powell's first speeches in South Down was well received by a group of farmers who had simply not understood that it had demolished the case for those guaranteed prices which were helping to keep them in business and which they therefore supported (Heffer 1998: 730). And the immigration issue was sure to command support from groups who were openly racist (which he denied being), favouring enforced repatriation (which Powell never did), if not open intimidation and black-shirt thuggery. However the popular response – expressed especially in the letters he received from constituents and non-constituents alike – convinced him repeatedly that his principles were consonant with those of the British people, with whom, for whatever reason, he remained obdurately popular. He achieved a particular demagogic success in awakening a response from the working-class Tory, who had always existed, but who in post-war Britain was a voice not easy to discern, while decades into his career it was to become deeply embarrassing for his left-wing opponents to see dockers demonstrating on a spontaneous basis in his favour.

Perhaps Machiavelli entertained similar populist feelings, nay illusions, as expressed in the peroratio to *The Prince*, which is a profession of faith in Italians far and wide, and also in a number of chapters of the *Discourses* where he expresses a confidence in democracy quite inconsistent with various cynical statements contained in the more famous work:[9] book 1, chapter 47 praises the people's judgement over particular issues – he has in mind their assessment of individual political figures – whereupon chapter 58 argues, using evidence from ancient republics such as Rome and Athens, that a *popolo* is 'wiser, more stable and of better judgement than a prince' (Machiavelli 1975: 313).

Such innate romanticism Powell certainly shared, both in terms of the concept in which it expressed itself ('the thread of a nation, the belief in a nation as the thing which explains and justifies everything'[10]) and his analysis of that concept: for 'a nation is not a rational thing. There is no rational basis for nationhood. What a nation is is what it feels itself to be, instinctively and emotionally.'[11] However meaningful, nay even dangerous, this concept may or may not be as a guiding principle, it certainly fits with several apparent truths whereby, for instance, intellectuality need well be no asset, at any rate for the Anglo-Saxon politician, and 'politics is about gut reactions', not intellectual issues.[12] Speaking more positively, one might see the transcending of logic and rational argument as not a dumbing-down of political discourse, but rather an expression of political intuition and leadership. Thus Bagehot argued, in a preamble to his study of *The English Constitution*:

> No orator ever made an impression by appealing to men as to their plainest physical wants, except when he could allege that those wants were caused by some one's tyranny. But thousands have made the greatest impression by appealing to some vague dream of glory, empire or nationality. The ruder sort of men ... will sacrifice all they hope for, all they have, *themselves*, for what is called an idea – for some attraction which seems to transcend reality, which aspires to elevate men by an interest higher, deeper, wider, than that of ordinary life.
>
> (Bagehot 1964: 63)

The problem with vague ideas, however, is that they are vague, and the problem with elevated interests is that they may not only transcend reality, but defy it. Hence it would have been no less revealing to survey popular understanding of Powellism in the twentieth century – what people thought he stood for, rather than what he actually proposed, why they supported him and not the main-stream Tories – than it is to trace the meanings assigned to Machiavellism in the sixteenth. In both cases one would surely encounter huge inaccuracies, though inaccuracies for which the figures so commemorated were, given a shared proclivity for paradox, at least in part responsible.

Nevertheless Machiavelli was far from being merely a Machiavellian, while Powellism, depending on how it is understood, may represent an equally distorting legacy. Moreover the terms as popularly used shared far less than did the men who sired them: Enoch resembled Niccolò, but he was no Machiavellian either. Thus is it interesting to observe that it was not to Machiavelli that Powell was likened by his contemporaries, but rather to Savonarola:[13] equally democratic, but puritanical, demagogic and prophetic with it. Again Powell was quite prepared to analyse his role as prophet, rather than political analyst:

> A politician crystallises what most people mean, even if they don't know it. Politicians are not word-givers. When they have spoken, individuals recognise their own thoughts. Politicians don't mould societies or determine destinies. They are prophets in the Greek sense of the word – one who speaks for another and gives words to what is instinctive and formless. Winston did this in the war. He crystallised a will which existed.
>
> (*Daily Mail*, 11 July 1968)

And his points are interesting, in that they cut across the conceited notion whereby a politician forms rather than responds to opinion: on the contrary, argues Kavanagh, 'A prerequisite for good political communications is to understand the thinking of the voters' (1995: 15), however emotional, prejudiced, and symbolic, rather than rational, this be. They also argue for a link of intuition and principle which binds speaker and public almost in defiance of the 'politics of permanent condescension' dominating televised rallies with their embargo on questions, and their ticket-only admissions policy (ibid.: 217, quoting Hugo Young).

Nevertheless, though Powell may have responded to latent moods rather than forming new opinions, he still knew how to draft an argument and to encourage, nay render inevitable, the enhancement of the principles he would begin by evoking. It stands on record that he deliberately peppered his speeches with controversial material, catching the eye with statements and examples which were slightly extravagant (for instance, the famous case of the old lady living in a street of 'noise and confusion' and populated exclusively by blacks, which old lady no investigative journalist could then find),[14] and no doubt with what he felt to be attractive and catchy phrases – if not actual buzz-words, then the kind of 'allusion' and 'embellishment' to which Watt referred. He is reported to have said, 'I deliberately include at least one startling assertion in every speech in order to attract enough attention' (Shepherd 1996: 343). More good marketing?

Another tactic was to set up logical or pseudo-logical alternatives which polarized the choices in any political situation, following which he would point up one of the alternatives as disastrous, so leaving the interlocutor (or audience) but one possible conclusion, which of course is the very conclusion he had predetermined all along. An example follows from the five crucial speeches which Powell made in 1970 (later published as a volume by his supporters) and which may indeed have won the Tories that election, even though Powell was not, of course, at the time a front-bencher, nor even *persona grata* with that bench:

> I declare, then, that in my judgement, based upon what knowledge I have of human nature and upon what observation I have made of events in the world, the prospective growth of the Commonwealth immigrant and immigrant-descended population will result in civil strife of appalling dimensions, and that institutions and laws, let alone exhortations, will be powerless to prevent. On the other hand, it is not in my judgement yet too late to prevent or greatly reduce those consequences [this by the relative damp squib of reducing immigrant numbers].[15]

So either increased control of immigration, plus encouragement for repatriation, or ... rivers of blood, and moreover rivers of blood which threatened black as much as white, 'for the outcome which I believe is portended would be at least as disastrous for the newcomers as for the indigenous inhabitants.'

What is intriguing is not merely the use of either/or dichotomies, but also the appeal to patriotism, and the emphasis on his own political experience, both of which we have seen, in Powell's case as in Machiavelli's, to be very genuine qualities – and qualities they were equally keen to market. Switching back five hundred years, we have Machiavelli writing a famous letter in 1527 – a date very late in his life – and in the specific context of a threat on the native country from foreign invaders, in this instance Bourbon's Imperial army which was to sack Rome only weeks later:

> I love my country more than I love my soul. And I tell you this from that experience which sixty years have given me, that I do not believe we have ever gone through such difficult straits as these, wherein peace is mandatory yet the war must be sustained.
>
> (Letter to Francesco Vettori, 16 April 1527)

So the wise and experienced Renaissance politician points out his dilemma: either continue the campaign, however ruinously, or face national disaster; and the perceptive and uncompromising modern politician points out his: either block immigration or face civil war.

The next speech, subtitled *The Enemy Within*, was delivered two days later, and amounted to an attack on enemies of Britain, be they left-wing extremists, student rebels, the IRA, or, it would appear, those dangerous fifth-columnists who were arguing for racial integration. The power of these forces, fomenting anarchy, brain-washing and discord, could be broken only by 'plain truth and common sense, and the will to assert it loud and clear .... Without that there is no escape from the closing trap; no victory over those who hate Britain and wish to destroy it.'[16] Again, notice the appeal to patriotic values, the insistence that there is an unseen threat of vast potential, but also a security that the threat can be nullified if the right alternative is chosen: that alternative being, curiously enough, a Tory vote next week – again something of a rhetorical bathos.

The following speech, delivered in the very week of the election, was in some ways the most interesting and the most significant, specifically because it addressed the question of conviction politics which I mentioned previously, and assaulted the consensus which had formed at that time between the major parties over the crucial issue of Common Market membership. What Powell demanded was that individual candidates declare, and that their potential electorate force them to declare, where they stood on this issue: for Europe or for Britain. At the same time he made his own anti-EEC position apparent and on the basis of similarly rigid choices. Was Britain to remain politically independent, or be reduced to the level of Staffordshire County Council? For 'In the Common Market ... government would not be a British government; it would be a continental government,' imposing on a country in permanent minority defence policy, taxation and conscription (since 'how can conscription not be involved?').[17]

The stated dichotomy is clear: 'these islands' are opposed to 'a sovereign authority of continental character, continental location and continental outlook', a closure which, incidentally, exemplifies the classic rhetorical pattern of the tricolon, but which of course pre-empts the possibility of a fusion of national with supranational perspectives, in other words that European outlook which Heath had been encouraging for decades. The choice is between sovereignty conserved and sovereignty abandoned, another knockdown argument, but one based on a very naïve distinction, given the dispersal of sovereignty which has always pertained to greater or lesser degrees in local, national and supranational structures: GATT, the international courts and the Geneva Convention are various examples one could cite.

Finally the last speech, which was delivered two days before the poll and is interesting for other reasons again than the rhetorical dichotomy which set head to head 'two futures for Britain, futures irrevocably, irreversibly different'.[18] Such a stark contrast was far from reality, given the party leaderships' consensus on so many major issues including, for instance, the mixed economy, Europe, the Atlantic Alliance and the nuclear deterrent. Nevertheless Powell saw the choices as radical and potentially disastrous: either a Tory victory, or total state control of the economy; either a Tory victory, or the loss of the nation's best – that is mass emigration of British-born families; either a Tory victory, or an end to private education, private health-care, in fact an end to individual liberty.

It is via a similar dichotomy that Machiavelli presents his underlying challenge to current political thinking and it resides in the professed imposition of realistic truth (*verità effettuale*) over fantasy (*imaginazione*) – as broached in the first paragraph of *The Prince* chapter xv, where the politician who abandons the former (that is, political praxis: 'what is done') for the latter (that is, ethical duty: 'what ought to be done') faces not survival but ruination. Moreover the moral chapters, following later and specifically related to the ethics of monarchic government, also use the *aut ... aut* formula: the Prince can be either generous or parsimonious, but generosity leads to excess spending, increased taxation, hatred and ruin; the Prince would ideally be loved and feared, but if a choice must be made between the two, then love is the worse political quality, causing the ruin of a Prince whom it leads to trust his subjects' words; the Prince should be a lion and a fox, using force or cunning as is required by a particular situation, for a wise monarch (*'uno signore prudente'*) cannot keep his word in all circumstances (Machiavelli 1961: ch. xviii). Rigid alternatives first divide his subject matter, then rigid alternatives impose his revolutionary political morality and, finally, rigid alternatives prevent the reappearance of traditional ethics which he has excluded: if men were all good, this precept would be invalid; but since they are evil, and would not keep faith with you, no more need you do so with them (ibid.).

Such and similar tactics may have built a popular response, but other considerations kept Powell away from that Tory leadership which he long coveted – was he, like Machiavelli's Savonarola, a prophet unarmed (Machiavelli 1961: ch. vi)? In these terms, though the rhetorical skills may have been admirable, the political strategy was wrong. Too ready to resign on principle (for example as junior minister under Thorneycroft in 1958, or as Conservative candidate in 1974 and on the day Heath called an election), so Powell was not the standard Tory pragmatist who would sooner ride out the storm of political conflict than take to the boats. To this extent Thatcher – another conviction politician, yet a superb marketeer as well – paid lip-service to Heathian policies in his cabinets and shadow cabinets, all the while forming her political (and ideological) power base. Then, her opportunity coming with his fall in 1975, she took power, and imposed policy afterwards: as Anthony Jay (1967: 11) opined, quoting Russell, 'important achievement is and will be almost impossible to an individual if he cannot dominate some vast organisation', and such were the arms that Powell lacked, at least at the crucial moments.

Paul Foot (1969) argued in *The Rise of Enoch Powell* that the stand on immigration which he emphasized in 1968, and retained thereafter, was in some ways the beginning of a campaign to exploit popular rather than party support in his own drive for ultimate leadership: for many of the ensuing years his popularity was higher than that of any right-wing opponent. However his refusal to stand as Tory candidate in the first 1974 poll lost him a vital opportunity to outmanoeuvre Heath in opposition and, when he returned to the Commons in the second 1974 election, it was as a Unionist MP without the Tory whip: no way to spring back to the Front Bench let alone into 10 Downing Street.

So Powell was destined to become a political outsider in a situation which reflected a deal of his influence and in which many of his policies (especially in economics and industry) were to become operative.[19] And, oddly enough, with the instauration of the last Florentine Republic in 1527, Machiavelli was similarly marginalized, even though it was a regime to which, given his principles, plus the dedication and experience manifest during the Soderini period, he must have felt strongly, if not intensely, committed. Being by now, however, too closely identified with that regime's opponents, the Medici – to whom, after all *The Prince* had been dedicated and perhaps even presented – he was once again, as in 1512, *persona non grata* with the governing power. He died but a few months later.

Notes

1 Taken from Gilbert, A. (trans.) (1989) *Machiavelli: The Chief Works and Others*, vol. 1, Durham, NC: Duke University Press, p. 82.

2 The term is owed in context to a personal letter of Powell dated May 1938.

3 See the notorious passage 'and as a woman she must needs be thumped and beaten ... ' (Machiavelli 1961: ch. xxv), cf. Powell's comments on 'a girl called "Fortune"' quoted in Heffer (1998: 127).

4 I have in mind the Orti Oricellari, the Florentine talking-shop to two of whose members the *Discourses* are themselves dedicated.

5 See especially *Discourses*, 2.2, on our effeminate world where submission is more highly praised than vengeance: Nietzsche argues a similar case in *Human, All Too Human*.

6 Speech in Bromley, 25 October, 1963.

7 See Heffer (1998: 881). He made the claim in 1984, four years after the event.

8 The original influence on his liberal economic theory was Friedrich von Hayek, with whose work he became acquainted while employed, after demobilization, by the Conservative Party Research Department (see Heffer 1998: 212).

9 For example: 'One can say this in general terms about people: that they are ungrateful, inconstant, play-acting and deceitful, fearful of danger, greedy for gain' (Machiavelli 1961: ch. xvii).
10 Interview of 1995 quoted in Heffer (1998: 5).
11 Interview in *The Guardian*, 22 February 1971.
12 Cf. Masters 1996: ch. 6 (first quote) and p. 145 (second quote). One recalls the smearing of both Wilson and Macleod as 'too clever by half', and the success of Reagan's so-called 'Aw shucks!' style of presidency, whereby he admitted being at a loss with finer detail.
13 For example, Crossman when asking of a Labour Party Conference in January 1967, 'Who is running the opposition?'
14 Speech in Birmingham, 20 April 1968.
15 Speech in Wolverhampton, 11 June 1970.
16 Speech in Birmingham, 13 June 1970.
17 Speech in Tamworth, 15 June 1970.
18 Speech in Wolverhampton, 16 June 1970.
19 The point was made by Peregrine Worsthorne in *The Sunday Telegraph*, 10 June 1979, that is following the first of Thatcher's electoral victories.

References

Agnew, J. C. (1986) *Worlds Apart: the Market and the Theater in Anglo-American Thought, 1550–1750)*, Cambridge: Cambridge University Press: 76.

Bagehot, W. (1964) *The English Constitution*, London: C. A. Watts: 63.

Bodin, J. (1966) *Method for the Easy Comprehension of History*, New York: Octagon Books. (In ch. 6, he somewhat grudgingly accords Machiavelli an analogous special mention.)

Brown, S. (1995) *Postmodern Marketing*, London: Routledge.

Daily Mail, 11 July 1968, as quoted in Heffer (1998: 474).

Dunning, W. A. (1905) *A History of Political Theories*, vol. 2, New York: Macmillan.

Foot, P. (1969) *The Rise of Enoch Powell*, Harmondsworth: Penguin.

Gilbert, F. (1965) *Machiavelli and Guicciardini*, Princeton, NJ: Princeton University Press: Introduction.

Hart, K. (1999) *Putting Marketing Ideas into Action*, London: Library Association.

Heffer, S. (1998) *Like the Roman: the Life of Enoch Powell*, London: Weidenfeld and Nicolson.

Jay, A. (1967) *Machiavelli and Management*, London: Hodder & Stoughton.

Kavanagh, D. (1995) *Election Campaigning: The New Marketing of Politics*, Oxford: Blackwell.

Kotler, P. and Armstrong, G. (1996) *Principles of Marketing*, London: Prentice-Hall, 7th edn.

Lewis, R. (1979), *Enoch Powell. Principle in Politics*, London: Cassell.

Machiavelli, N. (1961) *The Prince*, trans. G. Bull, Harmondsworth: Penguin.

—— (1975) *Discourses*, trans. L.J. Walker, London: Routledge & Kegan Paul.

—— 'Letter to Francesco Vettori', 16 April 1527, translated as 'Letter 332' in *Machiavelli and His Friends: Their Personal Correspondence*, J. B. Atkinson and D. Sices (eds), Illnois: Northern Illnois University Press, 1996: 416.

Masters, R. D. (1996) *Machiavelli, Leonardo and the Science of Power*, Paris: Notre Dame, IN: 146.

Najemy, J. (1993) *Between Friends*, Princeton, NJ: Princeton University Press.

The Observer, 29 January 1961, as quoted in Shepherd (1996: 217).

Shepherd, R. (1996) *Enoch Powell*, London: Hutchinson.

The Sunday Telegraph, 10 June 1979, as quoted in Heffer (1998: 823).

Tomalin, N., 'Patriotism based on reality, not on dreams', *The Times*, 2nd April 1964, p.13.

The Times, 7 March 1969, as quoted in Heffer (1998: 515).

THE SOLDIER DIES IN A DITCH, THE
LOVER DIES IN DESPAIR.

CLIZIA, 4.124[1]

15 Butchers, bunglers and Machiavelli

Italian political philosophy and the First World War

Martin Stephen

Introduction

The abiding presence of Niccolò Machiavelli can be seen in the links between the reputation and achievements of Machiavelli himself and an outwardly far-distant and very different figure, Sir Douglas Haig. Haig commanded British land forces on the western front for most of the First World War. Machiavelli could not have known of Sir Douglas Haig, and Sir Douglas Haig would have known of Machiavelli only by name. Placing the two side by side might seem to recreate the comic pairing of the Medici *condottiere*, Giovanni delle Bande Nere, and Machiavelli, when, after two hours of hopeless drilling by Machiavelli, it fell to the *condottiere* to restore discipline in the twinkling of an eye. Yet, if the meeting at the Orti Oricellari in 1516 that is the setting for *The Art of War* were to be recreated in 1918, it is likely that Sir Douglas Haig could take the place of the mercenary commander Fabrizio Colonna, as one of the most famous and respected commanders of his day.

The majority of this paper deals with the reputations of these apparently dissimilar men. Yet they are linked at the level of practical philosophy and their attitude towards military matters, in two beliefs in particular. In one such belief they were wrong. Machiavelli dismissed the power of artillery and modern technological developments in warfare, just as Haig felt the machine gun to be no real threat to a well-trained well-mounted horseman. In their idea of the use of cavalry both men were united. Haig was a passionate cavalryman, who took part in one of the British army's last great cavalry charges, at Kimberley in 1900. Despite stories to the contrary, Haig never believed in cavalry as the primary strike force in modern warfare. Rather he believed that it was the infantry who made the breakthrough and the cavalry who used their speed to mop up the remaining enemy. In Book III of *The Art of War* Fabrizio states 'they [cavalry] are more meeter to follow the enemy being discomfited, than to do anything which in the same is to be done, and they be, in comparison to the footmen, much inferior' (Gilbert 1965).

In a second belief they were right. Machiavelli dismissed the effectiveness of mercenaries, arguing instead for wars to be fought by local militias, amateur soldiers who would return to their peacetime professions once fighting was over. His reasoning was based as much on a concept of civic virtue inherited from classical authorities as it was based on military necessity. It also had the politician's fear of a standing army, suggested in *The Art of War* (Book I) by Fabrizio when he states 'if a king does not arrange things in such a way that his infantrymen are content to return home and to live off their trades during times of peace, he will of necessity come to ruin' (Gilbert 1965). Haig had no choice but to use the equivalent of Machiavelli's local militia. Little more than 100,000 troops were available from Britain's professional standing army in 1914, and their ranks were decimated by the early fighting.

Haig therefore fought the most successful land campaign in British military history with a conscript army whose 'Accrington Pals' and local loyalties made them exactly comparable to the militia envisaged and endorsed by Machiavelli. Haig's locally based militia fought the bloodiest campaign Europe had ever seen, both to victory and to a solution that saw not one serious mutiny, and brought a new meaning to the concept of the amateur soldier. Those who survived did go back to their peacetime jobs, where, of course, such jobs still existed. Machiavelli would have thoroughly approved of Haig's achievement with his conscript army. In Book VII of *The Art of War* Fabrizio distinguishes between 'those leaders who have accomplished great deeds with an army already organised according to its normal discipline' and 'those leaders who have not only had to overcome an enemy but who, before reaching that point, were forced to produce a good and well-disciplined army of their own; these men, without a doubt, deserve more praise than those who operated with good and disciplined armies' (Gilbert 1965). Haig had to create his own army and then see it to victory against some of the most professional forces in the world. Proper credit has rarely been given to him for achieving what Machiavelli spotted as a rare achievement five hundred years earlier.

Personalities and philosophies

Any comparison between the two men has to admit that Haig was a deplorably revolting human being. He neglected his children to the extent of turning them into vandals. He may or may not have used homosexuality as a path to favours, but certainly used his own private money to ease his path to promotion. He was sycophantic to royalty and used his connections there to go behind the backs of his fellow officers in order to sabotage their careers and to advance his own. General Kitchener (of whom Asquith said 'He is not a great man. He is a great poster') received this treatment when Haig was fighting alongside him and at the same time sending highly critical letters back to Sir Evelyn Wood, the Adjutant General. It was written of Haig (de Groot, 1988) that 'He was concerned mainly with his own progress, something from which he never more than slightly distracted.' He ordered the offensives that cost thousands of

British soldiers their lives. His diaries and wartime writings were edited subsequent to the war to prove that he was right.

Was Machiavelli an equally charming man? The gap of five hundred years means that we shall never know. As with Shakespeare, all we have are some of the words written by the man, from which we may deduce at great hazard the man behind the mask. However, it does seem clear that Machiavelli believed rulers were there to do the job for the people, not because they were thoroughly saintly, church-going and lovely people. He might have been highly amused by the extent to which history has failed to recognize that generals are appointed to win wars, not to save lives or to be angels landed on earth. Indeed, Fabrizio's description of his trade in *The Art of War*, Book I, suggests Machiavelli of all people would have known how to judge Haig when he says:

> nor has any good man ever taken it [warfare] up as his own particular profession. For a man will never be judged good who, in his work – if he wants to make a steady profit from it – must be rapacious, fraudulent, violent, and exhibit many qualities which, of necessity, do not make him good.
>
> (Gilbert 1965)

It was not that Haig lacked an apologist; it was rather that his finest apologist had the misfortune to be born over four hundred years before him, and was unknown to him.

Haig, Machiavelli and the truth

Haig's real mistake was to tell people the truth. De Groot (1988) quotes Haig as writing 'The aim for which the war is being waged is the destruction of German militarism. Three years of war and the loss of one-tenth of the manhood of the nation is not too great a price to pay in so great a cause.' It was the same mistake in principle, if not in practice, as was made by Machiavelli, who has a touching faith in mere truth being automatically persuasive. As with Machiavelli, Haig's unpalatable truths were the product of major historical changes. The First World War gave armies only part benefit of technology. It gave them the bolt-action rifle, barbed wire, machine guns and the exploding artillery shell. These, if used in conjunction with deep-dug trenches, were superb for a defensive war. To overcome these defences a number of additions were needed to the armoury. Radio communication, not land-line powered telephones, allowed commanders to order and direct their troops away from enemy concentrations and on to areas of weakness and simply to keep them under orders once they vanished over the top. Tanks were needed to crush the barbed wire and ride over the trenches. Aircraft were needed to strafe the enemy trenches when an attack was being launched and to bomb enemy artillery and machine gun enemy reserves and the transport that brings them.

None of these were there in 1914; precious few had arrived by 1918 in any meaningful sense. It was clear to any thinking person that the war of 1914 could only be won by a process of attrition. Attrition costs lives. It was a truth that a nation that launched a war without wishing to pay for it in the coinage that all wars demand, was not willing to face. Just so with Machiavelli, who told in *The Prince* a number of truths and found society attempting to paste flimsy moral denials over them, in the rush not to perceive what in reality all knew to be true. Both Machiavelli's society in the quality of its leadership and Haig's society in the quality of its generals wanted omelettes without breaking eggs. What is revealed in society's response to both men is the hypocrisy of those societies, not the hypocrisy of the men themselves.

Haig, Machiavelli and morality

It has been and remains a matter of acute academic debate whether Machiavelli ever truly meant to say that the end justifies the means. However, what he *did* say in *The Prince* – 'one must consider the final result' – summarizes exactly the philosophy of Haig. He believed that his conscript armies might well crumble under the continual pressure of war, and that what was therefore needed was 'The Big Push', the one great offensive that would end the war quickly. Ironically, the offensives on the Somme, at Passchendaele and elsewhere were designed to use lives now to save them later. Haig accepted that these offensives would create casualties. On balance he believed that the butcher's bill would be far less if one of these great offensives succeeded in smashing the German line and so ending the war. The final result would be less bloodshed and less threat of civil disturbance as a result of a war that had gone on too long at too great a cost.

Those who only half-read Machiavelli believe in an amoral figure for whom success and power outweigh any suffering caused to others in pursuit of that success. Exactly the same is believed of those who judge Haig apart from the facts of his life. The truth for both men is the same, namely their belief that a degree of suffering might well be essential if the greater good of the greater number is to be obtained. Both believed that, if the desired end was good and moral, the leader might have to act outside the conventional boundaries of traditional ethics. Perhaps the weakness of both men was that neither had experienced the type of bloody battle on which they wrote. Haig was a courageous soldier who had faced combat on numerous occasions, but who had never fought on anything like the killing fields of Loos, the Somme and Passchendaele. As Anglo (1969) comments, 'Machiavelli's experience of really bloody battles, such as delighted him in the safety of his study, was negligible'. Haig was nearer the front line than almost any other top commander in the war (he pioneered the use of a train in order to get closer to the action), but in Anglo's term Haig's command train was simply an extended study.

Politics and the man

Machiavelli and Haig lived in a world where politics and soldiering were inseparable. The difference was that, with Haig, the extent to which he was forced to
be a political animal has never been widely appreciated. Machiavelli existed in a
climate where the balance of power between the Soderini and the Medici
faction could be the deciding factor, not just in his career but also in his facing
torture. The equivalent for Haig was the battle between English politicians,
French politicians and generals, on the one hand, and the factions which would
allow the English generals to carry on the war as they wished. In effect, the
existing military establishment and its representatives in Government were the
equivalent to Haig of the Soderinis, the opposing politicians and French
generals the Medicis. A complicating factor was that the enemy had the
strongest recruit in the Prime Minister Lloyd George, desperate for a quick way
to end the war before the unpopularity of the casualty figures lost him his job.

Haig was never free to act on purely military grounds, with the interlinkage
between politics and warfare as strongly an influence on him as it had been
when Machiavelli wrote *The Art of War*. The Somme offensive was dictated in
two fatal areas by political considerations. Its timing was dictated by the need to
show willing to the French, who were starting to doubt the true dedication to
the war of the British. The position of the offensive was dictated by its being a
point in the line suitable for Anglo-French co-operation and not by tactical
considerations. Haig believed himself surrounded by a position for which
Machiavelli's Prince would have been well prepared. Haig was surrounded by
political enemies, in his own country and in France. These enemies, and Prime
Minister Lloyd George in particular, were intent on Haig's destruction. They
were also intent on pursuing policies that would either have lost the war, or lost
more lives, or both. Haig saw his survival as guaranteeing the best possible
outcome for the war. The stakes were so high that they justified, in his eyes at
least, almost everything that Haig did to achieve his own survival.

Folk history and the real thing

The final link between Machiavelli and General Haig is the large number of
people who have poured hatred and scorn on both men for what they are
perceived to have been and done, rather than what they actually said and did.
The historian Alan Clark credited to those on the German side the description
of English forces as 'Lions led by donkeys'. I cannot quote an original source
for this comment, as – though it is cited by Clark – I am not aware of the original source. As well as donkeys, the English generals have been described as
'butchers and bunglers'. It is frequently overlooked that no general on any side
found the key to breaking through the trenches until technology had advanced
to the levels found in mid-1918. It is also forgotten that the proportion of casualties to those serving in uniform was actually less than was the case for the
Peninsular War a hundred years earlier. Nor is it recognized that the British

Army was essentially a colonial army and colonial armies have a tradition of shepherding their men, because reinforcement can be up to three months away by troopship. Finally, numerous commentators have failed to acknowledge that the British army for most of the First World War was an untrained army which simply could not be handled with the techniques that were applicable to properly trained and fully professional troops.

Haig made numerous mistakes, but they were by and large not the mistakes of which he stands accused. The link with Machiavelli is clear. The clear moral dimension in his work has been overshadowed in popular culture at least by a pragmatism and concern with the end result that both distorts and misrepresents what was actually said. The story of the evil and unscrupulous Machiavelli and the blood-sucking incompetent Haig are too good not to be true – and therefore they must be made so. After all, historical accuracy is for boffins, not for real people.

Conclusion

I have concentrated here on the way in which a reputation for something evil can be acquired and, in so doing, treated Machiavelli and Haig as historical figures who have, in their differing ways, become folk myths. Two areas would repay further study. The first is whether Machiavelli's ideas might have helped Haig to an earlier conclusion of the war. There is some evidence that Haig did not have too little morality, as history has charged him with, but rather too much. There is every evidence that he would have benefited from a closer acquaintance with the purely political awareness of Machiavelli. The second is a wider comparison of Machiavelli with Haig on the grounds that, just as Machiavelli was seeking to come to terms with the existence of a new type of Prince, so Haig was forced to come to terms with a new type of General. Both were men with their feet firmly based in tradition, but with heads that could see clearly that tradition was no longer going to be enough for victory.

For those who market or manage the armed forces, a lesson does emerge from an examination both of Machiavelli and of Haig. The people at large are quite willing to accept war whilst it appears not to require anyone's death, or any sacrifice of morality. The only acceptable war is a clean war – and the only clean war would be one where hostilities were never declared or embarked upon.

Note

1   Cited in De Grazia, S. (1989) *Machiavelli in Hell*, Princeton, NJ: Princeton University Press, p. 122.

References

Anglo, S. (1969) *Machiavelli: A Dissection*, London: Victor Gollancz: 152.
Boraston, J. H. (ed.) (1979) *Sir Douglas Haig's Despatches*, London: Dent.

Bondanella, P. and Musa, M. (eds) (1979) *The Portable Machiavelli*, Harmondsworth: Penguin. (Used as the Machiavelli source wherever the passage is available.)

De Groot, G. J. (1988) *Douglas Haig, 1861–1928*, London: Unwin Hyman: 26, 242.

Gilbert, A. (1965) *Machiavelli. The Chief Works*, Durham, NC: Duke University Press. (Used as the Machiavelli source wherever the passage is not available in Bondanella and Musa 1979.)

Laffin, J. (1988) *British Butchers and Bunglers of World War 1*, London: Alan Sutton.

Stephen, M. (1996) *The Price of Pity: Poetry, History and Myth in the Great War*, London: Leo Cooper. (My comments on Haig rely heavily on this work.)

Terraine, J. (1990) *Douglas Haig, The Educated Soldier*, London: Leo Cooper.

FOR THERE IS SUCH A DIFFERENCE
BETWEEN HOW MEN LIVE AND HOW
THEY OUGHT TO LIVE THAT HE WHO
ABANDONS WHAT IS DONE FOR WHAT
OUGHT TO BE DONE LEARNS HIS
DESTRUCTION RATHER THAN HIS PRESER-
VATION, BECAUSE ANY MAN WHO UNDER
ALL CONDITIONS INSISTS ON MAKING IT
HIS BUSINESS TO BE GOOD WILL SURELY
BE DESTROYED AMONG SO MANY WHO
ARE NOT GOOD.

THE PRINCE[1]

16 Machiavelli and human nature

Robert Gutfreund

> Man acquires at birth, through heredity, a biological constitution which we must consider fixed and unalterable, including the natural urges which are characteristic of the human species .... The biological nature of man is, for all practical purposes, not subject to change.
>
> (Einstein 1949)

In this chapter I make three claims for the continuing relevance of Machiavelli for understanding human behaviour. First, I suggest that Machiavelli's concept of human nature retains an ongoing and enduring significance for contemporary political thought and public, political action. Second, that this concept – and a belief in an essentially unchanging human nature – is one that is shared with the philosophic and analytical assumptions which are found in both Hobbes and Freud. Finally, I maintain that, contrary to the widespread belief that such a fixed concept of human nature is a denial of the development of human potential and social progress, it is claimed that it is a necessary – though, of course, not sufficient – foundation for the continuation of individual liberty.

It is currently unfashionable to argue for a relatively autonomous concept of human nature that is independent of social and economic circumstances and institutional conditions. The widely accepted and often unquestioned philosophical assumption, so evident in the work of Rousseau and Marx and their remaining adherents, is that it is social circumstances which determine the nature of human nature and that, if only the 'right' changes were made in social and institutional arrangements, these will bring about significant changes in human behaviour. To some extent there is a truism here. The important objection to this approach, however, arises from the in-built belief that this process has no terminal point – a stage beyond which individuals may be impervious to directional, even directed, change. Most major political programmes appear to me either to be based upon a complete neglect of any consideration of human nature or to include an erroneous notion of man being subject to social forces which 'oversocialise' him (Wrong 1961).

It is clear to me and those who reflect upon this that every political philosophy is underpinned by at least a minimal conception of human nature; it follows from this that any political philosophy which does not take into account how human nature functions within the public – that is, political – sphere, cannot have claim to full coherence. As Scruton (1990) states, 'political philosophy is, at least in part, the elaboration of human nature in terms of which the sphere and aims of politics may be described'. All political and social concerns imply a view of a person and their potential development towards some optimum state of wellbeing which is the specific good – or end – they consider appropriate. Aristotle, one of the early political theorists to reflect on this, saw the purpose of life as the cultivation of human intellect and reason in pursuit of happiness, 'to the good which has the highest degree of finality' (Aristotle 1953: 36).

Every conception of human nature we hold confronts the individual as both objective and subjective phenomena – external to ourselves – 'out there' – and internal – within us. All our understanding invariably includes both descriptive and prescriptive dimensions; there can be no analysis of the social or individual circumstance that is 'free' of such evaluations. As the Kantian view implies, we do not merely describe phenomena in a neutral way; every description includes our own evaluative observations (values) on social phenomena and we hope others share our views. Thus 'truth' depends not only upon what is true for the individual – what corresponds most closely to his perceived sense of reality around him. But also any answer to the question 'what is Man?' presupposes – and is inseparable, if only implicitly, from beginning to provide an answer to – our key political question, 'what is good for man?' (Berry 1986: 31).

By contrast, for Christian philosophers, most notably Aquinas, 'the purpose of man was to acquire knowledge of God, His rules and obey His Commandments' (Aquinas 1959: 109). But theologians were also very concerned to subordinate both the individual and their political world to 'divine providence [which] imposes order on all things and manifests the truth of the Apostle's saying "All things that are, are set in order by God"' (ibid.). Within this theological context and frame of reference, primary political obligation does not belong to the temporal political world since 'not all that man has, or is, is subject to political obligation, hence it is not necessary that all his actions be considered worthy of praise or blame in the political community. But all that he is or can be, must bear a relationship to God' (ibid.). This subordination of the 'political community' to the deity and their earthly representatives was to have lasting effects – not always desirable – upon political philosophical discourse and practices.

Machiavelli, given his essentially democratic concerns, rightly rejected such claims by the deity to subordinate the political order to its vision of this and the 'other world'. As Skinner (1978: 183) states, Machiavelli 'has no hesitation in concluding that any attempt to employ a Christian scale of values in judging political affairs must be altogether given up'.

To accept any essentially fixed, unalterable view of human nature implies an inevitable restriction upon the whole Western political enterprise of unlimited faith in reason or even 'progress' since at least the French Revolution; though, in Machiavelli's concept of human nature, such limitation has been much in evidence well before then. One might add that, consequently, the entire 'Utopian' enterprise of unending and unhindered social and human improvement is brought into question. The rejection of what is, in my view, the false notion that men have the capacity to control fully the social world and are also fully in control of their own desires does make the Utopian enterprise in the final analysis untenable. Little wonder that Scruton (1990: 192) could be dismissive of Utopian sentiments: 'If you wish to believe something that flies in the face of all the known facts of human nature, you are best advised to believe it of the future, which is forever unobservable. In that way the implausible is made irrefutable.' And logically, this is the invariable and apologetic 'defence' of all the many failed social systems and political innovations since Machiavelli. The 'conditions' were not right, the organization was at fault, or there was too much interference by external and hostile 'enemies'. Rarely, if ever, is failure attributed to human nature and a resistant unwillingness to submit to totalitarian rule – the historically inescapable consequence of living under the authority of those who believe they have found the 'answers'.

By their persistent failure to fully acknowledge constraints upon progress set by human nature, Utopian theorists are in danger of subscribing to their theories by highly fallible intuition alone. Contrary to this, Machiavelli, in offering a science of politics (a concept much disputed!) attempted to base the foundation of the state on firmer bases than one reliant on intuition alone. He may have done much more than this, in that he represents the 'rise and development of a new doctrine, manifesting the spirit of an age, personified in a man' (Villari 1892). It is often unrecognized in political philosophical discussions that the acceptance of an intrinsic theory of human nature, which regards man as a social being requiring association with others, is at the same time tantamount to accepting a theory of necessary human and social conduct, in other words, an embryonic, developing theory of politics. However, as politics is an ongoing activity which occurs in the public realm, an organized mechanism and associated processes for peacefully resolving disputes between individuals and groups, it follows that human conduct can be changed. Unlike in the state of nature – the changing cycle of seasons, the freezing point of water or the laws of gravity – human conduct and hence political activities can, it is rightly held, be modified and subjected to human volition and direction. About this there exists considerable consensus. What has been and remains vigorously contested is the extent to which human nature determines the parameters of political and social change, or obversely, whether political and social change determines human nature.

My claim here is that there are aspects of human action which are impervious to any and every significant attempt at modification by political, public endeavours. On whichever bases we select our view of human nature (I hesitate, since human freedom is not boundless but is always limited by values, beliefs and feelings as well as social circumstances and the necessity to labour), we should acknowledge that this selection is itself determining the 'ought' nature of what is to be done in politics. What may be taken as real – in contrast to assumed –

indicators of such limitations? I will suggest that in the analysis of Machiavelli and Freud – and also significantly of Hobbes – there is a common, shared recognition that this limitation is imposed by inescapable dimensions of human nature beyond individual or even social control; and, especially in the work of Machiavelli, by the unpredictable nature of Fortuna (perhaps comparable to what was referred to as 'always an element of chance in history' by Marx, but conveniently neglected by his 'followers' to maintain the appearance of 'scientific socialism').

The foregoing may appear as a rather extended introduction to the subject of human nature and the title of this chapter. However, to develop more fully our understanding of Machiavelli's crucial achievement we need to comprehend some aspects of the philosophical background within and against which Machiavelli was writing – the competition between essentially secular Greek and Christian conceptions of human nature; temporal power and political ends focused upon this world and religious 'other-worldliness', the ends of which belong beyond this world. This 'tug of war' between what we would now call 'competing ideologies' persisted at least until the sixteenth century, when the insights of Machiavelli effected a far reaching transformation and radical shift in the West's conception of political discourse from the ideal to the real, from that which 'ought' to be to that which is existent. When these important, politically significant insights of Machiavelli were harnessed to the later writings of Hobbes, the 'old Christian-cum-Aristotelian metaphysics was simply played out' (Ryan 1973). Once this long established and pervasive tradition of political thought was undermined, if not entirely overturned, it was but a short theoretical step towards transforming the very institutional framework within which subsequent political reflection would in the future occur. Following their unavoidable confrontation with the synthesized radical critique and rationalist idealism of Machiavelli and Hobbes, the Deist, theological conceptions upon which political philosophy had hitherto been dependent could no longer be sustained or later even 'justified' in secular terms.

The transformation of the political and social order in the four centuries since Machiavelli were to be effected by dual stimuli emanating from the application of reasonable reason and a belief – or more precisely several beliefs – about the nature of eternal truths concerning justice and human liberty. These beliefs, when harnessed to the development of scientific and rationalist approaches to industry and work, permeated every aspect of human endeavour and strengthened the application of reason in politics. Rationalist beliefs in human potential are frequently reformulated into near messianic doctrines (in terms often of 'Left' or 'Right') and maintained, often contrary to all the evidence, with a tenacity almost impervious to human reason. Expressed in these terms, the assumed logic of 'historical movement' is often perceived, by the followers of doctrines, to reside in the dynamics of some historical unfolding towards a 'solution' to the identified 'problems' of political society almost independent of individual will or endeavour. It is by processes of such historical inevitability, as exemplified by Marx – and to a lesser extent Hegel –

who saw a 'rationally discernible development in history' (Plant 1973: 57) that human progress is seen to advance. History is deemed to possess some deep inherent logic and coherence, which it is claimed (and hoped!) can counteract the unpredictable, irrational nature of human nature.

It was believed throughout the nineteenth century that the emergence of a true, benevolent dimension of human nature has to await the abolition of the exploitative nature of capitalist relationships and the transcendence of human ignorance which has been maintained throughout history by what Marx was to term an 'ideology'. Both reformers and revolutionaries believed that, with access to appropriate knowledge and the effects of changing social circumstances – perhaps a shift in means rather than of ends – in other words by education and re-education, man would be enabled to follow the postulates of his 'real', 'true' human nature. Human potential would then be actualized in everyday experience rather than remain stifled in the daily contradictions which have been man's historical experience hitherto. The future – its uncertain and unknowable form notwithstanding – is deemed amenable to directional and intentional human modification. As one theorist has perceptively summarized it, 'an ideal promotes the conviction that reality could be other than it is and since an ideal furnishes a standard against which reality can be evaluated, an ideal serves as both incentive and partial guide for progress' (Kalin 1975: 200). Little wonder that there remains considerable disenchantment when daily political and social experiences do not match Utopian promises.

Machiavelli appears to me to have no prefixed notion of progress towards which individuals consistently strive, have to be cajoled or ultimately coerced. This absence of explicit Utopian visions enables him to focus upon everyday necessities. It also 'rescues' individuals from much inevitable disappointment that accompanies all such enterprises. If we can philosophically accept that 'one of the deepest human desires is to find a unitary pattern in which the whole of experience, past, present and future, actual, possible and unfulfilled is symmetrically ordered' (Berlin 1997: 180), then it can be said that Machiavelli has contributed to such a 'discovery'. He cast doubt over the long, historical claims of progress, not only in *The Prince* – which was after all one of many works offering 'advice' to rulers – but in the corpus of his work.

Central to this were three politically significant postulates. The first was a demonstration – one is tempted to say a 'proof', but that would take us into realms of methodology – that there exists an enormous gap in practical politics between overtly stated intention and social action, between proclaimed political ends and the actual opportunities or will for their realization. The actual pursuit of power is seen as the central motivating force in all political, public activities; and, although ideals are everywhere to be found, these are at all times but a subterfuge to camouflage this and the essentially violent nature of politics.

Machiavelli's second contribution, clearly developed from the first, was to identify a coherent universal concept of human nature and explore its implications for the political realm; he recognized both its potential and the limitations this imposed upon the pursuit of programmes in practical politics. The enduring modernity and continuing relevance of his approach influenced many nine-teenth-century and subsequent formulations of politics concerned with 'mass' movements, elite theories and the analysis of political behaviour. To give one example, it is rarely remarked how much Gustave Le Bon appears to follow Machiavelli's methodology by adopting a historical analysis and arriving at similar conclusions:

> It is not the facts in themselves that strike the popular imagination, but the way in which they take place and are brought to notice .... It is necessary that ... they should produce a startling image which fills and besets the mind. To know the art of impressing the imagination of crowds is to know at the same time the act of governing them.
>
> (Le Bon 1903: 79–80)

Faith in the idea of progress by changing institutions is scorned and dismissed as a 'grave delusion' consequent upon an excessive reliance on reason. And since 'the masses ... must have their illusion at all cost they turn instinctively to the rhetoricians who accord them what they want. The masses have never thirsted after truth – whoever can supply them with illusions is easily their master; whoever attempts to destroy their illusion is always their victim' (ibid.: 125–6). Most importantly, Machiavelli's realism represents a significant shift in political theory from what is widely *believed* to be, to what actually is *known* to be.

Finally, Machiavelli re-introduced into political theory the classical demo-cratic concept that political power ultimately resides in the people. We should hold him in high esteem for having liberated almost all Western political theory from those metaphysical, essentially theological restrictions which were the legacy of Judeo-Christian political doctrines. One may concur with Wolin's insight that Machiavelli had

> made the basis for the first great experiment in a 'pure' political theory [and] the manifesto which he drew for the new science reflected the belief that before political phenomena could be meaningfully analysed, they must be freed from the enclosing illusions woven by the political ideas of the past.
>
> (Wolin 1961: 198)

In this project he anticipated Marx – and in his analysis of human nature surpassed Marx's notion by far!

Central to Machiavelli's view of human nature was his vision of the political – most assuredly public – domain within which practical politics occurred. I have already suggested that Machiavelli separated the realm of politics from the realm of morality – the what 'is' from the what 'ought' to be. Whilst the latter always represented a preoccupation with the ends to which public life is directed, the former described a distinctive, accurate view of power relationships in a world of continuing violence and conflict. It is against such a background – of wars, calumny and intrigues – that Machiavelli's formulation of practical politics is most appropriately comprehended.

If Wolin's judgement that 'it has been and remains one of the abiding concerns of the Western political theorist to weave ingenious veils of euphemism to conceal the ugly fact of violence' (Wolin 1961: 220) has validity (and in my view it has much) then Machiavelli's theory of the role of human nature in politics is persuasive. He warns that 'Whoever desires to found a state and give it laws, must start with assuming that all men are bad and ever ready to display their vicious nature, whenever they find occasion for it' (Machiavelli 1950: Book I, ch. iii). In an analysis reminiscent of Hobbes, who elevated the maintenance of order as the supreme duty of government in the absence of which the war of each against all would ensue, Machiavelli recognizes that 'human desires are insatiable, (because their nature is to have and do everything whilst fortune limits their possessions and capacity of enjoyment) and this gives firm rise to a constant discontent in the human mind' (ibid.). Social order requires firm laws and strong leaders to enforce these, a fact vindicated by all the evidence around that 'men act rightly only upon compulsion; but from the moment that they have the option and liberty to commit wrong with impunity, then they never fail to carry confusion and disorder everywhere' (ibid.: Book 2, Preface). Driven by a constant striving for 'glory and riches' they 'succumb to the evil-readiness of men's nature' (De Grazia 1989: 79).

Machiavelli recognized that the political, public world consists of fleeting phenomena which could only momentarily be grasped within the timespan of the present – and once comprehended were almost immediately in the past, already a part of history as individuals begin to reflect upon them. He fully understood that in a world of ongoing change and flux, men continuously yearn for social and individual stability – it is continuity rather than change which appeals to their nature. In an important sense he anticipated Freud, holding that man's only hope of attaining a sense of stability was to invoke illusions about the nature of the real world. In trepidation of the unknown they cling to habits which have been outpaced by events, no longer in accord with political realities. Hemmed in by inexorable social circumstances and powerful individual ambition, men create an illusory, highly symbolic world of merely temporary, fleeting security. As Wolin (1961: 212) summarizes it, these were 'forms of illusion springing from man's tendency to project a world distorted by his own excessive ambitions, hopes and fears'. In my view, any changes in political and community arrangements would have only the most minimal effect upon such fears, a range of illusions remaining necessary. Thus, in Machiavelli's view, any sense of security experienced in the public domain is also illusory and is a causal factor in necessarily releasing in individuals what Wolin terms 'the psychological springs of ambition and domination'. In politics, he warns, it is not only against the unpredictability of circumstances, but also against individual motivations that the wise ruler has to guard since 'he must consider well the motives that have induced those who have favoured him to do so' (Machiavelli 1988: ch. xx).

There persists a duality of uncontrollable factors in Machiavelli's concept of politics and the nature of the political. First, there is that enduring dimension which arises from inherent human desire and ambition; second, there are those events which are an unavoidable consequence of Fortuna – and which cannot be known in advance. It is important not to confuse Machiavelli's notion of 'Fortuna' with another significant unknowable, that of a 'Divine Will': by locating his analysis within a historical context and mode of explanation, it is closer to Marx's concept of there always being 'an element of chance in history'. Since Machiavelli separated practical political activities from the realm of purposive political philosophy, one may wonder why his views on human nature are not fully recognized and given the serious political consideration they clearly merit.

There appear to me to be two main explanations. First, by recognizing that men often do not live according to those moral imperatives which are claimed to guide their public action, he has brought individuals closer to a sense of social reality and 'truth' than we might otherwise be. If Plato's analogy of the cave implies an ongoing human preference for myths and illusions (as surely it does), then Machiavelli's insights provide a further necessary dimension by pointing towards the true nature of daily political activity from which these essential myths have been removed. Of course, as befell the escaped prisoner in the cave, who is ultimately killed for relating his observations of the 'real' world, Machiavelli's critics often shudder at his insights. He offers little hope to political philosophers in terms of human advancement or 'progress', believing individuals to have far less control over their actions or ability to influence the course of events than they suppose or would prefer. In the cities 'civilisation is already corrupt', although there remains some distant hope since 'good laws bring good fortune and from good fortune results happy success in all enterprises' (Machiavelli 1950: Book I, ch. ix).

In Machiavelli's concept of a universal human nature, it is the unchanging and essential similarities between men, including their 'envious nature', rather than their differences which assume significance, 'for all men are born and live and die in the same way, and therefore resemble each other' (ibid.). It is crucially important for a political leader to be aware of human nature, for it is from such understanding that he will be able to judge and calculate whether it is better to be loved rather than be feared:

> Men are not as they are described by those who idealise them – Christians or Utopians – nor by those who want them to be widely different from what in fact they are and always have been and cannot help being, but seem to Machiavelli as 'ungrateful, wanton, false and dissimulating, cowardly and greedy ... arrogant and mean, their natural impulse is to be insolent when their affairs are prospering and abjectly servile when adversity hits them'.
>
> (Berlin 1997: 285)

Faced with the realities Machiavelli describes, public morality ceases to be the central focus of politics; the ruler is also (in part) released from any constraining private moral concerns and enabled to concentrate upon maintaining his position of public power. Ongoing vigilance remains necessary and, in a somewhat chilling and often misunderstood passage, he tells us that a prince

> who wishes to make a profession of goodness in everything must necessarily come to grief among so many who are not good. Therefore it is necessary ... to learn how not to be good and to use this knowledge and not to use it, according to the necessity of the case.
>
> (1988: ch. xv)

Whether one chooses to be good or not is seen to be determined by the social context and the requirement to act in the interests of the state – or, we may now claim, the institution, or enterprise. He does not extol us to behave in a bad way – only to learn when to do so as necessity demands.

In reflecting upon his work almost five hundred years after Machiavelli, we may speculate why, after all this time, we remain at least uneasy about him. One explanation is that, having separated politics from private morality, he further emasculated the influence of the Church in public life and thus extended our perception of living in a moral vacuum. Contemporary disquiet can be a response to his essentially pessimistic – or realistic – legacy which inspired the very influential 'Italian School' of political theory, and in particular its preoccupation with elites and the role of leaders. In combination – even more in synthesis – the orientations of V. Pareto (1935), G. Mosca (1939) and R. Michels (1966) continue to undermine the progressive beliefs of the 'Enlightenment' and the often exaggerated liberal claims by politicians even today of democratic and social progress. Within Machiavelli's work the centrality accorded to the analysis of power – especially 'naked power' (devoid of justice or morality) – has 'been treated once and for all' (Russell 1938: 98). Given our high aspirations for social and human progress it is little wonder that we still 'shudder' at Machiavelli's name because of our unassuaged and deeply felt realization that:

> the realities he described *are* realities: that men, whether in politics, in business or in private life, do *not* act according to their professions of virtue; that leaders in every field seek power ruthlessly and hold on to it tenaciously; that the masses who are coerced in a dictatorship have to be wooed and duped in a democracy; that deceit and ruthlessness invariably crop up in every state .... [Machiavelli] confronts us with the major dilemma how to adapt our democratic techniques and concepts to the demands of a world in which naked power politics dominate ... we hate and fear him because he has exposed our dilemma and made it visible to ourselves and the world.
>
> (Lerner 1950)

He has also, I suggest, destroyed for many the necessary human, if illusory, confidence that derives from the pursuit of social or individual ideals since, almost by logical definition, ideals cannot be realized. Of course, this is not a sufficient reason why human beings should not strive for attainable improvement, or attempt the rebuilding of past glories. Machiavelli's insights offer us all a powerful argument against every form of Utopian-induced 'social engineering', whether by self-appointed dictators or well-intentioned representatives of the industrial majority. Paradoxical as it may appear, this forms a basis for the realization of a large measure of human freedom.

My general unease with the claims of the idea of 'progress', particularly when these are formulated independent of social context and a theory of human nature, is the certainty with which an always uncertain and unknowable future is predicated. Every vision of the future is in some measure dependent upon a distinct perception concerning the present and a notional faith in possibilities. However, since the future is always uncertain and unpredictable, faith in the actualization of progress requires conviction concerning our abilities to 'humanize' human nature and determine social events. Our belief in these possibilities often subordinates reason or fails to contextualize human potential. This allows – even encourages – the inclusion of increasingly unreasonable, even irrational behaviour to enter into human affairs; from this, it is a short step to the justification of every vile act in the name of 'progress'.

As noted, Machiavelli's concepts of human nature and politics formed the bases of the whole 'Italian School' of political science which, when allied to Freud's social theories, did so much to undermine the nineteenth-century ideas of progress and, in particular, the Marxist enterprise. Indeed, I take the unfashionable view that, contrary to the widely held image that Machiavelli's analysis of human nature and politics led to Fascism, his ideas, and particularly when combined with Freud, are the main bases which preserved human freedom and the liberal principles of the Enlightenment.

We are familiar with Marx's view of human nature, wherein man is conceptualized as essentially in control of the social milieu. Marx's explicit theory of human nature which perceives man as integral to nature, that is to 'nature both as it exists *outside* man and as man's nature' (Geras 1983). For Marx there can be no isolated individuals, only a realization that, within the division of labour, social relationships take on an independent existence between individuals. 'The accidental nature of the conditions of life for the individual appears only with the emergence of the class ... ' (ibid.). But surely the 'element of chance in history' is ever present, as Machiavelli's discussion of 'Fortuna' shows and recent European events demonstrate, irrespective of the organizational form of society.

Although for Marx human nature is essentially responsive to social and particularly economic circumstances, the more relevant and persuasive explanation of human nature in the political realm is located in the work of Freud. Both he and Machiavelli demonstrate and compound an essentially fixed view of human nature. Even the important role of historical factors and social conditions, or elusive concerns about 'inter-subjectivity' or 'ontological affirmations' in Marx, cannot detract from or eradicate the relatively fixed phenomenon of internal drives in human nature, though their significance may be modified. Accordingly, the aggressive drives can be socially re-defined as a positive value, necessary for self- and species- preservation – as in wartime – or morally justified by socially sanctioned re-contextualization – as in marketing and economic competition.

I believe that if Machiavelli were alive today he would eschew the Marxist view of human nature in terms equal to those of Freud. There can be few more compelling or sustained rejections of the basis of the Communist view of human nature than that expounded by Sigmund Freud. Here is one of the most influential thinkers of the last two thousand years rejecting one of the more pervasive, politically influential movements of the twentieth century. This rejection is all the more powerful because it is based upon an entirely different and realistic conception of human nature and its potentiality.

In Freud's view man's nature has an innate 'inclination to aggression' which is impervious to significant modification. The historically developed Christian ideal to 'love one's neighbour as oneself … is justified by the fact that nothing else runs so strongly counter to the original nature of man' (Freud 1930). Freud shares a certain affinity of disbelief with Machiavelli when he (Freud) remarks 'so long as virtue is not rewarded here on earth, ethics will preach in vain' (ibid.). The influence of property is not entirely dismissed since 'a change in the relations to possessions would help more than ethical commands but this has been obscured by socialists who hold a fresh idealistic misconception of human nature' (ibid.). Unlike Marx, who remains rooted within the Greek, Judeo-Christian tradition of political and moral thought, Freud rejects much of this tradition and is less constrained – or impeded – in his analysis by a desire to fundamentally transform social conditions. He is less hindered by Utopian visions of future society and this enables him to be much more objective than Marx. Freud also understood himself in relation to the world. 'The time comes' he writes, 'when each one of us has to give up as illusions the expectations which, in his youth, he pinned upon his fellow men'; and yet retains the belief that 'it would be unfair to reproach civilisations with trying to eliminate strife and competition from human activity' (Freud 1930). There is here a recognition that both aggressiveness and the attempt to socially limit its expression are an ongoing feature of the human condition.

The following passage is the most unyielding and penetrating critique to undermine analytically the whole Marxian enterprise:

> The Communists believe that they have found the path to deliverance from our evils. According to them, man is wholly good and is well-disposed to his neighbour; but the institution of private property has corrupted his nature …. If private property were abolished, all wealth held in common and everyone allowed to share in the enjoyment of it, ill-will and hostility would disappear among men …. I have no concern with any economic

criticisms of the communist system; I cannot enquire into whether the abolition of private property is expedient or advantageous [in a footnote he calls attention to the 'miseries of poverty in my own youth'], but I am able to recognise that the psychological premises on which the system is based are an untenable illusion ... [since] in abolishing private property we deprive the human love of aggression of one of its instruments, certainly a strong one, though certainly not the strongest, but we have in no way altered anything in its nature. Aggressiveness was not created by property. It reigned almost without limit in primitive times when property was still very scanty and it already shows itself in the nursery.

(Freud 1930: 112–13)

Freud anticipated (generally accurately) how the new political system of Bolshevism (and indeed Fascism) would respond to the historical legacies which remain in all societies and the inextinguishable resilience of the aggressive dimension of human nature. In a manner reminiscent of Machiavelli, Freud judged that new holders of power would claim the necessity of punitive and repressive current measures to be justified by the ends:

... so long as men's nature has not yet been transformed it is necessary to make use of the means which affect them today. It is impossible to do without compulsion in their education, without the prohibition of thought and without the employment of force to the point of bloodshed.

(ibid.: 180)

He would maintain, along with both Plato and Machiavelli, that men need illusions and myths and Freud's work can best be understood by an attempt to analyse what his editor describes as 'the irremediable antagonism between the demands of instinct and the restrictions of civilisation' (ibid.).

It is misleading to charge Freud or Machiavelli, as many have done, with only providing a culturally specific account of human nature or a theory which applies to 'masculine' analysis only. Freud's statements concerning human nature and its relationship to society in *The Future of an Illusion* show a universality which transcends any narrow, single culture: 'one has to reckon with the fact that there are present in all men destructive and therefore anti-social and anti-cultural trends' (Freud 1927). Civilization could be fully viable only after the successful 'coercion and suppression of the instincts'. Although the suppression of instincts is attempted in every culture, this can never be completely effective and the inner drives of man continue to surface in violent episodes often manifested in the public domain. Whilst men possess the skills and means to extract and utilize wealth from nature to satisfy shared, collective human needs, they also require appropriate regulatory mechanisms to 'adjust the relations of men to one another and especially the distribution of wealth'. There is, Freud holds, an interdependence between the social production of wealth men extract from nature and their 'mutual relations [which] are profoundly influenced by the amount of instinctual satisfaction which the existing wealth makes possible' (ibid.). This is an unambiguous acknowledgement that differentials in the distribution of material wealth directly affect the extent of instinctual satisfaction, but it does not amount to an acceptance that an equal – or less unequal – distribution of wealth would eliminate the human tendency towards aggression.

Clearly, both Machiavelli and Freud regarded human aggressiveness and violence as a universal, trans-historical concept. The political significance of this is not only that it corresponds to a widely observed and sensed reality, but rather that it represents a distinct phase or point of 'arrival' in political thought. If accepted as everyday occurrence, it obviates the anxiety-inducing and forlorn, frequently encountered human quest for significant social amelioration in almost every dimension of the human condition; continued Utopian expressions of this quest are almost invariably dependent on an inadequate understanding of human nature. Despite his much greater optimism, John Stuart Mill shared Freud's view. 'Civilisation', he wrote, 'in every one of its aspects is a struggle against the animal instincts' (Wolin 1961: 318).

It is illuminating that, if from differing perspectives, both Machiavelli and Freud (Hobbes too – though space and occasion exclude him) consider social coercion as necessary. Freud held that repression of instinctual drives is a necessary pre-condition for the existence of 'civilisation'. Fundamental aggressiveness permeates and is manifest in the constant interplay of love and hate which continually struggle for ascendancy and control within the internal and external, social life of every individual; importantly, this often subconscious conflict is independent of and additional to the aggressiveness inherent in the striving for satisfaction of the sexual drive. This distinction is important since it avoids the centrality often accorded to the sexual dimension of Freud's analysis and negates much ill-informed criticism directed at Freud's theories of sexual development in infancy. In emphasizing a socially manifested drive to aggression, he refutes those critics who (in error) charge Freud with having focused primarily upon sexual drives. Further, by identifying aggression and the sexual drive as the main foci, it universalizes the appropriateness of the theory and 'rescues' it from accusations of being culturally specific.

This insight into understanding the limiting nature of political possibilities is crucial. Freud acknowledges that the demands of both the social structure and individuals seeking intrinsic inner driven satisfaction have to be reconciled. It is of course not only individual wishes, motives or desires which require to be accommodated in the political domain. Indeed, human desires and wishes are to a very considerable degree – never totally – socially determined and socially circumscribed. An exclusively psychologically focused theory of human motivation is inadequate for understanding political aspirations insofar as it fails to take into account the extent to which human desires are socially determined. Equally, a concept of human action excessively dependent upon a notional 'social construction of human nature' is also incomplete if it takes insufficient cognisance of 'forces in man that are resistant to socialisation'. Clearly, 'to

Freud, man is a *social* animal without being entirely a *socialised* animal' (Wrong 1961).

Why do these two complementary formulations of the genesis of human behaviour remain significant? I suggest that when synthesized into a coherent and developed explanation of human nature – Machiavelli's deriving from the 'ebb and flow of separate histories' and Freud's from 'the natural sciences' – they are an essential liberating device that rescues us from the constraining and often illiberal intentions of potential 'social engineers' and in particular from those who base their deep convictions exclusively upon economic, rational man. Human freedom, liberty and justice require not only a measure of equitable distribution in material circumstances but also the retention of a spirit of individual resistance to impersonal bureaucracies as well as collective and collectivist forces of every persuasion. In Machiavelli and Freud we can each discover an explanation and justification for our non-conformity and even resistance to authority.

Clearly, I have not attempted a 'new' theory – rather, to identify the constants of human behaviour. There is no sense of Utopian purpose in Machiavelli – no first, second, or even 'third' way. Those entrusted with or holding power are required to behave in a particular way if they wish to hold on to power. As a political scientist, his concern is about processes of power – the ends to which it is directed are the concerns of the moralist, or each of us as citizens. That innate aggressive drives are often directed into positive outcomes in the workplace is much in evidence; even the language of politics or human nature concerns are evident in managerial or marketing activities.

Perhaps I could suggest a number of possible implications for managers which may follow from the position adopted here. First, that in order to avoid unnecessary frustration, there should be no assumption that rational behaviour can be expected in the workplace at all times. There are very few people who have not on some occasion been exasperated and failed to make sense of why colleagues have acted in a particular way. On most occasions there is a reasonable and quite rational explanation. But there are also instances when explanation eludes us – we cannot locate the behaviour within a coherent, comprehensible framework. On such occasions, and at least until a better explanation is found, we should not assume rational behaviour at all times.

My second point is not entirely unrelated to the first – that in all human, socially constructed arrangements there exists an element of events which we cannot entirely predict. Thus, irrespective of how much we tried to anticipate the unfolding of future developments, there is always the likelihood that some circumstances we are unable to influence. The good manager has no reason to apportion blame or even accept responsibility for an inability to predict the future with precision. That it is so often predicted is quite fascinating!

Finally, Machiavelli confirms our experiences that not everyone around us is predisposed to be good or virtuous at all times – and that we need therefore to learn how not to be good when the occasion demands; and to act so without the damaging feelings of guilt that often accompanies 'unkind' acts.

Any manager alerted to these dimensions of political realities should be better prepared to understand – even tolerate – the action of his or her workforce. The cumulative effects of this ought then to be a significant and knowledge-based amelioration of individual anxiety and stress. If this could be further harnessed to a key political principle – of separating the public from the private domain, in effect the workplace from the home – who would predict the – dare I suggest – happy consequences?

Note

1   Taken from Gilbert, A. (trans.) (1989) *Machiavelli: The Chief Works and Others*, vol. 1, Durham, NC: Duke University Press, pp. 57–8.

References

Aquinas, T. (1959) *Selected Political Writings*, ed. A. P. D. D'Entreves, Oxford: Basil Blackwell.

Aristotle (1953) *The Ethics*, trans. J. A. K. Thompson, Harmondsworth: Penguin Books.

Berlin, I. (1997) *The Proper Study of Mankind*, London: Chatto & Windus.

Benthall, J. (ed.) (1973) *The Limits of Human Nature*, London: Allen Lane.

Berry, C. (1986) *Human Nature*, London: Macmillan.

Le Bon, G. (1903) *The Crowd*, London: T. Fisher Unwin.

Coser, L. A. and Rosenberg, B. (eds) (1969) *Sociological Theory*, London: Macmillan.

Einstein, A. (1949) 'Why Socialism?', *Monthly Review*, May.

Freud, S. (1927) *The Future of an Illusion*, in Freud (1981) vol. XXI.

—— (1930) *Civilisation and its Discontents*, in Freud (1981) vol. XXI.

—— (1981) *The Complete Psychological Works of Sigmund Freud, Standard Edition*, trans. J. Strachey *et al.*, London: Hogarth Press and the Institute of Psycho-Analysis.

Geras, N. (1983) *Marx and Human Nature – Refutation of a Legend*, London: Verso Editions and N.L.B.

De Grazia, S. (1989) *Machiavelli in Hell*, Princeton, NJ: Princeton University Press.

Hobbes, T. (n.d.), *Leviathan*, ed. M. Oakeshott, Oxford: Basil Blackwell.

Kalin, M. G. (1975) *The Utopian Flight from Unhappiness: Freud against Marx on Social Progress*, Totowa, NJ: Littlefields Adams.

Kepner, C. H. and Tregoe, B. B. (1981) *The New Rational Manager*, Princeton, NJ: Princeton Research Press.

Lerner, M. (1950) 'Introduction' to Machiavelli, N. (1950) *The Prince and Discourses*, New York: Modern Library.

Machiavelli, N. (1950) *The Prince and Discourses*, ed. M. Lerner, New York: Modern Library.

—— (1988) *The Prince*, ed. Q. Skinner and R. Price, Cambridge: Cambridge University Press.

Marx, K. (1963) *Selected Writings on Sociology and Social Philosophy*, ed. T. Bottomore and M. Rubel, Harmondsworth: Penguin Books.

—— (1964) *The Economic and Philosophic Manuscripts of 1844*, ed. D. J. Struik, New York: International Publishers.

Michels, R. (1966) *Political Parties*, New York: The Free Press.

Mosca, G. (1939) *The Ruling Class*, New York: McGraw Hill. (First published 1877.)

Pareto, V. (1935) *Mind and Society*, 4 vols., New York: Harcourt, Brace & Co.

Plant, R. (1973) *Hegel*, London: George Allen & Unwin.

Plato (1955) *The Republic*, Harmondsworth: Penguin Books.

Pollard, S. (1968) *The Genesis of Modern Management*, Harmondsworth: Penguin Books.

Russell, B. (1938) *Power – A New Social Analysis*, London: George Allen & Unwin.

Ryan, A. (1973) 'The Nature of Human Nature in Hobbes and Rousseau', in J. Benthall (ed.) *The Limits of Human Nature*, London: Allen Lane.

Scruton, R. (1990) *The Philosopher on Dover Beach*, Manchester: Carcanet.

Skinner, Q. (1978) *The Foundations of Modern Political Thought*, vol. I, *The Renaissance*, vol. II, *The Age of Reformation*, Cambridge: Cambridge University Press.

Villari, P. (1892) *Life and Times of Machiavelli*, London: T. Fisher Unwin.

Wolin, S. (1961) *Politics and Vision*, London: Allen & Unwin.

Wrong, D. (1961) 'The Oversocialised Conception of Man in Modern Sociology', *American Sociological Review*: 184–93; repr. in Coser, L. A. and Rosenberg, B. (eds) (1969) *Sociological Theory*, London: Macmillan.

6
End piece

I SEND YOU GIULIANO, SOME THRUSHES,
NOT BECAUSE THIS GIFT IS GOOD OR
FINE, BUT THAT FOR A BIT YOUR MAGNIF-
ICENCE MAY RECOLLECT YOUR POOR
MACHIAVELLI.

*A THIRD SONNET TO GIULIANO, SON OF
LORENZO DE MEDICI*[1]

17 The myth and reality of telling the truth
The legacy of Niccolò Machiavelli

Phil Harris

Niccolò Machiavelli died in relative poverty, a worn-out man who had wanted to serve his country for the previous twenty years, but had been excluded from public office because he had been associated with the previous Republican regime. He would have found it ironic that his name today is still remembered perhaps more for political duplicity than for his belief in a dynamically led republican civic society.

When he fell from power he retired to the country and wrote his famous works *The Discourses, The Art of War, The Prince*, as well as plays and prose. The first two works have had a major impact on our intellectual tradition, whilst the shorter and more rushed book *The Prince* has become a standard management text.

In the foreword to *The Prince*, Niccolò Machiavelli offers his book to 'The Magnificent Lorenzo Medici' as a guide to effective statecraft and, as some claim, a bid for recognition and possible re-employment. In the end piece, we offer up these works and ideas contained in this book to students and scholars in the style of Machiavelli to continue to explore his works for the benefit of marketing and management.

As we reflect on Niccolò Machiavelli, it is important to remember that he was very much a man of his times who believed in Virtue, Probity, Loyalty, Truth and Civic Values in a changing world and was aware of the light and the dark sides of power and, of course, marketing and management. Perhaps some of the first recorded thoughts and observations can be seen in the quote below.

> Among the many considerations that show what a man is, none is more important that seeing either how easily he swallows what he is told or how carefully he invents what he wants to convince others of.
> (Letter II, from Niccolò Machiavelli to a Chancery Secretary in Lucca, Florence, early October 1499)[2]

To Niccolò Machiavelli

Almost always, those who wish to gain a great person's favour come into their presence with such of their possessions as they hold dearest, or in which they see them take most pleasure. Thus, modern European Princes, depending upon their domain, can receive as gifts: academic books and papers, conferences to attend, international travel and distant visits, executive company cars, health insurance, enhanced pensions, the powerful body or sub-committee to sit on, the increased budget, share options and, of course, the villa in Tuscany or Provence. Some Princes have even the right to appoint the Head of the European Bank, or give honours such as gongs and peerages or even estates, and may hark after the ultimate trinket – a pro-Prince media.

Wishing thus, for our part, to come before you with some proof that we are your faithful servants, we have found among our treasures nothing we hold of more worth than the understanding of the truth via academic rigour and systematic enquiry. These ideas are developed from your own writings and deliberations, which have been cruelly debased by inferior critics and biased interests. To counter this we offer here in this seminar and associated small volume a selection of papers and people for you to consider. We most humbly judge these persons and work worthy to come into your presence and worthy of your intellectual consideration. We, of course, trust in you and your grasp of history and knowledge of political power, management and marketing educa-tion that you will accept them.

We recognize this book is unworthy to be given to yourself, yet we trust out of kindness you will accept it, taking into account that there is no greater gift we can present to you than the opportunity to understand, after a few hours of reading, everything we have learned from history and your teachings. We have undergone much travel, torment and experienced anguish over many months in putting together this seminar and associated work. Where possible we have tried to ensure the work is not over-ornamented with rhetorical turns of phrase, or stuffed with pretentious and magnificent words, or made use of allurements and embellishments that are irrelevant to our purpose, as many do. For our inten-tion has been that our volume should be without pretensions and should rely entirely on the variety of examples and the importance of the subject to win approval.

We hope it is not thought presumptuous for our gathering of late twentieth-century academics and thinkers to discuss your behaviour, thought and works and their contribution to our intellectual inheritance. Just as those who paint landscapes set up their easels down in the valley in order to portray the nature of the mountains and the peaks, and climb up into the mountains in order to draw the valleys, similarly, in order to properly understand the nature of truth, one needs to be aware of how the reality can be distorted for political reasons.

We therefore beg you to accept this little gift in the spirit in which it is sent. If you read it carefully and reflect on what it contains, you will recognize it as an expression of our dearest wish, which is that your true character and works are judged rather than the falsehoods and myths which have become associated with you. And if, high up at the summit as you are, you should occasionally glance down into these deep valleys, you will see you have put up with the unrelenting malevolence of undeserved ill-fortune.

Conclusion

As the inscription on Niccolò Machiavelli's tomb in Santa Croce proudly reminds us:

Tanto Nomini Nullum Par Elogium

'no epitaph can match so great a name'

Notes

1 Taken from Gilbert, A. (trans.) (1989) *Machiavelli: The Chief Works and Others*, vol. 2, Durham, NC: Duke University Press, p. 1015.
2 Taken from Atkinson, J.B. and Sices, D. (1996) *Machiavelli and his Friends: Their Personal Correspondence*, De Kalb: Northern Illinois University Press, p. 23.

Selected bibliography

Burd, Laurence Arthur (ed.) (1891) *Introduction to Machiavelli's Il Principe*, Oxford: The Clarendon Press.

Calhoon, Richard P. (1969) 'Niccolo Machiavelli and the Twentieth Century Administrator', *Academy of Management Journal* June: 205–12.

Coyle, Martin (ed.) (1995) *Niccolo Machiavelli's The Prince: New Interdisciplinary Essays*, Manchester: Manchester University Press.

Curry, Patrick (1995) *Machiavelli for Beginners*, Cambridge: Icon Books.

De Grazia, Sebastian (1989) *Machiavelli in Hell*, Hemel Hempstead: Harvester Wheatsheaf.

Etzioni, A. (1995) *The Spirit of Community*, London: Harper Collins.

Harris, P. and Lock, A. (eds) (1998) 'Machiavelli at 500', Conference Proceedings, Manchester Metropolitan University, 18/19 May 1998.

Jacobi, Derek (1996) *Machiavelli for Beginners*, Cambridge: Icon Books Audio Cassettes.

Kelly, G., Kelly, D., and Gamble, A. (eds) (1997) *Stakeholder Capitalism*, Basingstoke: Macmillan.

Mattingley, Garrett (1958) 'Machiavelli's Prince : Political Science or Political Satire?', *The American Scholar* 27: 482–91.

Olschki, Leonardo (1945) *Machiavelli the Scientist*, Berkeley, CA: The Gillick Press.

Parel, Anthony J. (1992) *The Machiavellian Cosmos*, New Haven, CT: Yale University Press.

Shea, Michael (1988) *Influence: How to Make the System Work for You*, London: Century.

Skinner, Quentin (1979) *The Foundations of Modern Political Thought*, Cambridge: Cambridge University Press, 2 vols.

—— (1981) *Machiavelli*, Oxford: Oxford University Press.

Strauss, Leo (1958) *Thoughts on Machiavelli*, Chicago, IL: Chicago University Press.

Thomas, M. J. (1999) 'Marketing Performance Measurement: Directions for Development', *Journal of Marketing Management*.

Villari, Pasquale (1888) *Life and Times of Savonarola*, London: Unwin.

Viroli, Maurizio (1998) *Machiavelli*, Oxford: Oxford University Press.

Machiavelli's works

Atkinson, J.B. and Sices, D. (1996) *Machiavelli and His Friends: Their Personal Correspondence*, De Kalb, IL.: Northern Illinois University Press.

Bondanella, Peter and Musa, Mark (1979) *The Portable Machiavelli*, Harmondsworth: Penguin.

Gilbert, Allan (trans.) (1958) *Machiavelli: The Chief Works and Others*, vols 1–3, Durham, NC: Duke University Press.

Machiavelli, Niccolò (1927) *Mandragola*, trans. S. Young, New York: The Macaulay Company.

—— (1961) *The Prince*, trans. G. Bull, Harmondsworth: Penguin.

—— (1965) *The Art of War*, trans. E. Farneworth, New York: Da Capo Press.

—— (1995) *The Art of War*, trans. P. Bondanella and M. Musa, Harmondsworth: Penguin.

—— (1996) *Discourses on Livy*, trans. H. C. Mansfield and N. Tarcov, Chicago, IL: Chicago University Press.

Wooton, David (1994) *Machiavelli: Selected Political Writings*, Indianapolis, IN: Hackett Publishing Company.

Machiavelli's life

Marchand, Jean-Jacques (1975) *Niccolò Machiavelli: I primi scritti politici (1499–1512): nascita di un pensiero e di uno stile*, Padova: Antenore.

Montevecchi, Alessandro (1972) *Machiavelli: la vita, il pensiero, i testi emplari*, Milano: Accademia.

Muir, Dorothy Erskine (1936) *Machiavelli and His Times*, London: W. Heinemann Ltd.

Ridolfi, Roberto (1963) *The Life of Niccolo Machiavelli*, London: Routledge Kegan & Paul.

Ruffo-Fiore, Silvia (1982) *Niccolo Machiavelli*, Boston, MA: Twayne.

Santi, Victor A. (1979) *La Gloria nel pensiero di Machiavelli*, Ravena: Longo.

Management

Butterfield, Herbert, Sir (1940/1962), *The Statecraft of Machiavelli*, New York and London: Collier Books.

Egan, C. and Thomas, M. J. (1998) *The CIM Handbook of Strategic Marketing*, Oxford: Butterworth-Heineman.

Fisher, Roger, Kopelman, Elizabeth and Kupfer Schneider, Andrea (1994) *Beyond Machiavelli: Tools for Coping with Conflict*, Cambridge, MA: Harvard University Press.

Harmon, Paul *The Executive*, available HTTP: <http://www.proaxis.com/~pharmon/contents.htm> (accessed 4 February 2000).

Harris, Phil and Lock, Andrew (1996) 'Machiavellian Marketing: the Development of Corporate Lobbying in the UK', *Journal of Marketing Management* 12 (4): 313–28.

Hulliung, Mark (1983) *Citizen Machiavelli*, Princeton, NJ: Princeton University Press.

Hunt, Shelby D. and Chonko, Lawrence B. (1984) 'Marketing and Machiavellianism', *Journal of Marketing* 48: 30–42.

Jay, Antony (1967) *Management and Machiavelli*, London: Hodder & Stoughton.

McAlpine, Alistair (1992) *The Servant : A New Machiavelli*, London: Faber & Faber.

History

Bondanella, Peter E. (1973) *Machiavelli and the Art of Renaissance History*, Detroit, MI: Wayne State University Press.

Christie, Richard and Geis, Florence L. (1970) *Studies in Machaivellianism*, New York: Academic Press.

De Sanctis, Francesco (1956) *Storia della Letteratura Italiana*, vol. II, trans. D. Jensen, Milan: Feltrinelli Editore.

Frederic II (1789) *Papers of the King of Prussia*, Berlin: 5–11, 86–94.

Gentillet, Innocent (1576) 'Discours sur les moyens de bien gouverner et maintenir en bonne paix un Royaume ou autre Principauté', trans. D. Jensen, (1960) *Machiavelli: Cynic, Patriot, or Political Scientist?*, Lexington: D. C. Heath & Co.: 375–81.

Gilbert, F. (1965) *Machiavelli and Guicciardini: Politics and History in Sixteenth-Century Florence*, Princeton, NJ: Princeton University Press.

Hale, John Rigby (1961) *Machiavelli and Renaissance Italy*, London: English University Press.

Kraft, Joseph (1951) 'Truth and Poetry in Machiavelli', *Journal of Modern History* 22: 109–111, 116–21.

Macek, Josef (1980) *Machiavelli e il machiavellismo*, Firenze: Nuova Italia.

Meinecke, Friedrich (1924) *Machiavellism: The Doctrine of Raison d'État and its Place in Modern History*, trans. D. Scott, New Haven, CT: Yale University Press, 1957.

Mosher, Michael (1998) *Machiavellian Politics and Japanese Ideals: The Enigma of Japanese Power Eight Years Later*, Cardiff, CA: Japan Policy Research Institute.

Raab, Felix (1964) *The English Face of Machiavelli: A Changing Interpretation*, London: Routledge Kegan & Paul.

Wells, Herbert George (1911/1966) *The New Machiavelli*, Harmondsworth: Penguin.

Political and social science

Althusser, Louis (1987) *Machiavelli, Montesquieu, Rousseau: zur politischen Philosophie der Neuzeit*, Berlin: Argument-Verlag.

Ascherson, N., 'The Indispensable Englishman', *New Statesman*, 29 January 1999, p. 25–7.

Buckler, Steve (1997) 'Machiavelli and Rousseau: The Standpoint of the City and the Authorial Voice in Political Theory', *History of the Human Sciences* 10 (3): 69.

Donaldson, Peter Samuel (1988) *Machiavelli and Mystery of State*, Cambridge: Cambridge University Press.

Earle, Edward Mead (1971) *Makers of Modern Strategy: Military Thought from Machiavelli to Hitler*, Princeton, NJ: Princeton University Press.

Faulkner, Tom (1994) *The Machiavellian Legacy*, Lewes: Book Guild.

Femia, Joseph V. (1998) *The Machiavellian Legacy: Essays in Italian Political Thought*, Basingstoke: Macmillan.

Ferrara, Mario (1939) *Machiavelli, Nietzsche and Mussolini*, Firenza: Vallecchi.

Fontana, Benedotto (1993) *Hegemony and Power: On the Relation between Gramsci and Machiavelli*, Minneapolis, MN: University of Minnesota Press.

Grant, Ruth Weissbourd (1997) *Hypocrisy and Integrity: Machiavelli, Rousseau and the Ethics of Politics*, Chicago, IL: University of Chicago Press.

Grillo, Ernesto (1928) *Machiavelli and Modern Political Science*, London: Blackie and Son.

Hariman, R. (1995) *Political Style: The Artistry of Power*, Chicago, IL: University of Chicago Press.

Jensen, De Lamar (ed.) (1960) *Machiavelli: Cynic, Patriot, or Political Scientist*, Lexington: D. C. Heath & Co.

Masiello, Vitilio (1971) *Classi e Stato in Machiavelli*, Bari: Adriatica.

O'Byrne, John (1996) *O'Machiavelli (or How To Survive in Irish Politics)*, Dublin: Leopold Publishing.

Pearce, Edward (1993) *Machiavelli's Children*, London: Victor Gollancz.

Plamenatz, John Petrov (1963) *Man and Society: A Critical Examination of Some Important Social and Political Theories from Machiavelli to Marx*, London: Longman.

Rauch, Leo (1981) *The Political Animal: Studies in Political Philosophy from Machiavelli to Marx*, Amherst, MA: University of Massachusetts Press.

Smith, Bruce James (1985) *Politics and Remembrance: Republican Themes in Machiavelli, Burke and Tocqueville*, Princeton, NJ: Princeton University Press.

Stell, Hans-Dieter (1987) 'Machiavelli und Nietzsche: eine strukturelle Gegenüberstellung ihrer Philosophie und Politik', published doctoral dissertation, Ludwig-Maximilians Universität zu München, Munich.

Biographies of contributors

Terry Berrow

Terry studied International Relations at the London School of Economics and Political Science.

After graduating, he undertook a Postgraduate Certificate in Education at Garnett College. He gained a Master's Degree in Political Economy from Birkbeck College in 1976. Between 1988 and 1989 he had a research sabbatical at The School of Slavonic and Eastern European Studies, looking at the major changes taking place in Russia and Eastern Europe.

In 1991 he moved to the University of Humberside's Business School, teaching political economy and business strategy. During this period he was seconded to work in Hungary as a lecturer/consultant on a project funded by The British Council, which introduced Hungarian academics to British higher education teaching methods and best practices.

Since March 1999 he has been at Southampton Institute of Higher Education as Senior Lecturer in Business Strategy. Currently he is researching into the major changes taking place in Ikarus, an Hungarian bus manufacturer, in the context of the economic transformation taking place in Hungary.

George Bull

George Bull is an author, publisher and journalist who has divided his working life between editing and writing on economic and financial subjects, and historical studies.

His books include *Michelangelo: A Biography*, *Inside the Vatican* (translated into Italian, German and Japanese) and his translations from Italian of works by Machiavelli, Cellini, Vasari, Aretino, Pietro della Valle, and Castiglione.

He was foreign editor at the *Financial Times*, editor-in-chief of the *Director* magazine and now edits *International Minds*, *Insight Japan* and the *Euro-Japanese Journal*. He is President of Central Banking Publications Limited.

Richard Elliott

Richard Elliott is Professor of Marketing and Consumer Research in the School of Business and Economics at the University of Exeter, and a Fellow of St Anne's College, Oxford. He was formerly University Reader in Marketing at Oxford University, where he was a Deputy Director of the Said Business School. He worked in brand management with a number of multinationals. He was Marketing Director of an industrial plastics company and Account Director at an international advertising agency, where he managed the Colgate-Palmolive account. He entered higher education as a mature student and read Social Psychology at LSE and has a PhD from the doctoral programme in management at the University of Bradford Management Centre.

He has acted as a consultant for a wide range of companies including Mars Confectionery, British Airways, Royal & SunAlliance, Asda, Young & Rubicam, Nokia, British Nuclear Fuels, Smurfitt, Volvo, Bass, P&O, Kingfisher, United Biscuits, The Bay Radio and GEC. He is a visiting professor at ESSEC, Paris, Lancaster University and Thammasat University, Bangkok and has also taught at the London Business School, University of Dar es Salaam, St Petersburg Business School, and Warwick University.

He has published over 75 research papers in such journals as the *Journal of Consumer Research, International Journal of Advertising, European Journal of Marketing, Journal of Marketing Management, Advances in Consumer Research, Journal of Consumer Policy, Journal of the Market Research Society,* and *Journal of Product and Brand Management.* His research interests include socio-cultural aspects of advertising, brands and self-identity, the development of consumer culture and dysfunctional consumer behaviour.

Robert Gutfreund

Robert Gutfreund is a Senior Lecturer in the Department of Applied Community Studies at the Manchester Metropolitan University and an Honorary and Visiting Professor of Sozialpadagogik at the University of Applied Sciences in Hildesheim/Holzminden/Gottingen, Germany.

He left Budapest, where he was born in 1938, immediately after the war and settled with his mother in north-east England. He left school in Wallsend at 15, moved to London and undertook an apprenticeship, qualifying as an electrician in 1959 before National Service in the Royal Engineers.

On leaving the Army, he worked as an electrician for a year before training at the National College for the Training of Youth Workers. He returned to the north-east as the first full-time Youth Worker in the service of Durham County Council. He moved to London and later took a part-time one-year route for professional workers to obtain University entry qualifications and gained entry to the University of Durham in 1968. He read Sociology, although soon became more attracted to political theory. On graduation he obtained a post in the Youth and Community section at the then Manchester Polytechnic.

He finds teaching adults stimulating, and obtained a Master's Degree from the University of Salford for a thesis in deviancy theory in 1977. More recently, studies at the University of Manchester have led to a Doctor of Philosophy Degree, which argued against every form of community-orientated politics, each perceived as anti-democratic. He has written a number of articles on education and on youth issues and policies.

Phil Harris

Phil Harris was the prime conspirator behind organizing the *Machiavelli at 500* seminar held in Manchester in May 1998. Phil is Chairman of the Academy of Marketing, the professional body for marketing researchers and educators in the UK. He is also a member of the Senate and Council of the Chartered Institute of Marketing as well as being a Fellow, and is a board member of the American Marketing Association. Phil is Co-Director of the Centre for Corporate and Public Affairs at Manchester Metropolitan University, a research centre supported by Granada Group, United Utilities, Manchester Airport, PricewaterhouseCoopers, Shandwick, Mirror Group and various charity and public sector organizations. He is the author, with Frank McDonald, of the text *European Business and Marketing: Strategic Issues* (Sage) and of *Political Marketing* (Butterworth Heinemann) with Dominic Wring.

His main research interests are political marketing, political lobbying, strategic marketing, stakeholder marketing, European marketing and economic regional development. His doctorate is on the role of political lobbying as part of modern marketing practice.

He was responsible for co-ordinating the largest ever research project on private/public urban regeneration using the media as a stimulus (Granada Community Challenge) and has carried out work on using marketing to counter car crime and drug abuse. In addition, he has been a regular consultant to a number of blue chip companies, SMEs, charities and public sector interests over the last decade.

He has a business background of marketing and public relations management for ICI in the petrochemical, pharmaceutical and plastics industries and has current consultancy and research interests in government affairs, and in industrial and regional development.

He is the joint editor with Danny Moss of the *Journal of Public Affairs*. He has been an external examiner at a number of business schools across Europe, notably in Spain, France and Belarus. He is actively involved in developing transitional economic programmes in management throughout Central and Eastern Europe. He is author of over a hundred articles in the above areas, a member of the editorial boards of the *European Journal of Marketing* and *Journal of*

Marketing Management. He is a past Vice-Chairman of the Liberal Party and fought the 1992 General Election and the 1994 European campaigns. He has a penchant for Great Western Railway steam engines, real ale and Florentine steaks.

Andrew Lock

Andrew Lock is Pro-Vice-Chancellor and Dean of the Faculty of Management and Business at the Manchester Metropolitan University where he also holds a personal chair. His first degree was in French from the University of Leeds and he holds a Masters and PhD from London Business School. He was previously at Kingston Polytechnic (now Kingston University) and was visiting assistant professor at the University of British Columbia. He is Chairman of the Association of Business Schools, an auditor for AMBA and EQUIS and a fellow of the Chartered Institute of Marketing, the Royal Statistical Society and the Institute of Direct Marketing.

Current research interests are in political marketing, marketing communications and data-driven marketing models. His published work has appeared *inter alia* in *Journal of Marketing Management, European Journal of Marketing* and *Journal of the OR Society*.

Alistair McAlpine

Born in London at the Dorchester Hotel during 1942, Alistair spent his youth in the country. At 13 he went to Stowe, where he had an academic career distinguished only by an almost total failure to pass any exams. Many years later it was discovered that he suffered from dyslexia.

After a summer holiday at the age of 16, he started work on one of his family's building sites. In time he was entrusted with the management of a number of these sites. It was perhaps the happiest period of his life. He enjoyed the company of the men who worked there and the task of getting a building erected in an orderly manner.

In 1964, he became a director of the family's company. A lifelong collector of all manner of things as disparate as rare chickens and Venetian trade beads, it was about this time that he began to collect paintings by the New York Colourists and the American abstract expressionists. Also, sculpture by young English sculptors. He was on the council of the Contemporary Arts Society, the Institute of Contemporary Arts and the English Stage Company at the Royal Court Theatre. By accident he became involved in politics, the politics of Europe, becoming treasurer of the European league for economic co-operation in 1974 and then Joint Vice-Treasurer of the Keep Britain in Europe Campaign. In 1975 Margaret Thatcher invited him to become treasurer of the Conservative Party. After the election in 1979 he was given the post of Deputy Chairman of the party as well as continuing on as Party Treasurer.

At that time he was a strong supporter of Margaret Thatcher and he is still an unrepentant Thatcherite. He retired as Deputy Chairman in 1982 and then Party Treasurer in 1989. Since then he has written a number of books: *Letters to a Young Politician, Journal of a Collector, Collecting and Display, Once a Jolly Bagman, From Bagman to Swagman* and *The New Machiavelli.* He lives in Venice.

Beatrice Rangoni Machiavelli

Beatrice Rangoni Machiavelli was born in Rome, Italy, where she still lives. She studied physics and political science at the university in her home town.

She was first appointed a member of the Economic and Social Committee by the European Union Council of Ministers in 1982, and was reappointed in 1986, 1990, 1994 and 1998. She is a member of Group III (Various Interests) of which she was President from October 1990 until October 1998. The European Economic and Social Committee is an Assembly of 222 representatives of economic and social groupings in the Member States and forms an integral part of the European Union institutional machinery. She was elected President of the European Economic and Social Committee on 14 October 1998, by a majority of 90 per cent by secret vote.

A journalist by profession, she was editor-in-chief of the weekly *La Tribuna* for 10 years. She was also Italian correspondent of the magazine *Women of Europe*, a European Community publication appearing in nine languages. She also edits the magazine *Libro Aperto*, a liberal-leaning journal of political ideas.

She has regularly taken part in television debates and written numerous essays and articles on social affairs, economic matters and women's issues.

Mrs Rangoni Machiavelli heads the Italian Council of the German Friedrich Naumann Cultural Foundation and represents the Italian Consumers Council at European level. She is also a member of the presidency of the Italian branch of the European Movement and a member of the executive board of the Atlantic Treaty Association (ATA), the Italian Society for International Organization (SIOI) and the European Press Association. She is Vice-President of Liberal International (World Liberal Union); Member of the Council of the European Liberal, Democrat and Reform Party (ELDR); Member of the Bureau of ANDE (Italian League of Women Voters) of which she was President from 1977 to 1986.

Mrs Rangoni Machiavelli speaks Italian, French, English and German.

Kevin Moloney

Kevin Moloney of Bournemouth University teaches and researches the public affairs aspects of public relations and how they relate to journalism, marketing and politics.

He has looked at lobbyists for hire (1996, Dartmouth Press) and is working on *PR: the spin and the substance – a re-evaluation* for Routledge. He has also written on teaching public relations in UK universities and on the work of cultural spin doctors for TV adaptations of the classics.

Before teaching, he worked for twenty years in PR.

John Parkin

John Parkin is Senior Lecturer in the French Department of Bristol University where he has worked since 1972. His first degree was in French and Italian (Oxford, 1968) and his PhD (Glasgow, 1973) was on the subject of French Machiavellism in political and military writing in the Renaissance. He has taught courses in French and Italian Renaissance studies for much of his career and published articles concerning the political thinking of writers such as Étienne Pasquier, Jean Bodin and Montaigne, always with regard to their reflection of new currents in political thinking, particularly as stimulated by Machiavelli's writings.

In 1995 he contributed a chapter to a volume, edited by Martin Coyle and entitled *Niccolò Machiavelli's The Prince: New Interdisciplinary Essays* (Manchester University Press). This piece applied a Bakhtinian approach to the topic of dialogue in Machiavelli's work, dialogue being both an essential concept within Renaissance rhetoric and one of the key themes of Mikhail Bakhtin's contribution to twentieth-century philosophy. The patterns of rhetoric in Enoch Powell's political discourse, highly analogous to those of Machiavelli, were the subject of Parkin's contribution to the 1998 *Machiavelli at 500* colloquium in Manchester Metropolitan University, which conference has inspired this publication.

Parkin's interest in Bakhtin grew out of Rabelais studies, however, to which he has contributed several articles and chapters, as well as books on structures of variety in Rabelais' text, and on his influence on Henry Miller. In 1997 he published (with the Edwin Mellen Press) a study of six modern humour theorists, including Bakhtin himself, and his most recent work is an edited volume entitled *French Humour* (Rodopi, 1999). This work extends his own theories of humour, as influenced by Bakhtin, in chapters which examine Medieval polemics against marriage, the link between Rabelais and Bergson, and the satire of Jean de La Bruyère.

Despite being a student of Machiavelli, Miller and Rabelais, he has been happily married for 26 years to Eileen Parkin, MA Glasgow. They have two daughters, Antonia and Leonie, both of Oxford University.

Jayne Pashley

Jayne Pashley originates and went to school in Yorkshire (Doncaster, to be precise) and obtained her first degree in Business at the Manchester Metropolitan University, in 1994. She then engaged in a year of travelling, not just the conventional destinations, but also the Everest Base Camp trek in

Nepal, then Vietnam, Kampuchea and Burma, where she managed to get herself arrested two hours north of the capital and escorted back under armed guard! Time profitably spent in Hong Kong doing teaching and consultancy was followed by a journey home by rail through China.

Jayne took a research post in administration in the University of Aberdeen, mainly concerned with developing educational links between a variety of enterprising courses in the university and local industry and commerce. She then joined their Students Union to set up, from scratch, a service which provided introductions between employers and students for part-time work. Joblink was one of the pioneers in this field, and job-shops and agencies are now proliferating in the university world.

Picking up her postgraduate IPD on the way, she is currently employed by the City of Edinburgh Social Work Department, as Personnel Officer in Employee Relations Development, undertaking action research in personnel and adding to the jigsaw of her career in Human Resources. She is enthusiastic about travel, food, art, theatre, fitness and all of life's explorations.

Maureen Ramsay

Dr Maureen Ramsay is Senior Lecturer in Political Theory in the Department of Politics at the University of Leeds. Her teaching and research interests are in normative political philosophy applied to issues of social justice, theories of justice and feminist theory.

She has written three books, *Human Needs and the Market* (Avebury, 1992), *What's Wrong with Liberalism: A radical critique of Liberal Political Philosophy* (Leicester University Press, 1997) and with Lionel Cliffe *Democracy and the Politics of Lying* (Macmillan and St James's Press, 1999). The latter is both a theoretical exploration of the Machiavellian problem of means and ends in politics and a critical assessment of cases where governments have allegedly lied to the public.

Other work relating to Machiavelli includes 'Machiavelli's Political Philosophy' in M. Coyne (ed.) *Machiavelli: The Prince as Cultural Text* (Manchester University Press, 1995) and 'Machiavellianism' in *Encyclopedia of Applied Ethics*, vol. 3, Academic Press (1998).

Patricia Rees

Patricia is a Senior Lecturer in Management at the Manchester Metropolitan University. After her first degree in Politics she worked in the timber and publishing trades. She took a MBA at Manchester Business School and returned there to carry out research into the human aspects of computer design (including expert systems).

At the Manchester Metropolitan University Patricia's interests turned to marketing, particularly marketing in the Not for Profit sector, which is the subject of her PhD. Her research into UK local government is leavened by forays into Machiavelli, Milton and political marketing. She was deputy chair of the Academy of Marketing conference in 1997 and on the organizing committees of several other conferences. She has been a visiting lecturer at universities in Prague and Bratislava and she is a member of the Strategic Planning Society, the Academy of Marketing and the British Academy of Management.

Interests include playing the clarinet and boating in the Lake District.

Ken Simmonds

Ken Simmonds is Professor of Marketing and International Business at London Business School. He is known worldwide for his publishing, teaching and consulting in both fields. He established marketing at Cranfield School of Management and held the first Chair of Marketing at Manchester Business School before moving to London in 1969. He has also been a faculty member at Harvard, Indiana and Chicago Universities and taught as a visitor in many countries. He is currently Vice-Dean of Senate of the Chartered Institute of Marketing.

His directorships have included British Steel Corporation, EMAP plc, MIL Research Group plc and Aerostructures Hamble plc. He was board-level adviser to Reed International for many years. He currently sits on five boards of smaller companies in which he is also a shareholder.

Prior to his academic career, Ken worked for 10 years in various finance and commercial positions in New Zealand. Moving to the United States, he became one of the first three consultants starting the Arthur D. Little, Inc. management consulting practice. Subsequently he joined Harbridge House, Inc. and then moved to Europe to open its first office there. Later he was on the advisory board of MAC (now Cap Gemini). He has undertaken numerous top-level consulting projects for corporations and clients have included many large multinationals, including IBM. He has, however, devised creative strategies for firms of all sizes in a wide variety of industries and services. In addition, he has run top executive programmes in thirty countries for over 100 firms, including ITT, Monsanto, Raytheon, ICI, British Petroleum, General Motors, Philips, Cadbury Schweppes, Ciba-Geigy, Shell and IBM.

Ken's qualifications include a master in Commerce from Wellington, New Zealand, a doctorate in Business Administration from Harvard Business School and a PhD in Economics from London School of Economics. As well as being a leading marketing authority, Ken is a fully qualified accountant (FCA, FMCA, FCIS, JDipMA) and pioneered the field of Strategic Management Accounting.

Ken's leading US graduate textbook, *International Business and Multinational Enterprises* (written with Stefan Robock), is in its fourth edition. *Strategy and Marketing*, his casebook in marketing, is in its third edition. He was also Editor-in-Chief of the *International Journal of Advertising* for 15 years and serves on the review boards of twelve journals.

Martin Stephen

Martin Stephen is High Master of the Manchester Grammar School and, before that, was Head of The Perse School in Cambridge. His first degree was in English and History from the University of Leeds, which he chose as a rebellious teenager because none of the people he knew at school were going there. He read for his PhD from the University of Sheffield.

He has published 15 books, divided between literature and military history. His most recent is *The Price of Pity: History, Literature and Myth in the Great War* (Leo Cooper), for which the greatest accolade was being savaged by Alan Clark, MP. He is editor of the widely-acclaimed new anthology of First World War poetry, *Never Such Innocence*, now in its third edition as the Everyman *Poems of the First World War*. Also in its third edition is his classic undergraduate textbook, *English Literature* (Longman). His military history is co-published in the USA by the Naval Institute Press, most notably *Sea Battles In Close Up: Major Naval Battles of the Second World War* (Ian Allan/Naval Institute Press).

As testimony to declining standards in journalism, he writes regularly for *The Daily Telegraph, The Times, The Guardian, The Independent* and the *Daily Mail*, as well as for educational journals. He is a regular contributor to Radio 4's *The Message* and a number of other radio features, and his impact on the programmes in which he appears can be gauged by the fact that he was one of the first people to appear on the ill-fated *Anderson Country* on Radio 4.

He hates potted biographies, and only releases them to publishers in the hope that they boost the meagre sales of his books. His family cannot see why their details are of any interest to anyone else and he is too vain to release his date of birth, though he was undoubtedly still living when this was written.

Brian Stone

Brian Stone graduated from LSE with a joint honours BA degree in Philosophy and Economics in 1961. He then spent eight years in the advertising industry, progressing from his first post in the TV commercial department of Procter & Gamble, via advertising agencies, to being the executive producer of a small Dutch TV company. His diploma in Business Administration at the Manchester Business School acted as a foundation for three further years of research in occupational culture. He was then appointed Manager, Management Training Courses at Williams & Glyn's Bank, now Royal Bank of Scotland, where for eleven years he designed and ran management and business development courses. On leaving the bank, he was elected Fellow of the Chartered Institute of Bankers, for whom he then acted as founding Chief Examiner in Supervisory Skills.

Since 1984 he has been on the academic staff of the Manchester Metropolitan University, in the Department of Business Studies, where he is Course Leader on the BA (Hons) Business degree, and Co-ordinator of Management Development.

He designs courses in business skills, and co-ordinates the design and management of all his department's courses on the subject. He has taught management development and management skills at all undergraduate levels, and also advanced organizational behaviour and analysis at undergraduate and postgraduate levels. He is particularly interested in the design of practical, assessed student exercises, such as live business consultancies, which combine the experience of real-world business activity with the academic development of intellectual capacities to a good honours degree level. He has published textbooks and distance-learning texts, and several journal articles, in the subject of business skills development and course management.

Michael Thomas

Professor Michael Thomas is President of the Market Research Society; was Chairman of the Chartered Institute of Marketing in 1995; Chairman of the Marketing Education Group 1983–7; has built a new Business School in Gdansk, Poland 1991; was awarded the Order of Merit (Commanders Cross) of Poland in November 1994.

He travels regularly as Visiting Professor to the Universities of Georgetown, Indiana, Syracuse and Tennessee (USA), Karlstad and Linkoping (Sweden), Helsinki School of Economics (Finland), the University of Malta, and the National Economics University in Vietnam. He is an active author (*Gower Handbook of Marketing*, 4th edition, now published in Polish and Romanian; *How to Prepare a Marketing Plan*, 5th edition, 1998; *Handbook of Marketing Strategy*, 1998; *International Marketing*, 1998). He is also Editor of *Marketing Intelligence and Planning*, and on the Editorial Board of the *Journal of Marketing Management* and the *Journal of Brand Management*.

He is a frequent visitor to the Asia-Pacific Region, as well as to the USA (he is on the board of the American Marketing Association – Marketing Management Division). He dwells between the Scylla of modern marketing and the Charybdis of postmodernism, watching birds to keep his sanity.

Dominic Wring

Dominic Wring is Lecturer in Communication and Media Studies and a member of the Communication Research Centre, Loughborough University. A graduate of the Universities of Nottingham and Cambridge, he has also taught at several institutions including Anglia, Cambridge and Nottingham Trent.

His research interests include political marketing; the management of parties; and the political attitudes of young people. Outputs on these and other topics have appeared in a variety of publications, including the *Journal of Marketing Management* and *European Journal of Marketing*.

Dr Wring has completed a monograph, *Marketing the Labour Party*, for Macmillan. The book assesses the way in which the party has developed as a campaigning organization, since its formal entry into the electoral arena at the beginning of the twentieth century right through to the stunning landslide victory of 1997. Together with Phil Harris, he is currently writing a textbook on political marketing for Butterworth Heinemann. A regular media commentator on political and social affairs, Dr Wring was the youngest member of the twenty-strong Reuters' panel of experts assembled in the run-up to and during the last British general election. Currently Vice-Chair of the Academy of Marketing Specialist Interest Group on Political Marketing, he also co-convenes the UK Political Studies Association's Media and Politics Group.

Index